INVENTING GEORGE WHITEFIELD

INVENTING
George Whitefield

Race, Revivalism, and the
Making of a Religious Icon

JESSICA M. PARR

University Press of Mississippi / Jackson

www.upress.state.ms.us

The University Press of Mississippi is a member
of the Association of American University Presses.

Copyright © 2015 by University Press of Mississippi
All rights reserved
Manufactured in the United States of America

First printing 2015

∞

Library of Congress Cataloging-in-Publication Data

Parr, Jessica M.
Inventing George Whitefield : race, revivalism, and the making of a
religious icon / Jessica M. Parr.
    pages cm
Includes bibliographical references and index.
ISBN 978-1-62846-198-5 (cloth : alk. paper) — ISBN 978-1-62674-495-0
(ebook) 1. Whitefield, George, 1714–1770. 2. Presbyterian Church—
Great Britain—Clergy—Biography. I. Title.
BX9225.W4P15 2015
269'.2092—dc23
[B]   2014031686

British Library Cataloging-in-Publication Data available

For DJ and Lily, with love

CONTENTS

3   Introduction

11 CHAPTER ONE
    Origins of an Icon

38 CHAPTER TWO
    The World Is My Congregation

61 CHAPTER THREE
    That Province, Under God, Will Flourish

81 CHAPTER FOUR
    In the Footsteps of the Pilgrims

107 CHAPTER FIVE
    Inventing George Whitefield

126 CHAPTER SIX
    A Transnational Icon

155 Epilogue

159 Acknowledgments

163 Notes

209 Bibliography

229 Index

INVENTING GEORGE WHITEFIELD

INTRODUCTION

> we have strayed from the Immortal's ways
> And worship with a dull and senseless mind
> Idols, the workmanship of our own hands,
> And images and figures of dead men.[1]

> for, in truth, an image is only dead matter shaped by the craftsman's hand. But we have no sensible image of sensible matter, but an image that is perceived by the mind alone: God, who alone is truly God.[2]

This project began on a rainy London summer afternoon in 2008 while I was carrying out research in the Fulham Papers and the Records of the Society for the Propagation of the Gospel (SPG), both at the Lambeth Palace Library. In 1726, letters between the bishop of London and various Anglican clergymen in the American colonies surveyed planters' attitudes toward missionary work among slaves.[3] Most of the correspondence indicated that the planters opposed catechizing their slaves, as there had long been questions over whether English law permitted the permanent enslavement of Christians. This was all connected to the process of race making in the British Atlantic World, which—as scholarship by Clive Webb, Roxann Wheeler, Colin Kidd, and other show—was heavily predicated along protoracial religious lines up into the late eighteenth century.[4] While the Yorke-Talbot Opinion of 1729 effectively ruled out baptism as a path to freedom, attitudes were slow to change. As the research continued into the controversy over converting slaves, the name of an eighteenth-century evangelical Anglican missionary, George Whitefield, frequently appeared.

This controversy moved beyond questions of manumission into debates about whether Africans were suited (morally and intellectually) for religious instruction and whether conversion might make slaves rebellious. Even more worrying for slave owners was the conversion of slaves to an emotional form of religious practice in an age where emotion, or "enthusiasm," was often tied with sedition. Ultimately, in part due to Whitefield's successful efforts at converting slaves, another debate erupted between evangelicals like Whitefield and a mainstream Anglican establishment that was displeased with the popularity of evangelicalism. Because Whitefield preached that all mankind had freedom in the eyes of God, many planters also feared (and rightfully so) that his preaching might inspire activism directed toward political freedom.

Whitefield is a bit of an enigma. The obstacles to understanding him result from the absence of Whitefield's personal records, the complexities of eighteenth-century revivalism, and a legacy obscured by a devoted following that continued to revise his memory and legacy long after his death. He also published broadly. His writings were, in many cases, ambiguous and sometimes contradictory. This left his image open to wide interpretation and use by an enormous audience.

There have been magnitudes of volumes devoted to Whitefield over the years: Who was he? What did he stand for? What was his influence? Previous studies have supposed him as a so-called Pedlar, or salesman of popular religion, a showman, a revolutionary, and an American founding father.[5] He certainly excelled both at showmanship and promoting his religious ideologies. And while Whitefield could be construed as revolutionary in terms of his prolific influence on eighteenth-century religious culture (and beyond), the present consideration of Whitefield does not see him as a founding father. This is in part due to his death in 1770. Also, Whitefield occasionally spoke of France and Jacobite Scotland through a lens of anti-Catholicism, but Whitefield primary concerned himself with eternal matters.[6] On the other hand, Whitefield's flare for drama and his widespread publishing and missionary undertakings do factor into this assessment of "the Grand Itinerant."[7]

With all the attention Whitefield has received, scholarly and otherwise, what was striking was the limited scholarly attention paid to his conflicted relationship with the multitudes of slaves

Introduction

that he helped to covert, and with slavery itself. Whitefield was well-known for his caustic 1740 rebuke of southern (mostly Anglican) planters for their treatment of their slaves, and more particularly for their failure to ensure their religious instruction.[8] Yet little has been written on the subject since Stephen J. Stein and David T. Morgan published articles in the early 1970s.[9]

In the end, the sources did not support a volume devoted exclusively to Whitefield's ties to slavery. Nonetheless, it was clear that slavery constituted, unarguably, an important part of understanding Whitefield. And so began a new project: one that would hopefully contribute further to the discourse about who Whitefield was and what he meant for the religious culture of the eighteenth-century British Atlantic. The result is a book which argues that he should properly be understood as a religious icon of the British Atlantic World but that also explores Whitefield's understudied influence on evangelical beliefs about slavery, race, and religion as part of his iconic image.

John of Damascus was one of the first theologians to define (and defend) icons in the Christian sense. St. John of Damascus, as he is more commonly known, was the first Christian theologian to produce a serious and systematic study of images.[10] In his approach, political pressures "determined what precisely required clarification."[11] In response to critics of holy images, he wrote "things which have taken place are expressed by images for the remembrance either of a wonder, or an honour, or dishonour, or good or evil, to help those who look upon it in after times that we may avoid evils and imitate goodness."[12]

Although it is unlikely that Whitefield was well-read enough in theology outside of revivalists like William Law to be aware of the concept of "Imitatio Christi," his writings—and many of those of his followers about him—projected Whitefield in a manner that was very much suggestive thereof.[13] In many cases, the writings allude to scripture that draws parallels between Whitefield and Jesus. Some have chalked Whitefield's illusions up to his youthful exuberance and suggest that he later apologized, for both prior actions and the intemperance of some of his followers.[14] Nonetheless, such an apology is unlikely to have made much of a difference. It was precisely Whitefield's boldness that allowed him to

Introduction

captivate the audiences he did. If anything, an apology would have been received by his followers as an example of Whitefield's grace, piety, and humility but changed little else. Certainly, his efforts to model the benevolent, Christian slave owner after his prior criticisms of southern planters were met with derision and charges of hypocrisy.

What all of this did was to provide a framework to try to make sense of a nebulous, expanding, providential (protestant) British Atlantic that cried out for clarification and structure. Many Protestant denominations shared some common ground, but it was a diverse religious movement that would undoubtedly benefit from a central figure to unite its masses. In the spirit of the First Great Awakening (and indeed, subsequent Great Awakenings), this figure was ideally one universally recognized but not seen as a member of the hierarchy of any particular denomination. Many Protestant churches—especially in the New World—fiercely guarded their congregational autonomy. A religious icon, therefore, had to convey piety while avoiding anything that smacked of pope or bishop. That was one thing that many mainstream Protestants—evangelical or otherwise—could agree on, and why Whitefield was cautiously welcomed by staid New England clergymen like Congregationalist Benjamin Coleman, as well as by New Lights like Jonathan Edwards.

By the start of the nineteenth century, the example that Whitefield had set for revivalists possessed two dimensions. First, he modeled defiance against religious elites, placing more of a role into the hands of the common man. Ordained but unschooled preachers were more commonplace, and some even held leadership roles. Among their number were Bishop Francis Asbury, the Reverend George Liele, and the Reverend Andrew Bryan.[15] Second, Whitefield's modeling of Christ and projection of himself as an exemplar of piety offered a new model of Christianity in which common people could "mold Christianity in their own image," though tensions remained regarding church governance and hierarchies.[16]

As the vast historiography of early revivalism, which incorporates important contributions by scholars Patricia Bonomi, Jon Butler, Mark Noll, Frank Lambert, Thomas Kidd, and others

Introduction

demonstrates, even the mere pinning down and defining the Great Awakening is a difficult task. The clarification that an iconic Whitefield offered was a model by which a diverse group of observers could find spiritual fulfillment in an emerging, diverse, and nebulous religious culture. Owing to the extent of his missionary tours, the pervasiveness of his published sermons and pamphlets, and the persistence of his legacy (if sometimes fractious), Anglican missionary George Whitefield served that role for Early Modern evangelicals. Although ordained as an Anglican, Whitefield's propensity for preaching and writing to broad audiences and the public projection of piety that offered hope to the masses made him an ideal fit for that role.[17] So, too, did his frequent public challenges to the Anglican hierarchy over its moral authority and his advocacy for religious toleration.

It is no accident that evangelical Christianity took off in the British Atlantic around 1739, just as Whitefield's missionary career took off. Whitefield embodied a religious culture that he helped to shape and promote. It was not a religious culture that was embraced by all inhabitants of the British Atlantic World, but it was, nonetheless, significant.

For those whose religious beliefs fell outside of the Anglican community, Whitefield was an icon of religious toleration (even if he was not always consistent in his own practices). His popularity soared in a period where the more orthodox forms of Protestantism (notably Anglican, but also the more staid New England Congregationalists) clashed with a new, popular sort of Protestantism that undermined any chance of a single denomination capturing a majority stake in the souls of the New World.[18] It was a popular, evangelical Protestantism that defied denominational lines (unlike later revivals), promoted a religious experience based on the heart rather than the head, and profoundly changed the nature of pastor-congregant relationships.[19] The evangelical religious culture that emerged in the 1730s can also be characterized by extensive missionary activities that were not sanctioned by a national church, the emphases on atonement for sin and the Bible, and particularly on the conversion experience. The conversion experience was arguably the most important facet of the religious culture that Whitefield represented.

Evangelicalism also expanded ongoing discussions about religious toleration and whether this new, unstructured, and sometimes raucous form of worship would ever be accepted. Because of the aforementioned connections between emotion and sedition, evangelicalism tested the bounds of eighteenth-century toleration. Whitefield, among other things, embodied this discourse over toleration. Icons are meant to draw inspiration and devotion to the ideas behind them.[20] To his followers, and even to some of those who disagreed with his theology, Whitefield was a symbol of a post-Reformation struggle in the British Atlantic World to define the bounds of religious toleration.[21] An avowed Anglican who insisted that he was no schismatic, his frequent challenges to the moral authority of the Anglican hierarchy nonetheless served as a model for religious practice which put the emphasis on the relationship between God and individual.[22] It was a paradigm that, during the First Great Awakening, transected denomination and essentially eliminated hierarchies, what Nathan Hatch has called "the Democratizing of (American) Christianity," a true sort of religious toleration.[23] Because there was an established national church in Great Britain, the "democratization" of religion was much more tempered there than across the Atlantic, but Whitefield's influence was still keenly felt.

To slave owners and slaves alike, Whitefield also represented the duality of Christianity in the lives of slaves. For those who opposed slavery, his preaching about equality in the eyes of God inspired antislavery sentiments. Black abolitionists invoked his preaching. White abolitionists invoked his early criticisms of slavery. And although many a southern planter doubted his sincerity, Whitefield was also a model of proslavery paternalistic slavery, one wherein the master professed to be concerned with his slaves' well-being (spiritually and otherwise) but who saw no contradiction between slave owning and his faith.

As an icon, Whitefield was at times undoubtedly contradictory, but icons are invariably the creation of people. Whitefield had a considerable hand in the creation of his own image, but he was unable to exert complete control. The image that became iconic was shaped through a mix of visual culture and text, predicated on a British Atlantic print network that pre-dated Whitefield but grew exponentially during the eighteenth century.[24] Many of his writings were autobiographical in nature and laced with biblical imagery, with the intention of projecting a pious, humble, and Christlike figure. They were meant to inspire his followers to his example and to give hope to potential converts. Although at times his writings were ambiguous and inconsistent, Whitefield's followers used them to shape the iconic Whitefield they wanted. Some of the outcomes were precisely as Whitefield designed; others were unanticipated.

The erosion of Whitefield's reputation as a mainstream Anglican—which occurred early in his career—was essential to his transformation as an icon. Loosely organized around his published journals, the present book follows his career, explaining how local geography and politics, as well as imperial politics, shaped his image. His death at the age of fifty-five, absent any clear and permanent alliances with a particular church (in spite of his insistence that he was an Anglican) was the final element in his transformation to iconic status. Subsequent to his entombment in the basement crypt of the Presbyterian church whose founding he influenced, his tomb became a site of pilgrimage. His followers from across the Anglo-American world scrambled both to defend his legacy and to claim a piece of it as their own. Although his posthumous disciples largely agreed on his importance as a central figure of religious toleration (and liberty in what became the United States), the way he was read as an icon varied considerably, sometimes conflictingly.

The Second Great Awakening provided a rich backdrop against which his iconic status could continue to develop. Denominational lines became much more important than they had been during the First Great Awakening, yet Whitefield was still relevant as a unifying symbol to Methodists, Baptists, Presbyterians, and other Protestants. The Second Great Awakening included efforts to reach out to the unchurched, often in revivalist camp settings. As a forebearer of itinerancy and open-air preaching, Whitefield was an obvious source of continued inspiration, as the myriad of visitors to his crypt, often with ritualistic prayer over his bones, can attest. Whitefield was an important figure in the discourse over American religious culture and religious liberty, and one who factored into the vigorous debate over the role of religion both in the American Revolution and in the politics of the Early Republic.[25] Yet he also remained an international figure whose tomb continued to draw pilgrims from overseas. His iconic image took on new meanings according to time and place.

The complexities of each subsequent wave of revivalism means that Whitefield has remained an attraction and inspiration for evangelical Christians across denominations and centuries. Each subsequent revival brought a new set of political and social issues, wherein participants reproduced Whitefield's writings while sermons contributed new biographical accounts that reaffirmed his legacy as a figure who could center discussions of both personal religious experiences as well as concerns about piety as a whole.

This book could have evolved into multiple volumes processing the significance of what he symbolized through the present. Instead, it ends with the decline of the Second Great Awakening, as his followers processed his death. With the image-conscious Whitefield no longer around to play a role in forming his own image, his followers adopted that role. The results, as in life, were mixed and at times contradictory. Britons claimed as their own a religious icon that the Anglican establishment had utterly rejected approximately thirty years before. American followers tended to assert Whitefield's American-ness because of his influence over religious life in the colonies. High profile black followers like Olaudah Equiano and John Marrant, as well as a few white followers like Anthony Benezet, emphasized a spiritual and political freedom his preaching implied for slaves, while others rejected the idea that Whitefield supported antislavery sentiments. Whitefield had evolved beyond influential preacher into a symbol that could be co-opted or, for opponents of revivalism, scorned in the tradition of iconoclasm, even as the iconoclasm of the Protestant Reformation had long since passed.

CHAPTER ONE

Origins of an Icon

*E*arly in the nineteenth century, an English admirer of George Whitefield's stole Whitefield's humerus bone from his coffin and sent it in a parcel to England. The gruesome parcel's recipient, a Mr. Bolton, had expressed a desire to "obtain a small memento of the great preacher," but he later saw the theft of Whitefield's bones as paramount to sacrilege and returned it to its resting place in the crypt of the Old South Presbyterian Church in Newburyport, Massachusetts.[1] A procession of two thousand admirers of Whitefield followed the bone through the streets of Newburyport as it was returned to its crypt in 1837.[2]

The reburial of bones of a religious icon, reclaimed from Britain, can be construed as an exercise in nationalism.[3] This incident shows the tension between revivalists who "claimed him" for the providential future United States and those in the country of his birth, who never forget that Whitefield was an Englishman. Just as he had no permanent ties to a specific denomination, he was no longer fully British. Yet in part because he died before the Revolution, he was not quite American either. Instead, he became a religious icon—one with multiple layers of significance—across the Atlantic World.

Whitefield's transformation to iconic status began in earnest with the start of his missionary career in 1738. It was a journey that he chronicled in his multipart autobiography, beginning approximately ten years after his first travels to the American colonies. Most icons are painted, but Whitefield was an icon created of textual images, many of them created by Whitefield himself. His writings began with a recounting of his birth and early life, from "imprudent" youth into religious life as a young man.

Whitefield's autobiographical accounts emphasized his journey to religious life, much like the Gospels.[4] They used a philosophical dialogue that was intended to communicate the details of the subject's life and used the individual's life as ethical instruction.[5] Some theologians argue that the New Testament is not a study of ethics itself, but Jesus is universally viewed by Christians as a moral teacher. As such, the New Testament tends to be used to teach biblical ethics.[6]

Whitefield's writings should be understood along a similar paradigm, in that they are a philosophical dialogue, centered on an individual (himself), and intended to convey Whitefield and his life as a model for biblical ethics. In fact, he specifically projected himself as Christlike, and the writings of his supporters, even to the twenty-first century, have frequently followed suit. After his death, his devotees' writings served as a defense of Whitefield and the ideas he represented as well as an effort to preserve his memory.[7]

Whitefield was born in Gloucester, England, on the sixteenth of December 1714, the sixth child and fifth son of innkeepers Thomas and Elizabeth Jenks Whitefield. His father died two years after his birth. Whitefield noted that his mother "was used to say, even when I was an Infant, that she expected more Comfort from me than any of her other Children."[8] The lofty expectations placed on Whitefield were related both to his father's premature death and to chronic ailments that Whitefield claimed his mother endured for a year after his birth.[9]

Later in life, Whitefield tended to emphasize his humble tradesman's background. While his own actions were not always devoid of boastfulness, Whitefield believed that Christians should humble themselves before God, and themes of humility and also of the potentially corrupting power of wealth frequently appeared in his sermons, and most famously in his sermon "The Pharisee and Publican," where he discusses the motives of men for prayer and the importance of humbling oneself before God as a necessity for achieving true Grace.[10] Whitefield's emphasis on his roots as an innkeeper's son in his widely read autobiography was significant because it allowed him to project a humble and pious public image.

In Whitefield's accounts of his life, he emphasized his birth in an inn, just as Christ was born in an inn. His was a tradesman's beginning, just as Christ had been a tradesman—a carpenter. While Whitefield had a number of wealthy patrons, many of his followers had come from humble backgrounds, so identifying with their modest roots allowed Whitefield not only to project himself as a model of true Grace, but also positioned him to build a greater rapport with such would-be converts.

Following her separation from Whitefield's stepfather, his mother moved from the family's inn when Whitefield was about sixteen years old. His first conversion experience came at Saint John's Church when he visited an older brother in Bristol. He later said he felt God speaking through him, describing his experiences in Bristol as a sign that he was intended for a higher purpose than innkeeping.[11] Two months later, Whitefield returned to visit his mother in Gloucester. As fate would have it, a former classmate, who was a servitor at Pembroke College, Oxford, came to visit Whitefield and his mother at this time. The classmate described the servitor program, which allowed him to discharge his college expenses and to earn a small wage by performing menial tasks for the wealthy students. Elizabeth Jenks Whitefield immediately seized upon this plan, reportedly crying out, "This will do for my Son! Will you go to Oxford, George?" According to Whitefield, he replied, "With all my Heart."[12] The former schoolmate immediately prevailed upon those who had helped him to help Whitefield attain a servitor's position of his own.

When Whitefield entered Pembroke, just shy of eighteen, he was among the most fiscally humble of students. The master of Pembroke had, contrary to expectation, accepted Whitefield's application to become a servitor on the recommendation of a family friend. Young Whitefield waited on young men from wealthy families, waking them, running errands, serving at parties, polishing their shoes, and even completing their assignments. Being a servitor was a thankless job that meant reporting errant classmates who violated their curfew to the college master. The gentlemen students retaliated by "chasing the servitors though the college halls, clanging pots and candlesticks in imitation of a fox hunt."[13] Whitefield described the students he worked for as "being so extravagant in their living that it unfitted them for prosecution of their proper studies."[14] Whitefield also found that his workload effectively prevented him from joining other students in "excesses of riot," because he spent so many hours alone at his studies that his limbs were "benumbed."[15] His criticisms of his wealthy classmates were a part of Whitefield's careful construction of a public image of piety and humility, in this case playing the Plebian to his wealthy classmates' Pharisee.[16]

It was at Pembroke College that George Whitefield solidified his interest in ecclesiastical life and also became attuned to the extensive religious commercial print network. He could read the religious volumes that shaped his outlook, including *Mr. Law's Call to a Serious Devout Life*, of which he had known prior to university, but could ill-afford.[17] He began to pray daily and to receive the weekly sacrament at an Anglican church near the college, as well as at Oxford Castle, where "the despised Methodists" received communion once a month.[18] Whitefield noted that his sympathies for the Methodists pre-dated his days at Pembroke College. He used to regularly defend them to the other Pembroke College students—to the point where he was rumored to be one of them.[19]

Methodism, a movement of Protestant Christianity that originated in Great Britain, began as a small movement with an aim of reforming the Church of England. John and Charles Wesley, who were early mentors to Whitefield, were key figures in its founding and particularly in writing its tenets. The name "Methodist" evolved from a derisive nickname by its opponents, who scoffed at the "methodical" approach its followers took to religious life. In its early years, its followers hoped to reform the Church of England, as its early leaders saw schism from the Anglican Church as undesirable.

Whitefield began his acquaintance with the Wesleys shortly after he matriculated at Pembroke. He was at St. Mary de Crypt Church to receive the Holy Eucharist one day, when a young woman from a local workhouse attempted to take her own life by slitting her throat.[20] Whitefield notified Charles Wesley of the attempted suicide, believing the Wesleys were "ready to do every Good Work."[21] In an effort to remain modest, he asked not be identified, but the Wesleys soon learned his name. Whitefield, before this known to Charles Wesley as a solitary figure whom he had seen walking the town's streets alone, received an invitation for breakfast the following morning. Whitefield gratefully accepted Wesley's request, as he was looking for more friends who shared his growing religious devotions.[22]

From then on, Whitefield saw Charles Wesley regularly. Wesley lent him an array of important religious tomes, including works by George Byron Koch, William Law, and Henry Scougal. Koch was a seventeenth-century theologian whose 1680 book, *What We Believe and Why*, served as a personal guide for the Wesleys and their followers. William Law was an eighteenth-century English theologian whose writings, and particularly *A Practical Treatise on Christian Perfection* (1726) and *A Serious Call to a Devote and Holy Life* (1728), were incredibly influential to the Wesleys, Whitefield, and other important figures in early revivalism. Henry Scougal was a seventeenth-century Scottish theologian whose writings, including *The Life of God in the Soul of Man* (1677), were, like Law's, important influences upon Whitefield, the Wesleys, and other early revivalists. Religion, as Scougal described it, meant church attendance, harming no one, and maintaining regular prayers, as well as performing acts of Christian charity toward less fortunate neighbors.[23]

Although he was still an Anglican at this point, Whitefield's consumption of this body of literature, so influential to the Methodist revivals in Great Britain, serves as an early indicator of the later decline of his reputation within the Anglican Church. The idea of Christ within influenced Whitefield's belief in the conversion experience, which was one of the ideas that eventually cost him his good standing with the Church of England. Scougal's writings about Christian charity were another idea that, when Whitefield implemented his own charitable causes, undermined his reputation at Pembroke and beyond.

Whitefield credited Wesley's friendship, and his generosity with his personal library, for helping him, Whitefield, to understand "what true religion was."[24] As Whitefield was exposed to the ideas of New Birth and Good Works, his religious fervor deepened, although his own New Birth differed from that of his Methodist contemporaries.[25] This difference can be attributed to Whitefield's desire for a public, pious image. In order to sell both his image and the New Birth, he needed his conversion to be a public event.

He achieved this by producing public accounts of his conversion experiences in his journal, the two installments of his autobiography, his sermons, and other religious tracts. These publications served as fodder for Whitefield's detractors, but they also carried considerable weight among his followers, reappearing in multiple editions.

Whitefield's association with the Wesley family cost him socially and otherwise. His classmates scorned him, even occasionally throwing dirt on him. The projection of Whitefield's public ridicule, and particularly of having dirt thrown at him, had a biblical significance of which Whitefield would have been entirely aware. There are a number of biblical accounts of Early Christians being subjected to this sort of scorn because of their faith. David, for example, was showered with dirt and pelted by stones as he walked along with his followers.[26] These sorts of images cast the profoundly image-conscious Whitefield as a martyr for his faith and resonated with his followers. Members of Pembroke College's administration and faculty were also hostile to Whitefield's entanglements with the infamous Methodists. The master of Pembroke threatened to expel him because of the work Whitefield undertook among the poor under Charles Wesley's influence.[27] Neither was Whitefield's family, having heard "concerning" reports from Oxford, pleased with the religious turn his life had taken.[28]

Owing to a period of illness, Whitefield took a few months away from Oxford. He continued to read regularly and, in a fashion, to minister to the poor and the sick.[29] His religious beliefs began to solidify, and he began to see them as an orthodox interpretation of the doctrine of the Church of England.[30] This set the stage for his future perception of himself as a reformer within the church, rather than as a schismatic. Later, his fervent embrace of New Birth theology and his lack of polish both proved to be obstacles to gaining recognition as a respectable member of the Anglican clergy.

Approximately nine months after he left Oxford, during his visit home, he began to think about receipt of his Holy Orders, which frequently depended on the right connections and were not guaranteed. He prayed regularly and wrote to friends, soliciting their prayers that he be permitted to enter the ministry, though he later claimed he prayed not out of a desire to enter the ministry, because it would be impious to desire that.[31] Bishop Benson of Gloucester laid hands on him on June 20, 1736, although he was then two-and-a-half years under the canonical age of twenty-four. In 1738 he had to return to England from his first voyage to the colonies in order to formally receive his priest's orders from the bishop of London.[32] Whitefield noted in his autobiography that he believed God had sent him a dream prior to receiving his call before the bishop, letting Whitefield know that ordination was to occur.[33] Lady Selwyn, a member of one of Gloucestershire's more prominent families, had recommended Whitefield's ordination to the bishop and made Whitefield a gift of "a piece of gold" some days beforehand.[34] The bishop reportedly told young Whitefield that "he had heard of his Character and liked his behaviour at Church."[35] Bishop Benson also told Whitefield that "he would ordinarily not ordain anyone under the age of twenty-three, but thought it his duty to ordain him whenever he came for Holy Orders."[36]

Whitefield resolved to present himself for Holy Orders at the next Ember Day, though the matter of "what part of his Lord's Vineyard [he] would be sent to labour first" remained "in dispute."[37] Because of his young age, the Anglican Church in Great Britain did not immediately assign him a pulpit. Instead, for the time being he remained in Oxford at the behest of John Philips, a wealthy English merchant, who offered him thirty pounds a year to tend to the spiritual needs of the prisoners in Oxford and others in the Wesley brothers' absence.[38] Whitefield also preached his first open-air sermons.[39] At this point, as a young minister, he had not yet developed much of a reputation, either among the Anglicans or other religious denominations; nonetheless, these open-air sermons were a precursor of his itinerancy, a practice that only expanded after his travels to the colonies. Relatively early in his career, however, a series of events unfolded that would put him on the path he would follow for the rest of his life.

In 1735 Whitefield's mentors, John and Charles Wesley, traveled to Georgia at the request of Governor James Oglethorpe, who was in need of a minister to head a parish in the new settlement of Savannah. The Wesleys' visit lasted only a few months. John fled to England following a scandal involving the niece of a Georgia magistrate, Thomas Causton. Plagued by allegations of sexual misconduct and disputes with a number of important colonial officials, Charles Wesley had already departed Georgia.[40] Though their mission was unsuccessful, the Wesleys remained interested in furthering missionary work in Georgia.

Whitefield wrote of their mission as a success, noting they had planted a "small grain of mustard-seed" that had "grown into a great tree . . . and fill[ed] the land."[41] As a result of the circumstances that led him to missionary life, Whitefield quickly came to believe that God "had called him to publick work."[42] Captivated by a number of letters that the Wesley brothers had sent him from Georgia, Whitefield decided that he should undertake missionary work in the colonies. After careful vetting by Oglethorpe, Edward Gibson, the bishop of London, and the archbishop of Canterbury, Whitefield embarked on his first voyage to the Americas in 1738. This was the beginning of a life's journey that led him to travel to the Americas seven times and to produce an estimated eighteen thousand texts, some 78 percent of which were published.[43] From the beginning, Whitefield's mighty publishing labors were an integral aspect of the creation of his public image.

The initial phases of Whitefield's transformation into a public icon of revivalism involved both a change in his relationship with the Church of England and what he came to mean for religious diversity at a time when freedom of religion was the subject of considerable debate in both Great Britain and the colonies. As Whitefield began to preach first in Great Britain and then in its colonies, he fully desired to promote religious diversity. He sought, and achieved, large audiences for his religious message. Perhaps naively, Whitefield was also quite keen to maintain his standing as a reputable member of the Anglican community, even while seeking the broadest audience possible and promoting religious toleration. In the long run, these two goals were not compatible. As his success in evangelizing grew, he faced more contention from the ecclesiastical authorities of the Church of England on both sides of the Atlantic.

The religious tolerance with which Whitefield was concerned stemmed from seventeenth-century English notions that individuals ought to be able to choose their church and their minister without interference by government.[44] Religious freedom was seen as a right of English citizens, though by the time of Whitefield's career, the "liberty of conscience" of the English Civil War had become a much less radical concept.[45]

The question of to whom religious tolerance should be extended and how far that toleration should go was complicated. John Locke tied the idea of tolerance into English liberty. "Our Government," Locke wrote in his 1690 pamphlet, *Letter Concerning Toleration*, "has not only been partial in Matters of Religion, but those also who have suffered under that Partiality."[46] Locke blamed "the narrowness of Spirit" of those who wrote to "vindicate their own Rights and Liberties" that were "suited only to the Interests of their own Sects" as the "Principle Occasion for our Miseries and Confusions."[47] In other words, divisiveness and bigotry was counter to English interests and undermined true liberty.

Locke exported his ideas on tolerance to some of the British American colonies. The Fundamental Constitutions of Carolina, which he had authored twenty-one years earlier, barred the use of religious assembly as a venue for seditious speech but also declared, "No person of any other church or profession shall disturb or molest any religious assembly."[48] The colony's proclivities evolved largely for pragmatic reasons, just as Whitefield would later embrace religious tolerance. Carolina's charter needed to embrace religious tolerance because of the colony's religious diversity. If the Lords Proprietors failed to acknowledge these varied beliefs in the early days of settlement, the colony would have had little chance of attracting settlers. Still, it was a limited sort of tolerance. Carolina's Lockean toleration did not extend to anyone deemed subversive by colonial authorities.[49]

In spite of what, by Whitefield's own account, was a relatively happy and fulfilling time preaching in Great Britain, Georgia remained on his mind. In mid-December 1736, he received word that his friend Charles Wesley had returned from Georgia. Wesley, who undoubtedly wanted to escape rumors of his scandalous tenure in Georgia, had returned to England in search of "labourers." A letter from his brother, John Wesley, echoed this sentiment, but appealed to Whitefield directly: "God shall stir the Hearts of some of his Servants, who putting their Lives in his Hands shall come over and Help us, where the Harvest is so great and the Labourers so few. What if thou art the Man, Mr. Whitefield?"⁵⁰ Whitefield quickly resolved to travel to Georgia, with the understanding that he would need to return to England after a time to take his ministerial orders. He made a visit to Oxford to say goodbye to his friends and visited Gloucester to see his family and to receive the blessing of its bishop. The bishop told him that he approved of Whitefield's decision, having little "doubt but God would 'bless [him]' and that [he] should do much Good abroad."⁵¹

Whitefield made an additional trip to Bristol to visit some other relatives. There, he offered lectures at St. John's Church and St. Stephen's at the invitation of the parish ministers. According to Whitefield, these lectures, which emphasized the New Birth, drew considerable attention to the as yet relatively unknown young minister. The doctrine of the New Birth, or regeneration, which is the antecedent to modern born-again Christianity, draws inspiration from a number of biblical passages, particularly John 3:7: "Ye must be born again."⁵² As the Wesleyan Methodists practiced it, adherents of the New Birth doctrine believe that for a person to be a true follower of Jesus, he or she must undergo a conversion experience. The person was then, as John Wesley described it, "born of God, born of the Spirit, in a manner which bears a very near analogy to the natural birth."⁵³ Those who experienced conversion frequently described it as though a light came through them, causing them to view sin and salvation in a new way.⁵⁴ This New Light doctrine rankled many in the Anglican clergy as well as the clergy of more traditional dissenter or Old Light sects as a threat to their authority.⁵⁵ For Whitefield to preach this doctrine presented a considerable problem for his reputation as an Anglican clergyman, but it also helped shape him into a symbol of revivalism.

Whitefield needed to receive formal approval from Oglethorpe and the bishop of London for his plans to go to Georgia. Whitefield survived Bishop Gibson's scrutiny, noting particularly the bishop's concern not to send anyone of "sinister views," a reference to Gibson's distaste for Methodism.⁵⁶ At this point, Whitefield could still pass as an Anglican clergyman in good standing with the church, since he was not yet all that well-known.

Whitefield's growing popularity, his appeal to dissenters, and particularly his preaching about New Birth began to draw the ire of Bishop Gibson. The Bishop's ability to censor Whitefield at this time was limited, since there had been no formal complaints against him by a member of the Anglican clergy. Since the regeneration, or New Birth doctrine, was not yet a consistent part of his preaching, Anglican clergymen in good standing in the Church of England still defended his character. Moreover, since a license was not required to preach in Georgia, there was little purpose in denying Whitefield a license to preach unless the bishop wanted to make a political statement. That Georgia was a new colony, with little in the way of a strong, formal political or ecclesiastical authority yet in place, worked in Whitefield's favor. Both Whitefield and Bishop Gibson were acutely aware that the bishop's hands were largely tied in the absence of complaints or substantive evidence of radical behavior.[57]

While the bishop could not officially sanction Whitefield, the latter's preaching did not escape controversy. Shortly after his audience with the bishop, two Anglican clergymen summoned Whitefield to tell him that he could no longer preach in their parishes unless he would "renounce that part of [my] Sermon on Regeneration."[58] Whitefield declined to meet their demands and saw the hostility against the dissenters as counterproductive.[59] He argued that the way to bring them over was "not by Railing and Bigotry, but by Moderation and Love."[60] For Whitefield and his followers, as well as many New Lights generally, the goal was to be able to practice religion unmolested by government and the state church, the Church of England. They firmly believed that religious liberty meant that one's beliefs need not be "certified by the state" and that one could change church or chose one's minister without fear of persecution.[61] Whitefield also saw preaching about regeneration as necessary to advance "the true religion" and as part of his "responsibility to maintain the community of believers in the one, true mode of faith."[62] Whitefield believed that he should be able to preach about regeneration and justification by faith without jeopardizing his standing as a minister in the Anglican Church, even though neither was consistent with church doctrine. In practice, preaching this nonstandard doctrine, which was common among eighteenth-century revivalists, was incompatible with standing as a respectable Anglican clergyman. Both Anglicans and dissenters had proclivities toward asserting that they spoke the "only legitimate form of religious truth," but his preaching of dogma commonly associated with dissenters while performing as an Anglican marked a rise in Whitefield's embrace of latitudinarian theology.[63] Whitefield attributed at least some of the hostility against him to "Godly jealousy" over his success.[64] Some of Whitefield's admirers echoed his claims that he was an object of jealousy and a victim of a bigoted Anglican hierarchy, establishing him as a martyr of sorts.[65] One pro-Whitefield magazine published an image of him on a cushion, with a "bishop looking enviously over [his] shoulder," and labeled a "Mitred drone."[66] The image, which has not survived to modern day, appeared in a newspaper that had solicited a recalcitrant Whitefield to sit for a picture. Whitefield saw the publication of this sardonic picture as little more than an effort to stir up trouble. Nonetheless, it demonstrated that Whitefield was gaining significance as a symbol in the discourse about toleration and religious culture.

Upon consultation with friends, Whitefield acquiesced to sit for a picture for the offending publication in hopes that he could regain control over his image and repair the damage from the earlier image. Whitefield was keenly aware that images could be read as text and were thus another means to shape, or in this case rehabilitate, his public reputation.[67] Unfortunately, sitting for a new picture failed to quell the outrage the first picture had caused.[68] Just when his situation in Great Britain hit a fevered pitch, Whitefield finally received the call for departure to Georgia in December 1737.

Whitefield boarded the ship *Whitaker* two days later, on December 30, though the vessel did not set sail until January 6. Whitefield spent much of the eight days leading up to departure reading, writing in his journal, and preaching aboard the ship's deck and at a local church. The journal he kept was eventually published, initially as excerpts and eventually in full volumes, as part of his commercial campaign for his public image.[69] Just days into the voyage, Whitefield counted approximately twenty catechumens (not baptized, but undergoing religious instruction) from among his fellow passengers. He began to read nightly prayers to the *Whitaker*'s captain.[70] Whitefield's growing friendship led the captain to invite Whitefield to lead regular prayers and public

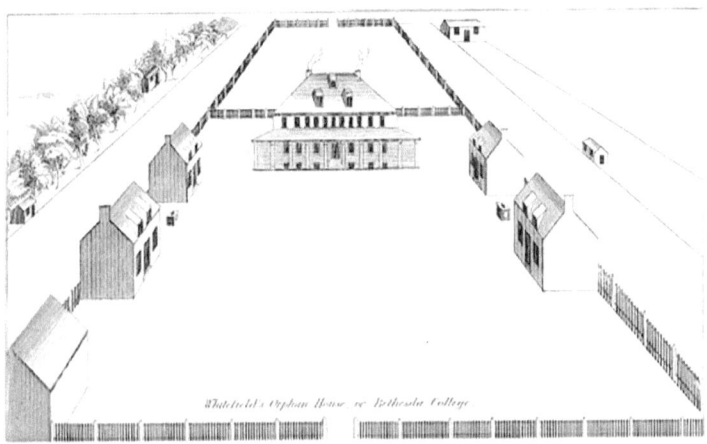

Bethesda Orphanage (Savannah, Georgia), as it would have appeared in George Whitefield's Day. Courtesy of Ed Jackson.

worship on the *Whitaker*.[71] Through his travels, he also became the figurehead of a growing provincial community that looked to him for religious guidance and defended him from his critics.[72] His followers were interconnected across the British Atlantic World both through personal contact and the sale of his writings.[73] While his followers never matched Whitefield's level of publication, they did tap into the connections he created, resulting in several letters and pamphlets that defended him against critics.

Whitefield finally arrived in Savannah, Georgia at around seven in the evening on Sunday, May 7, 1738. The British had colonized Georgia only five years prior to his arrival, based on plans laid out by James Oglethorpe. The positive political ramifications of Oglethorpe's proposal pleased King George II, who granted a charter for the lands between the Savannah and Altamaha Rivers and promptly named the newly chartered colony after himself.[74] Georgia's 1732 charter named a London-based board of twenty-one men to serve as overseers of the colony, with James Oglethorpe as its first governor.[75]

Official settlement began in February 1733 as a modest colony of forty-four men, twenty women, twenty-five boys, and seventeen girls, which then grew rapidly. Some of the earliest settlers included convicted criminals, sentenced to transportation. Colonial Georgia

Origins of an Icon

James Edward Oglethorpe. Drawing by Samuel Ireland.
© National Portrait Gallery, London.

was, in many respects, a frontier between the Spanish American settlements in Florida and Georgia's much more established, wealthier colonial "sibling," South Carolina.[76] Its government was weak, scandal-prone, and plagued by corrupt and ineffectual officials. Thomas Christie, the colony's recorder, for example, had a reputation for "signing anything when drunk."[77] Colonist John Terry wrote, "I long very much to get out of Savannah, for there are here Human Snakes, much more dangerous than the Rattle ones."[78] Oglethorpe and Georgia's trustees hoped that religion might bring a degree of order to the colony and help to mitigate the corruption and chaos, which is why missionaries like the Wesleys and Whitefield received invitations to set up missions there.

Settlers in Whitefield's Georgia also lived for its first six years under a near-constant state of fear and expectation of war with

Spain.[79] Any report of Spaniards, and particularly Spaniards and their Yamasee Indian allies, was cause for alarm, as Georgia's settlers fully expected a Spanish invasion.[80] By the time of Whitefield's arrival, colonial Georgia's economy had deteriorated significantly. Many Georgia settlers were fleeing to Carolina in search of land, slaves, and trade. Between 1737 and 1741, it is estimated that Georgia's population may have dropped drastically, from five thousand to five hundred settlers.[81] In spite of the chaos, Whitefield reported that he was received with "great civility."[82] Georgia's colonial leadership saw missionaries like Whitefield as a potential break on the colony's decline, and the trustees were determined not to give up on the colony despite its failure to prosper.[83]

Whitefield had high hopes for Georgia's religious and economic development. He was quick to dispel speculation by some back in Britain that the colonists in Georgia had, as a whole, been idle. He saw considerable progress and praised the work of John Wesley, writing that "his name is very precious among the people; and he has laid such a foundation, that I hope neither men nor devils will ever be able to shake."[84] He was, however, disheartened at a lack of resources in the colony that particularly disadvantaged the children. This conclusion strengthened his resolve to construct a long-planned Orphan House in Savannah, with the hope that those of means would give charitably toward its support.[85] Like his missionary work in Oxford, Bethel Orphan House became a vehicle by which Whitefield could publicly express his religious message, writing of it in his journal, publishing accounts of it in newspapers and other periodicals, and speaking of it in his sermons in Britain and the colonies.[86]

His new life in Georgia was not without its challenges. Like many eighteenth-century clergymen, Whitefield was hostile to religious viewpoints that directly undermined, or that he perceived as undermining, his work. One incident, approximately a month after his arrival, led to a confrontation with a parishioner who was "broaching many heretical doctrines" and "particularly in denying the eternity of hell torments."[87] This parishioner exemplified one of the challenges to a philosophy of religious toleration calling for individuals to choose their own religious paths without interference from ecclesiastical or civil authorities.[88] He confronted the parishioner but was unable to convince the recalcitrant man of the veracity of eternal torment. When the parishioner asserted that "he believed that it was his duty to inform mankind, that they were to be annihilated," Whitefield stripped him of his eligibility to receive communion.[89]

Whitefield expressed surprise at being received openly by the Freemasons and wrote favorably of them in his journal, though he did not recognize them as Christians.[90] He also took inspiration from the "order and industry" of the Salzburger settlement and characterized its participants as "worthy of God's assistance."[91] He tended to publically admire Protestant sects who posed no threat to him, but not to recognize their religious ideologies as equal to his own.[92] Whitefield was particularly heartened with the Salzburgers' orphan house, and he donated to it some of his own stockpile of supplies intended for his own planned orphan house.[93] His reactions to both the Salzburgers and the Moravians echoed those of James Oglethorpe, John Wesley, and his friend Benjamin Ingham, who called the Moravians "the most useful and the holiest society of men in the whole world."[94]

During this first missionary trip to the colonies, Whitefield also visited South Carolina. Among all the colonies, South Carolina was second only to Rhode Island when it came to religious toleration.[95] Though officially an Anglican colony, the grant called for the allowance of "indulgences and dispensations in religious affairs" and stated that "no person ... was to be molested for any difference of speculative opinions with respect to religion, provided he did not disturb the peace of the community."[96] The colony's approach to religion was promising, in that it suggested Whitefield could propagate his religious messages without interference by South Carolina's local government.

The religious toleration extended by Carolina's government did not mean that each sect received equal favor from the proprietary government or that churches always lived in harmony with each other.[97] In 1727 a quarrel broke out between the French Huguenot settlers and the Anglicans. The Huguenots believed that the Anglicans, spurred by Commissary Alexander Garden, were "molesting them."[98] The Huguenots were not the only ones who complained of opposition. Everyone with suspected or confirmed Jacobite ties faced rampant hostility, including opposition to their appointment to any position of leadership.[99] Quarrels from the old world thus spilled into the new. However, dissenters enjoyed positions of influence in the government and were also seen by the proprietors as "men of honor, loyalty and fidelity."[100] This worried those in London who wanted to create an Anglican Church in the colonies in the image of the church in England.

The colony's inclinations toward religious toleration, along with its shortage of Anglican clergy in South Carolina, also meant that many clergy in the Anglican community back in Great Britain saw the colony as a maelstrom of immorality, marked by "idleness, drunkenness and swearing."[101] To quell "immoral behavior" and to undermine the influence of dissenters, the Society for the Propagation of the Gospel (SPG) sent missionaries into the region.[102] Concern over the dominance of dissenters also motivated the creation in 1698 of an act of Parliament "to settle a maintenance on a minister of the Church of England in Charlestown."[103] Despite all these efforts, there was only one Episcopal church, compared to three dissenter churches, for the from five thousand to six thousand white inhabitants of South Carolina in 1704.[104] It is therefore wholly unsurprising that Whitefield's latitudinarian approach to religion later resulted in considerable problems for him among the local ecclesiastical authorities appointed by the Church of England.

Of further significance to Whitefield's experiences in South Carolina was the installation of his future adversary, Commissary Garden, in Charles Town as the bishop of London's representative in 1719. Garden's installation occurred just as the colony was transitioning from proprietary to royal government, resulting in an increase in the sorts of formal government and church structures with which Whitefield frequently clashed. This period marked a buildup in forts and churches—especially Anglican— and the creation of formal colonial governance modeled after the British Constitution. By early 1734, Bishop Gibson understood that a growing Anglican population in the colony would require additional parishes.[105] A dearth of ordained, licensed Anglican ministers of "suitable moral character" to serve this growing Anglican population, however, sometimes led to fighting between Anglican parishes over the ministerial services of a single minister.[106] It was therefore not surprising that when he visited the colony during his first missionary tour, Whitefield reported the meeting as having gone well and wrote of being received "in a most Christian manner" by Garden and several others.[107] Whitefield was not yet controversial enough to raise the concerns of a commissary who was worried about the paucity of Anglican ministers. Whitefield's stay in Charles Town was also brief, and it marked the end of his first missionary tour in British America, which he declared "an excellent school to learn Christ in."[108] His first missionary visit would, however, be his last tour in the colonies that went unmarked by controversy.

Whitefield's initial missionary work lasted just three months. He sailed for England early in September 1738, reaching the coast of Ireland on the morning of November 16. In spite of the controversy that had erupted shortly before his departure back in January, Whitefield in his journal described his reception by the bishop of London and the archbishop of Canterbury on Saturday, December 9, as "favorable," though he did not elaborate on the details of the meeting.[109] Since Whitefield clearly wished to preserve his ties to the Anglican Church and avoid appearing to be at odds with the Church of England's hierarchy, it is unlikely that he would have reported in his journal any tensions that may have occurred during their meeting. To reveal clashes with the bishop of London would have undermined his credibility as an Anglican and might have given credence to claims by his growing number of critics that he was a schismatic. Since he was very conscious of his public image, mentioning clashes in a journal that he routinely made public would have been entirely counterproductive.

He began publishing the journal in 1738, just after his return from Georgia. Altogether, there were seven journals, which were initially published separately between 1738 and 1741 and sold by subscription and through booksellers and printers throughout Britain and the colonies. Whitefield's journals were an essential part of his public relations campaign, in which he chronicled his missionary labors.[110] They were an example of the development of his public image, a "shadow of the good things to come," through an extensive commercial religious printing network that spanned the Anglo-American world.¹¹¹ Together with his two autobiographies, these journals projected an image of a pious, humble, and charitable crusader for religious toleration. They enabled him to assert considerable influence over his public image and to counter criticisms.¹¹² The success of his publicity campaign, though, meant that he encountered additional opponents who recoiled against him not only as an individual, but also because of what he was coming to symbolize.

On his second day back in London, Whitefield found that five churches refused to permit him to preach and that "some of the clergy, if possible, would oblige [him] to depart out of these coasts."¹¹³ Rather than evidence that he was inciting schism, as his critics so frequently charged, Whitefield saw these interactions as positive publicity for his message. Public discourse, in print and otherwise, brought further attention to himself and his work, even if he could not always control what was said as the result of this discourse.

Because fewer churches now welcomed him, Whitefield began preaching to relatively modest audiences at alternative venues, such as at the Fetter Lane Society, which until around 1740 enjoyed a close relationship with John Wesley and the Methodists, as well as at the Crooked Lane Society and the Crutched Friars' Society in London.¹¹⁴ Around this time, Whitefield published a pamphlet on the subject of religious societies, which he compared to early meetings of "Primitive Christians" who had gathered secretively in such settlings to evade persecution.¹¹⁵ It was language commonly used by dissenters advocating religious toleration. In 1696 Quaker William Penn, for example, wrote and published a pamphlet in which he described Quakerism, which was the target of considerable persecution in England, as a "revival" of Primitive Christianity, or Christianity in its purist form.¹¹⁶ In invoking the term *Primitive Christianity*, Whitefield also sought to brand his religion as a pure form of Protestant religious practice as well as to legitimize the practice of preaching outside of a church. In invoking himself again as Christlike, he projected himself as the ultimate Primitive Christian. In this pamphlet, Whitefield also made the argument that, if a group of five or more could gather in a private vestry, then it was also "lawful" for a group of five or more to gather in a private home, thus asserting both biblical and ecclesiastical legitimacy for these gatherings.[117] Neither for the first nor the last time, Whitefield publically suggested hypocrisy on the part of critics.

Whitefield's audience members included Anglicans, Methodists, and Quakers.[118] He still saw himself as an Anglican but increasingly tended to ignore denominational lines when preaching, even if he did not always wholly agree with the ecclesiastical interpretations of his listeners.[119] Indeed, while Whitefield "found the Quakers' foundation to be all wrong," he admired the "purity of their spiritual side."[120] Whitefield's spirit of practicality influenced his attitude toward preaching to interdenominational crowds, but some who heard him speak also blamed him for inciting religious division in Great Britain. One reviewer noted that he

> was not a stranger to those causeless divisions among you, occasioned by Mr. Whitefield's doctrine ... which have even drove some of you into despair, and have caused others ... to think their eternal happiness forfeited, though a want of those feelings which he prescribes as the necessary ingredient for a good Christian.[121]

The anonymous antirevivalist writer responded negatively both to Whitefield's Calvinism and to what he saw as the dangers of Whitefield's emphasis on the importance of the New Birth, or conversion experience, for true grace. He believed that Whitefield's teachings could lead "really pious and well-meaning people," good Christians in his eyes, to doubt their faith and their hope for salvation after death.[122] He continued, "I shall leave it to you to think whether any doctrine, attended with such melancholic and frightful consequences, can be a means of promoting the glory of God and benefiting mankind. I doubt not but you will think in the negative."[123] Statements like those of the anonymous writer demonstrate not only contemporary criticisms of the New Birth doctrine and reveal one of the problems inherent in creating a provincial network out of a large and deeply divided transatlantic community. His followers saw him as a man to whose message they could relate, even if they were of another denomination. His detractors saw him as inciting confusion in a world where there was no consensus about toleration or what constituted "true religion." Figures like Whitefield suggested to Britons that they had another choice than the Church of England.

On January 14, 1739, having reached the canonical age, Whitefield was formally ordained at Christ Church in Oxford. He preached twice that day.[124] He praised God for "enabling him to preach with the demonstration of the Spirit, and with power," and wrote that God "quite took away my hoarseness, so that I could lift my voice like a trumpet," which, in the context of Abrahamic tradition, plays on imagery of Gabriel, or God's messenger. In doing so, Whitefield established himself as part of the "true customs" necessary for iconification, and also invoked the "use of scripture of shapes and forms to convey a faint conception of God," described as a fourth category of icon by St. John of Damascus.[125] This imagery, the emotional, extemporaneous style of preaching, together with his taste for extempore prayer, would contribute to the many, almost unrelenting charges of enthusiasm and sedition that Whitefield faced throughout his career.[126] It was common to many evangelical preachers of the Great Awakening in America, such as the American-born, Yale-trained Jonathan Edwards (1703–1758). Edwards, the grandson of eminent Connecticut Congregationalist preacher Solomon Stoddard, was one of the most influential colonial-born revivalist preachers. He was dismissed from his parish in Northampton, Massachusetts, in 1750, in part due to his support of the conversion experience, or New Birth, as a requirement for full church membership.[127] Like Edwards, Whitefield understood that "colonial ministers of evangelical temperament appealed to the emotions of their people as the quickest way to conviction of sin and conversion" in an era where preoccupations with "God and sin" were giving way to the rationalism of the Enlightenment.[128] Edwards and Whitefield were both "deeply conscious even as saved of a persisting sense of sin and guilt."[129] Edwards was also said to encourage emotional outbursts as a sign of true conversion early in his evangelical career.[130] Rather than condemning this enthusiasm, Whitefield, Edwards, and other evangelists saw it as a "remarkable outpouring of God's grace."[131]

Whitefield's growing propensity for preaching to gatherings outside established churches, which he documented extensively in his journal and were well publicized in the newspapers, quickly became problematic. The fact that private religious societies frequently played host to his sermons in England during this period was the source of at least one documented canonical complaint.[132] The complaint labeled the meetings as secretive, seditious, and contrary to the Church of England, a charge that Whitefield denied. He asserted quite adamantly that the gatherings were only intended as fellowship-building and were not schismatic.[133] He chafed at what he saw as the hypocrisy of the clergy who "charge me carelessly with schism and being righteous overmuch" and yet did not consider "that the Canon of our Church forbids our clergy to frequent taverns, to play at cards or dice, or any other unlawful games."[134] Whitefield frequently responded to criticisms of his ministry by pointing out what he saw as inconsistencies between the behavior of Anglican clergymen and authority figures and Church Canon. This was one of many occasions in which Whitefield challenged the authority of members of the Anglican clergy.[135] Through these challenges, he made a public example of those who failed to live up to the pious model that he set in his autobiographies and his journal, particularly in contrast with the image he presented of himself as an indiscrete youth who had found "true religion" as an adult.[136] These challenges also reinforced Whitefield's determination to project himself as a pious Anglican who faced resistance from hypocritical critics as he tried to steer the Church of England in a more moral direction by example, a veritable paragon, or icon, of religiosity that would resonate in an uneven providential landscape.

A few days after facing this charge, Whitefield and John Wesley met with two clergymen of the Church of England who were opposed to their New Birth doctrine. It was at that meeting that Whitefield first recognized that the New Birth had become a fundamental difference between him and his opponents and not one that could readily be overcome. In spite of this theological difference over New Birth doctrine, Whitefield still saw himself as a loyal member of the Church of England's clergy. He met with the bishop of Gloucester on February 6, 1739, reporting in his journal that the bishop warmly received both him and John Wesley and commended their missionary work in Georgia.[137] And on occasions when his Anglicanism was challenged, he took these challenges public on both sides of the Atlantic. For example, late in 1739, he received a letter from the bishop of Gloucester admonishing him to "preach to the congregation which was entrusted to his care."[138] The bishop's warning to Whitefield was intended to deter Whitefield's itinerancy, but it was also an indicator that his conduct had strayed considerably from that sanctioned by the Church of England. Whitefield was, in all likelihood, fully aware of the fact that fewer respectable Anglican pulpits were open to him, so the bishop's message was twofold: Whitefield could either start functioning as a respectable Anglican or else desist from the ministry altogether. In response, Whitefield wrote a public letter to the bishop, thanking him for his concern but denying the charges that he violated church law and telling the bishop that "he [the bishop] equally offend[ed] when he preach[ed] outside his Diocese."[139] As with most letters to the bishops, he signed the letter "from your Lordship's obedient Son, and Obliged Servant."[140] In doing so, he was performing the part of the loyal Anglican clergyman, showing deference to church hierarchy, although publication of the letter could hardly be seen as deferential.[141] Whitefield would eventually grow so bold as to tell his adversaries of his intentions to publish their correspondence.[142]

In the case of the letter to the bishop of Gloucester, which appeared in the *Boston Evening Post* on November 19, 1739, Whitefield—in comparing the bishop's actions—not only (subtly) challenged the bishop's moral authority, but also underscored his argument that his actions should not be seen as radical.[143] Similarly, in February 1739, he wrote and made public a letter to the bishop of Bristol, protesting the decision of the chancellor of Bristol to bar him from preaching in a church to benefit the Orphan House. The chancellor had characterized him as a dissenter and a preacher of "false doctrine," but Whitefield responded that

> though many are brought to the Church by my preaching, not one has been taken from it. The Chancellor is pleased to tell me my conduct is contrary to the Canons; but I told him those Canons which he produced were not intended against such meetings as mine are, where his majesty is constantly prayed for, and everyone is free to see what is done.[144]

Whitefield signed his letter, "Your Lordship's dutiful son and servant," but he did not record the bishop's response.[145] Either he never received one or the bishop's response was less than favorable to Whitefield's claims that his preaching did not undermine the church. By this time, Whitefield believed that the church should take note of his success and join in it, rather than attempting to hamper it.

In May 1739, Whitefield began plans for a second trip to the colonies. He expected to sail to Pennsylvania aboard the *Elizabeth* and then preach his way southward, back to Georgia.[146] Some British supporters, who had followed reports of him in the press, proposed to join him in Georgia. Among them was Joseph Periam, a mental patient in London's Bethlehem Hospital, who had been confined there by his family for being "*Methodically* mad" after fasting, praying loudly in public, and giving his clothes to the poor.[147] These were the same sorts of activities Whitefield had engaged in during his own "awakening" at Oxford. Whitefield, unsurprisingly, championed Periam's request to follow him to Georgia, a request that was granted by Periam's family and doctors.[148] Whitefield here offered encouragement to followers who met resistance from their families and also demonstrated to the readers of his journal how he took care of his "flock."

During this period, Whitefield also corresponded with a number of field preachers, with whom he clearly identified.[149] He blamed the clergy who denied him the use their pulpits for his itinerant preaching: "I have no objection against, but highly approve of the excellent Liturgy of our Church, would ministers lend me their churches to use it in. If not, let them blame themselves, that I pray and preach in fields."[150] Once again, Whitefield's published journal modeled a public challenge to the clergy, contributing to his transformation into an archetype of religious liberty that had already taken root in America. These clergymen having effectively forced his hand, he painted himself both as a victim of religious bigotry and one who was entirely reasonable and justified in his actions, rather than the dangerous radical that his critics made him out to be. These sorts of exchanges would only increase over the course of his career.

In early June 1739, Whitefield said goodbye to his London friends and began a short, pre-voyage preaching tour of England en route to Liverpool, where he was to meet his ship. Although Whitefield's plans to set sail for the Americas were temporarily thwarted by embargoes due to the War of Jenkins' Ear, his popularity in both the colonies and Great Britain was growing.[151] While waiting to depart, he preached. After one sermon, he claimed to have received letters from congregants who "came to hear [him] out of bad motive, but were appended by the free grace of Jesus Christ."[152] This was a signal, both to Whitefield's followers and to his opponents, of the power of "true grace" to overcome bigotry. To his opponents, and particularly those in the church hierarchies, this was a signal that he could not be stopped. To his supporters he portrayed a rapidly expanding provincial community whose power would to continue to grow while winning over critics. In late June, he wrote that "wherever I go, people fly to the doctrine of Jesus Christ. 'My sheep,' says our Lord, 'hear My voice. A stranger will they not follow.'"[153] About ten days later, in Bristol, he noted bells ringing, which he took to be in homage of his visit. "I was received as an angel of God," he wrote. That night, he preached to a group of about six or seven thousand.[154]

Emboldened by his growing popularity, Whitefield began to challenge not only the ecclesiastical authorities but the civil authorities as well. In early July 1739, the Gloucester town bailiff sent constables after Whitefield under orders of a local judge, who thought to charge him as a vagrant. Whitefield claimed that the magistrates did not have the authority "to stop [his] preaching, even in the streets, if [Whitefield] thought it proper."[155] In practice, however, Whitefield's bravado did have its limits. On the advice of Benjamin Seward, his more cautious friend and supporter, Whitefield preached in Seward's fields that evening, evading the jurisdiction of the local civil authorities.[156]

This experience in Gloucester was the first of many such conflicts with civil authorities. Later that month, he made public, via his journals, an exchange of letters with John Abbot, mayor of Basingstoke. Abbot wrote Whitefield a letter warning him against preaching in the town and causing a disturbance. Whitefield challenged Abbot to find a law against his meetings and charged him with presupposing that Whitefield had sinister motives rather than waiting to see if a problem arose. Abbot was unable to

Origins of an Icon

Enthusiasm Display'd: or, The Moor Fields Congregation. [England]: Publish'd by C. Corbett according to ye late Actt P, 1739 August 20. Engraving. Library of Congress Prints and Photographs Division, Washington, D.C.

produce a specific law but voiced his objections to preaching on unconsecrated grounds. In the Anglican tradition, preachers typically confined their activities to a church and followed a protocol that included use of the Book of Common Prayer. Whitefield did not adhere to these expectations, preaching in an unknown supporter's private field that night, against the advice of a friend and supporter. Fearing legal retribution, he cut short his evangelizing tour and returned to London to wait out the embargo on voyages to the colonies.[157] He would go on to have similar confrontations in the colonies, notably with Commissary William Vessey of New York and Commissary Garden in South Carolina. He continued to generate controversy for the duration of his life, to be sure, but this facet of his transformation remained more or less constant after his falling out with Commissary Garden.

On Tuesday, August 14, 1739, he boarded the ship *Elizabeth*, bound for Philadelphia.[158] The *Elizabeth* reached that city on Saturday, November 3, 1739. On his second missionary expedition, which lasted through June 1740, Whitefield would ignite a maelstrom in the colonies.[159] Colonial newspapers were filled with advertisements of Whitefield's latest journal publication and of his upcoming sermons. Announcements of his impending arrival in the colonies were circulated well in advance, and some colonial newspapers had been printing largely favorable accounts of his preaching in Great Britain for the better part of a year.[160] These newspapers were also full of advertisements for copies of his sermons.[161] His press in Great Britain, on the other hand, was considerably less positive, as he was viewed by many there as an unscrupulous nuisance.[162] The transformation of his image took place on both sides of the Atlantic. By that point, Whitefield's willingness to preach to anyone prompted constant criticism.[163] Itinerancy meant that his reputation and sermons were directed toward people he had never met, the result being that his influence expanded beyond that of a conventional minister, an expansion that was essential to his iconification. It also made him less orthodox in the eyes of the Anglican Church, where the hierarchy expected its clergymen to restrict their preaching activities to sanctioned pulpits. His Anglican respectability unraveled relatively quickly after his return from his first missionary tour.[164]

Because the rhetoric of religious toleration was so complex and evolving, there was much debate about whether Whitefield was a positive figure for religious toleration. In the colonies, there were some appeals, which included those of fellow revivalist preachers Jonathan Edwards and Gilbert Tennent, for Christian unity.[165] In practice, there was no true freedom to practice one's faith without the public judgment of others, as antirevivalists lamented.[166] To dissenting antirevivalists, the proclivity of Whitefield's visits to created division in communities undermined the spirit of religious toleration. He would continue to evolve into an icon through subsequent missionary tours, though by his death, his iconic image extended well beyond debates over religious liberty.

CHAPTER TWO

The World Is My Congregation

*I*n May 1738, George Whitefield secured passage aboard the *Elizabeth*, along with an entourage of eleven friends and supporters. Later tours led him back not only to South Carolina and Georgia, but also to the Middle Colonies and New England. As Whitefield became entrenched, and indeed synonymous with the religious culture of the First Great Awakening, he acquired greater popularity and found more opportunities for transdenominational encounters. His activities during these tours also escalated the controversy surrounding him and alienated him from key figures in the hierarchy of the Church of England. The events of this second tour denoted not only the unraveling of his reputation as an Anglican, but also the continued rise of his public reputation to the point where numerous members of the Anglican hierarchy felt compelled to respond to it. They responded not merely to Whitefield the individual, but to what he came to mean as an icon of revivalism.

When Whitefield arrived in the Americas for his second missionary tour, he brought aboard the *Elizabeth* boxes filled with copies of his own printed sermons, journals, letters, and prayers, as well as other evangelical pamphlets, including hundreds of copies of William Law's *Treatise on Christian Perfection*. Two of these pamphlets were particularly influential in Whitefield's own conversion to what he considered true Christianity.[1] With his talent for advanced promotion, these tours heightened his popularity and exposed him to even wider, more diverse audiences.

Whitefield's first stop on the second tour was Pennsylvania. By the time he arrived in 1739, Pennsylvania was a crucible of Quakers, German Moravians, Scots-Irish Presbyterians, and Pennsylvania

Dutch. This amalgam of faiths and nationalities all lived under William Penn's philosophy of liberty of conscience. The Quakers had long been persecuted by the English and were keenly sensitive to anything suggestive of religious persecution. Penn pointed out the hypocrisy of those who separated from the Church of Rome and then imposed a national religion on others, calling it "unchristian and unnatural."[2] Drawing from the rhetoric of the English Civil War, he also argued that "God required us to serve him, without endangering our undoubted birthright of English freedom."[3] He saw religious liberty rooted not only in God's law, but also in English law, though some in the colony complained of a Quaker hegemony. Anglican minister William Smith, for example, referred to the Philadelphia Yearly Meeting as the Quakers' "political cabal."[4]

Like Whitefield, Penn was intensely concerned with the religious morality of the colonies.[5] Also like Whitefield, his proclivity toward religious freedom was limited to Protestantism; he harbored a staunch dislike of the Roman Catholic Church. Some of Penn's aversion to the Catholic Church was rooted in the Inquisition and the church's "imputing all the blood of poor Protestants to some unwarrantable civil score," effectively overstepping civil law.[6] Penn's ideology was, no doubt, shaped by his childhood during the reign of Oliver Cromwell and by being the son of a naval officer engaged in Cromwell's campaigns against the Irish. He believed that Catholic practices were "opposed to scripture" and opposed particularly with the notion that doctrine rested "upon the single edicts of the pope."[7] The power held by the pope also ran against Penn's belief in the flaws of humankind. And, in an argument that was entirely compatible with Whitefield's goal of making religion accessible, he argued against the Roman Catholic Church's practice of rendering mass and prayers entirely in Latin, which was largely "unknown to many millions of souls."[8]

Pennsylvania and the Middle Colonies were in a period of rapid population growth at the time of Whitefield's arrival, the increase estimated at a 530 percent increase for the white population between 1710 and 1760.[9] Immigration added a large number of Germans and Scots to the existing Swedish, Dutch, and English populations, in part owing to the work of philanthropic societies.[10]

Consistent with the circumstances of the colony's founding, religion and politics were "more closely intertwined in Pennsylvania than in any other colony."[11] They were so intertwined, in fact, that when it came to organizing for the colony's defense, Governor Charles Gookin addressed the problem of improving security "without engaging any Man against his religious Perswasion an obvious reference to the colony's pacifist Quaker and Moravian populations.[12] Pennsylvania was particularly known for its religious toleration, which was reinforced by a 1709 law. On a local level, after James Logan became mayor of Philadelphia in 1722, he even empowered religious societies in Philadelphia, like the ones Whitefield had preached to in London, to buy and hold land. This went beyond the right to choose one's faith, since religious freedom did not mean equal rights to property.[13]

The colony's emphasis on religious toleration made it a particularly good arena for Whitefield's challenge to religious and civil authorities. Given the tendency of Whitefield's preaching to stir up considerable passion in his followers, however, Pennsylvania's sensitivity to religious squabbling meant that his detractors still had clear grounds, rooted in the law of the colony, to criticize Whitefield.

Whitefield reached Philadelphia on Saturday, November 3, 1739. He reported being warmly received by Penn, the commissary, and other members of the colonial government.[14] Prayer, and several disputes with local clergy about "justification by faith"—which, like the liberty of conscience, was another legacy of the English Civil War—occupied Whitefield's first few days back in the colony.[15] The meetings with colonial authorities included Quakers, Presbyterians, and Baptists. During this stopover in Philadelphia, he also made the acquaintance of Presbyterian Gilbert Tennent, a friend of James Erskine, whose writings Whitefield found inspirational.

The Tennents—Gilbert and his father, William—with whom Whitefield aligned himself, were leaders of the New Siders, or New Lights. New Lights favored revivalism; Old Lights were suspicious of it. The schism occurred along both class lines and cultural lines. The Old Siders were typically born and educated in Scotland, while New Siders were typically younger, born in the colonies, and tended to resist the hierarchical structures of more "conservative elders" whom they saw as out of touch.[16] It is not surprising that Whitefield and the Tennents became allies, despite their denominational differences. His relationship with the Tennents was one of mutual convenience into which Whitefield entered during his travels in the colonies, though it would come to cost his reputation with the Anglican clergy in the colonies.[17] The Tennents were also welcoming to Whitefield, as Presbyterians in the colonies in this period tended toward interdenominational cooperation with a variety of other Protestant sects. Until denominational lines became more rigid in the 1830s, during the Second Great Awakening, the Board of Directors for the Presbyterian Church in British America frequently included members from other denominations.[18] A well-known evangelical figure and proponent of the doctrine of the New Birth, Whitefield would have been seen as a vital ally by the Tennents.

Whitefield's initial perception of the colony was entirely positive. "Many have been quickened and awakened," he wrote, "to see that religion does not consist in outward things, but in righteousness, peace and joy in the Holy Ghost."[19] In spite of his doctrinal disagreements with the Quakers, he saw their trembling in the course of prayer as a manifestation of their awakening and experience of true faith. The convergence of multiple denominations also clearly heartened him, but he began to speak openly about his concerns with the Anglican clergy in the colony, calling their principles "unchristian."[20]

Whitefield's arrival in Philadelphia was announced in newspapers around the colonies.[21] Public responses to Whitefield in the colony were mixed. One follower was moved to pen a poem in response to Whitefield's preaching, a form of veneration to an emerging icon. The poem, published more than once after Whitefield's visit, described how he changed the church experience for his followers. Whitefield, the author wrote, "comes with Zeal divine ... In whose strict Life the Christian Graces shine, In doctrine sound, in Faith and Virtue strong, With soft Persuasion dwelling on his Tongue."[22] The author referred to Whitefield's oft-questioned character and suggested that it was superior to that of previous ministers:

> He comes by Heaven's Command, to chase away,
> Those Mists and Clouds that long have hid the Day:
> to pull a long prevailing error down,
> Which takes from off Emanuel's Head the Crown:
> To rouse with an awakening Trumpet, those,
> Who sat supinely in a false Repose.[23]

The anonymous writer clearly referenced what he believed to be his own conversion experience after hearing Whitefield. More significantly, in his use of "He comes by Heaven's Command" and his references to "Emanuel's Crown," the writer mimicked Whitefield's own language, in his journal and his autobiographical publications, in which he presented a Gospel-like image for himself. Whitefield's own language was reproduced in the writing of his followers, demonstrating just how successful he was at promoting it. It also showed that Whitefield now embodied a Christian ideal for his audience, an ideal that would survive, and indeed, continue to evolve long after his death.

One less favorable response came by way of a letter from some Presbyterians, who challenged some of the doctrinal and scriptural interpretations that Whitefield had expounded both in print and in preaching. Whitefield responded, point by point, in a letter that he subsequently published. For example, they corrected his assertion "that Adam was adorned with all the Perfections of the Deity."[24] Whitefield countered that it was a "wrong Expression" and that he would correct it as "all the moral communicable Perfections of the Deity."[25] His response to the letter was published in *General Magazine*. In it he condescendingly suggested that his critics were put up to their criticisms by their pastors and implied that, if such was the case, theirs was an act of cowardice. "They had better have spoken out," he wrote, "I should as readily have answered them as you."[26] In his response to these critics, he repeatedly referred to his conversion experience, noting that "the Lord's dealing with me was somewhat out of the common Way. . . . Our Lord was pleased to enlighten me by Degrees."[27] While Whitefield was not yet embroiled in the controversy over the conversion experience of ministers, he was already asserting the authority of his own conversion as evidence of his expertise in "true Grace" and that his interpretation was the true religion. This letter was advertised for sale in the *Pennsylvania Gazette* in November 1740.[28]

Whitefield had been in Philadelphia for only a week when he left to accept the invitation of a Mr. Noble to bring his missionary tour to New Jersey. Early in the eighteenth century, the settlements of East and West Jersey merged, having come out from under their proprietary governments in 1702. The period between approximately 1707 and Whitefield's arrival was marked by a rising English influence in agriculture, writing, and even speaking habits. The colony was also becoming more Anglican as the Church of England increased its presence there through the efforts of the SPG. Dutch Reformists, Scottish Presbyterians, and Congregationalists all railed against the rising influence of the Anglican Church.[29] This controversy simmered at around the same time a pamphlet circulated in England titled *The Rights of the Christian Church Asserted*.[30] This pamphlet, based on a sermon preached by English deist writer Matthew Tindall, alarmed the Anglican clergy because it argued that "the Church of England—as by law established—is a mere creature of the people and civil power, and the independent power of the clergy contrary to the ancient laws of the land even in Popish times."[31] In the colonies, where the line between church and state was not entirely clear and the Church of England was attempting to establish spiritual authority, ideas like Tindall's were particularly threatening because they undercut the church's authority (though they were potentially subversive to clergy in other sects as well). It was significant that Whitefield's teachings were already starting to emphasize the importance of the conversion experience for the achievement of true grace. While he did not yet explicitly argue for the necessity of conversion among clergy, the popularity of his teachings still implied problems for ministers who did not favor the New Birth. Since religious toleration in places like Pennsylvania suggested that parishioners had the right to choose their religion without interference by ecclesiastical or civil authorities, it meant that these parishioners might either abandon their church in favor of a new Whitefieldian one or replace their existing minister in favor of a new one. Tensions between the Anglican Church and other denominations led Congregationalists to join Philadelphia's Presbyterian Synod, which was dominated by the Tennents.³² Thus, it was to a very conflicted colony that Whitefield arrived in 1739.³³

William Tennent's son, Gilbert, also a Presbyterian minister, joined Whitefield on most of his journey through the Middle Colonies. Whitefield went on to New Jersey, arriving in Burlington on November 13, 1739, to preach to a mixed crowd. Whitefield was told that it was common, in these situations, for "dissenters and conformists" to "worship at different times, and in the same place."³⁴ Whitefield wrote in his journal, "Oh, that the partition-wall were broken down, and we all with one heart and one mind could glorify our common Lord and Savior Jesus Christ!"³⁵ As parts of the journals appeared in excerpted form in the newspapers, Whitefield's evocation of (Protestant) Christian unity can be understood as a public expression of his goal of creating a providential community, bound together by his religious vision.

While en route to New York, Whitefield first heard Gilbert Tennent preach, and he was moved, saying that "he convinced me more and more that we can preach the Gospel of Christ no further than we have experienced the power of it in our own hearts."³⁶ Whitefield believed that only those who were among "the converted" could legitimately preach the truth. Loosely interpreted, this idea privileged the conversion experience over other ministerial qualifications, a feature of revivalist culture in the latter parts of the First Great Awakening and into the Second Great Awakening. Whitefield's eventual public defense of Tennent's assertions that the conversion experience was essential for ministerial effectiveness played an important role in making critics of those who might otherwise have welcomed his message of religious toleration but who detested revivalism's tendency (and Whitefield's) to inspire untutored itinerants, as well as challenges by parishioners, to the teachings of their ministers.

News of Whitefield's travels abounded in the colonial papers, with reports either "filled with admiration" or scathing in tone.³⁷ Magnus Falconar, a supporter of Whitefield's, published a letter to "the Inhabitants of New-York" in Philadelphia's *American Weekly Mercury* to counter claims by Anglican clergyman Jonathan Arnold that Whitefield was a "deceiver" and preached "false Doctrine."³⁸ Falconar argued that Arnold was unable to "fix upon any one point of Doctrine" against Whitefield.[39] He also responded to Arnold's charge that Whitefield was "ignorant" by accusing Arnold of "the grossest of Ignorance ... for there's none so Ignorant as they who do not know it; and if the Blind lead the Blind, they'll both fall into the Ditch."[40] Falconar was "hopeful" that "good Christians that heard [Whitefield] will be very far from charging him with the least appearance of Deceit or false Doctrine."[41] Like other Whitefield supporters, Falconar imitated Whitefield's language, painting a public image of Whitefield as more knowledgeable and doctrinally sound than his opponents.[42]

The colonial Anglican clergy reported Whitefield's activities on his tour back to the bishop of London. Archibald Cummings, commissary of Pennsylvania and rector of Philadelphia's Christ Church, told the bishop that "for the sake of peace" he had permitted Whitefield to preach from his pulpit, but he also described Whitefield as "enthusiastically mad."[43] In 1737 Cummings preached a pair of sermons about the "Danger of Breaking Christian Unity." In one he expressed his belief that toleration, as practiced in Philadelphia, had gone too far: "The Liberty of every Man's serving God in his own way, being now stretch'd beyond due measure, will, 'tis to be feared, ending not serving him at all, at least in public."[44] Appended to this sermon was a letter to the bishop in which Cummings expressed concerns about defiance by another preacher and about the preservation of Christian unity. In it he described an incident wherein a parishioner brought "some Gentleman" to his house and effectively asked about Cummings's sanction to preach in Philadelphia. The unnamed gentleman said to Cummings, "You are not Rector of this Church. This is no Parish."[45] Cummings took this gentleman's comments as an "insinuation" that the bishop's authority to assign preachers "did not extend to Philadelphia."[46] This rejection of the authority of the bishop marked a tension between Anglican and dissenter communities and a challenge that the Anglican Church faced in expanding in a predominantly dissenter colony suspicious of strong external structures like the Church of England. The first letter pre-dates Whitefield's arrival in the colonies. Nonetheless, Cummings's letter about placating Whitefield's followers and "keeping the peace" almost certainly meant that Cummings also saw Whitefield as a force subversive to

Christian unity as well as potentially schismatic. Philadelphia was still predominantly a dissenter society at this time, so Cummings and his Anglican brethren had to tread carefully. Whitefield's supporters were able to influence the appointment of colonial clergy, so it was imperative for these clergy not to alienate them.[47]

Early in the fall of 1739, Whitefield moved on to New York. The decade leading up to Whitefield's arrival was marked by an effort by both English civil powers and the ecclesiastical authorities of the Anglican Church in New York to solidify their power in the colony. As early as 1706, the Presbyterian Reverend Francis Makemie had warned his parishioners and readers against "Pernicious Doctrine, and Principles; any thing to the disturbance of the Church of England or of the Government."[48] By the 1730s, prayers and reports of the activities of Trinity Church, the primary Anglican Church in New York, filled columns in the New York newspapers.[49] Newspapers were part of the colonial community and served as an important means to disseminate ideas about religion, public morals, politics, and manners.[50] Much as Whitefield used newspapers to this end, churches used newspapers—though on a smaller scale than Whitefield—to promote themselves within the community. Although an Anglican, the appearance of Whitefield at this juncture, with his mass interdenominational appeal and unorthodox preaching, posed a formidable competition for those who hoped to draw a majority of church membership to the Church of England.

Whitefield's arrival in New York was reported in newspapers around the colonies.[51] Given the church's desire for dominance and its insecurity about its own influence in the 1730s, it is wholly unsurprising that Whitefield's reception by New York's Commissary Vessey contrasted sharply with his experiences in Philadelphia. Vessey had been instrumental in building and expanding Trinity Church, the first Anglican church in the colony, as well as expanding the colony's small Anglican population.[52] Whitefield's report on meeting Vessey, appearing in his journal of this missionary voyage printed in 1741, said that "he seemed to be full of anger and resentment."[53] It demonstrates that Vessey was well aware of Whitefield's reputation and, no doubt, his extensive publications. For his part, Vessey preemptively denied Whitefield use of his pulpit because he saw Whitefield's activities as undermining his own. At their initial meeting, Commissary Vessey also requested Whitefield's Letters of Orders, then his license. Whitefield told him that he had left his Letters behind in Philadelphia. Drawing on his experiences prior to his departure on his first voyage to Savannah, Whitefield challenged the commissary's authority, answering that "he never heard that the Bishop of London gave any license to anyone who went to preach the Gospel in Georgia; but that I was presented to the living of Savannah by the trustees, and upon that presentation had letters Dismissory from my lord of London."[54] Whitefield thus not only challenged the commissary, but by invoking his own rapport with Bishop Gibson, Whitefield asserted his legitimacy. To those reading his journal, this exchange was intended to reaffirm that Whitefield was a reformer rather than a schismatic. It also painted Vessey as one not entirely familiar with church policy and how the church operated its missions in the colonies. This was a big problem for a church official who was appointed, in part, to oversee Anglican missionary efforts in the colonies. It painted Vessey as an out-of-touch interloper, and it pandered to those among Whitefield's followers who distrusted external structures in their church governance.

Whitefield further antagonized Vessey by calling him out as a hypocrite when the commissary charged him with breaking his oath and the Canon. He reminded the commissary that his own frequenting of public houses violated the Canon. Once again, by reproducing this exchange in print, Whitefield painted himself as the true upholder of church doctrine and morals. Vessey angrily accused Whitefield of "making a disturbance in Philadelphia," a common charge made by Whitefield's critics.[55] They suggested that, rather than protecting religious morals, he sowed division wherever he went and was ultimately harmful to the religious culture of the colonies. Whitefield replied that his "end in preaching was not to sow divisions, but to propagate the pure Gospel of Jesus Christ."[56] Whitefield called Vessey a bigot and told him that he, Whitefield, was "no respecter of persons; if a bishop committed a fault, I would tell him of it; if a common clergyman did not act aright, I would be free with him also, as well as with a layman."[57] Once again, he played the propagator and upholder of true religion.[58] The commissary finally told Mr. Noble, the gentleman who had sent for Whitefield, to find him a pulpit. This version of events, described in Whitefield journal, was intended to signify Whitefield's ostensible victory against Vessey.

Two days later, Whitefield remarked that he saw his sermon on regeneration, first published in 1739, advertised in a New England paper.[59] The publication of this sermon made Whitefield more widely known but undermined his assertions of Anglicanness. Moreover, the sermon's publication came on the heels of Whitefield's public quarrel with an important colonial leader of the Church of England. Its publication produced at least one response in the *Gentleman's Magazine* by an unnamed letter writer, who asked Whitefield to clarify what the doctrine of the New Birth, or regeneration, meant for religion. The writer was not caustic like other Whitefield critics but expressed concerns about its consistency, first with Whitefield's message that "all mankind might enjoy equal blessing," which had implications for enslaved followers and also tended to contradict his otherwise Calvinistic doctrine.[60] Second, the writer, who clearly had some humanist inclinations, asked Whitefield to explain how the New Birth, or regeneration, was consistent with "the Natural Powers of the Understanding and Moral Agency."[61] He did not see regeneration as "sensible" or rational, demonstrating the tension between the old religious ideology of those concerned with evil and damnation and the newer, more rational ideology shaped by the Enlightenment.[62]

Whitefield's tour concluded with Whitefield, Gilbert Tennent, and their like-minded brethren promising to "remember each other publicly" in prayers.[63] This was significant, because Whitefield's preaching emboldened Gilbert Tennent's supporters in their growing rift within the Philadelphia Synod.[64] Whitefield went on to preach at Germantown, Pennsylvania, two days later, reporting that many in his audience of six thousand were moved to the point of tears. By his account, his audience included people from fifteen denominations, among them a Swiss minister and followers who had been "banished from Switzerland for preaching Christ."[65] Whitefield met many other European immigrants who reported similar experiences of exile, bonding both to him and to each other over his work and even translating it into other languages to bring it to a broader audience.⁶⁶ This helped expand Whitefield's influence even further across linguistic and ethnic lines. By this time, subscriptions for his volumes of sermons and journals exceeded two hundred.⁶⁷ Those of Whitefield's followers who had the financial means could pay to receive copies of these writings every time a new edition was printed.

During the first half of December, Whitefield traveled southward, to Virginia.⁶⁸ At Upper Marlborough, Virginia, he commented on his fears about the spread of deism in the colony.⁶⁹ Deism featured a rational approach to spirituality.⁷⁰ In this period, it was, in part, a reaction against the high Calvinism espoused by Whitefield and others.⁷¹ As such, its spread and, more generally, the rationalism of the Enlightenment, had the potential to undermine his message about the importance of godliness and the dangers of sin and eternal torment.⁷² A rise in its popularity could make Whitefield's work at conversions harder.

Not every eighteenth-century minister saw deism, knowledge of God, and natural philosophy as being in conflict. Both John Wesley and Cotton Mather published tracts on natural theology.⁷³ In doing so, Wesley and Mather, both of whom believed in godliness and the dangers of sin, expanded, rather than contracted, their audiences in an age where revelation found itself in direct competition with reason.⁷⁴ Whitefield did not embrace Enlightenment rationalism, but his pragmatism did lead him to an unlikely friendship with deist Benjamin Franklin. Franklin, a shrewd businessman, did not agree with Whitefield's theological beliefs but was so impressed with Whitefield's ability to enrapture large crowds that he began printing and distributing many of Whitefield's religious tracts.⁷⁵ The friendship and partnership between the two men illustrated how shared support for religious liberty could bring together even those whose personal religious convictions were diametrically opposed.⁷⁶

Deism was one of two obstacles faced by Whitefield in Virginia. The second was that Virginia was the most Anglican of all the colonies. The Virginia Charter instructed the colony's founders "to settle 'the true' [church as] established within our realme of England," and an Anglican chaplain was among the arrivals on the first ships.⁷⁷ Regular church attendance was compulsory; under

English law, those who failed to attend were subject to fines of one shilling per absence and twenty pounds for a month's absence, and that law extended to colonial Virginia.[78] Parents who refused to baptize their children in "the orthodox, established religion" by a "lawfull minister" were subject to a fine of two thousand pounds of tobacco.[79]

Like many colonies, Virginia experienced a shortage of ordained Anglican ministers, and at times Anglican clergy in the colony bemoaned a lack of spiritual morality.[80] Still, though plagued by a shortage of qualified clergy, a lack of support from the Society for the Propagation of the Gospel, and frequent bickering among clergy, politicians, and members of the planter elite, the Anglican Church's dominance in Virginia never faltered. Virginia's colonial rulers were notoriously intolerant of dissenters. They were few in the colony before the mid-eighteenth century, in part because the assembly ordered all dissenters out of Virginia in 1642. This, if it did not remove them entirely, did silence them.[81] Local ecclesiastical authorities kept a close watch on the orders and licenses of clergy working to "restrain the irregularities of the Clergy without meddling with the Laity."[82] Upon a subsequent visit in 1741, Whitefield would note that there were "no dissenters from the Established Church, except a meeting or two of Quakers."[83] Virginia also reenacted English laws that imposed fines, imprisonments, and civil disabilities on Roman Catholics who failed to take oaths of supremacy and allegiance to the English crown and church.[84] Quakers fared even worse; their books were banned and their meetings sharply repressed after 1659, and fines of one hundred pounds were levied against those who permitted their meetings.[85] It was a theo-political environment entirely hostile to Whitefield's goals.

Whitefield managed to make inroads in the colony, but he had difficulties in being accepted as an Anglican minister. A few days into this first tour of Virginia, he remarked upon the backlash against his transdenominational appeal: "If I talk of the Spirit, I am a Quaker; if I say grace at breakfast, and behave seriously, I am a Presbyterian. Alas! What must I do to be accounted a member of the Church of England?"[86] This spoke both to his pride in his ability to reach across Protestant sects and to his exasperation at not being recognized as a loyal Anglican. Given the colony's staunch Anglican identity, it is perhaps unsurprising that he felt compelled, in his journal, to play up his dinner with Virginia's commissary, saying that James Blair "received him with joy and asked him to preach."[87] He spent a total of eleven days in Virginia before heading further south to the Carolinas.

Whitefield and his party reached South Carolina on New Year's Day, 1740. Four days later, they reached Charles Town to news that his preaching had "mightily [grown] the Word of God" in New York.[88] Commissary Alexander Garden was out of town, so Whitefield was unable to seek permission to use a pulpit. Instead, he preached in a dissenting meetinghouse a day after his arrival in the city. He found the excesses in dress and behavior of those in his audience troubling: "I question whether the court-end of London could exceed them in affected finery, gaiety of dress, and a deportment ill-becoming persons who have such Divine judgments lately sent amongst them."[89] Whitefield chose their finery as the subject of his sermon, but his message was apparently not well received. He reported that "I seemed to them as one that mocked."[90] Whitefield's decision to speak about the excessive display was consistent with his long-standing concerns about the corruption of wealth. It was also indicative of his failure to take into account that his audience was comprised of planter elites, who were unlikely to be terribly accepting of his criticisms of their style. Revivalism, as preached by Whitefield, clashed with the development of high British culture (expressed in the colonies through refinement), which was central to planter class society.[91]

Whitefield continued on to Georgia, where he spent about six weeks before returning to Charles Town. His reception by Commissary Garden was cool, compared to their meeting in 1738. Garden's change in demeanor toward Whitefield was, in part, due to the latter's association with Tennent and the Philadelphia Synod of the Presbyterian Church. The previous summer, Garden had attempted to attain Anglican orders and an SPG missionary appointment for Robert Moir, a former member of the clergy of the Church of Scotland. His efforts were met with considerable opposition, and Garden blamed the local Presbyterians for "exciting prejudice" against Moir.[92] Whitefield's sermons in Pennsylvania and New Jersey had helped to bolster the Presbyterian insurgents, as well as many revivalists in these two colonies. The issue of itinerant preaching by those whom Whitefield had helped to inspire came to the surface.[93]

Whitefield's caustic criticism of southern planters also figured into Garden's change in deportment. In 1740 Whitefield published a letter in the *South Carolina Gazette* in which he castigated planters for their treatment of their slaves and identified it as a cause for the Stono Rebellion of that year.[94] He saw God's judgment in Stono and a number of other recent misfortunes to plague the colony: "Their houses have been depopulated with the Small Pox and Feaver, and their own Slaves have rose up in arms against them."[95] Garden, who had married into Charles Town's politically powerful and slave owning Guerard Family, counted many other prominent and influential planter families from among his congregation. When Whitefield's letter was published, Garden criticized it sharply, calling it "dangerous to Publick safety."[96] Garden took Whitefield's remarks personally and dedicated much time over the next decade to the (unsuccessful) destruction of Whitefield's character and credibility.

When the two men met in 1740, the commissary charged Whitefield with "enthusiasm and pride" and with "speaking against the generality of the clergy."[97] Garden referred not only to Whitefield's letter to the planters, but also to the myriad of letters, newspaper articles, pamphlets, and sermons in which he had criticized the conduct of various clergymen who spoke out against him. Further inflaming matters was the fact that only months earlier, Hugh Bryan, a follower of Whitefield's, had published a letter in the *South Carolina Gazette* that accused South Carolina's Anglican clergy of "violating their Canons daily."[98] Evangelical Christian Hugh Bryan was a wealthy planter, former assemblyman, former vestryman, and a member of South Carolina's colonial elite.[99] Bryan's letter "urged all to repentance, but singled out especially the ecclesiastical and civil authorities—even the king—and enjoined them to all 'humble themselves.'"[100] Whitefield helped Bryan edit this letter prior to its publication. As a result, the two men faced charges, though Whitefield made bail and his attorney was allowed to represent him in court, in absentia.[101] Given the letter's mention of both clergy and king, it is hardly surprising that they were labeled "enthusiasts."

Because of its association with the Roundheads of the English Civil War, enthusiasm was an even more serious charge than being a schismatic, as it suggested sedition on the part of the accused. Though no punishment was recorded, Garden saw the Bryan letter as "the latest Whitefieldian blast at the establishment" and "denounced it as scurrilous Libel."[102] Whitefield denied Garden's charges of enthusiasm and asserted his modesty, citing, as an example, a letter he sent to the bishop of Gloucester, but Garden scoffed. Whitefield then tried to assert his legitimacy by virtue of his Letters Dismissory from the bishop of London. This only infuriated the commissary, who forbade Whitefield to speak in any pulpit.

Whitefield replied that he "should regard that as much as I would a Pope's bull" but then asked Garden, "But, Sir ... why should you be offended at my speaking against the generality of the clergy; for I always spoke well of you!"[103] Whitefield believed that if Garden did not see himself as guilty of Whitefield's complaints, he should not take offense to Whitefield's comments. Whitefield inflamed matters further by asking the commissary, "Have you delivered your soul by exclaiming against the assemblies and balls here?" When the commissary declined, furious at Whitefield for catechizing him, Whitefield replied, "I shall think it my duty to exclaim against you."[104]

This exchange was a crucial development in the controversy over whether Whitefield was, in fact, Anglican, as well as an important step in his transition into an icon of revivalism. His argument with Garden, who was in many ways the ultimate anti-Whitefield iconoclast, was the latest of many instances where Whitefield portrayed his opponents as hypocrites or bigots who failed to live up to the religious standards of the Anglican Church leaders. It was advantageous for Whitefield to portray Garden as jealous and insecure. Doing so had the potential to undermine Garden's character in the eyes of Whitefield's followers and potential followers. In his depictions of his dispute with Commissary Garden, Whitefield was performing as a proverbial David, standing up to Goliath.

The Whitefield-Garden quarrel played out in print in grand, theatrical form on both sides of the Atlantic and through a furious exchange of letters between Commissary Garden and the bishop of London, as the commissary brought streams of charges of enthusiasm against Whitefield. Garden's campaign to discredit Whitefield was an effort to unravel the pious, humble, Anglican public image that Whitefield constructed for himself through the commercial press into an icon of sedition and discord. It was also an effort by Garden to establish himself as the true representative of Anglicanism. In October 1740 alone, Garden published six letters against Whitefield that, among other points, criticized Whitefield's doctrinal interpretations and referenced what Garden regarded as the insulting letter that Whitefield had written about Archbishop John Tillotson's comprehension of true Christianity.[105] Referring to his "rather railing Accusation against the Clergy of the Church of England in general, and the present Bishop of London in particular, of their teaching false Doctrine," Garden noted apparent contradictions in Whitefield's own preaching.[106] For example, Whitefield insisted that "Justification by Faith" alone was necessary for true grace. This came from a theological idea originating with Martin Luther and his meditations on the Book of Romans: "For in the gospel the righteousness of God is revealed—a righteousness that is by faith from first to last, just as it is written: 'The righteous will live by faith.'"[107]

Garden, on the other hand, believed that good works, the person's external acts, and adherence to the sacraments were significant in their candidacy for salvation. In his open letter, Garden noted that Whitefield had referenced good works in one of his own sermons and called upon Whitefield to explain his inconsistencies.[108] In a subsequent letter, Garden also accused Whitefield of slandering clergy in his claim that they did not preach the true doctrine, and he asked Whitefield, "What Evidence have you therein brought to support your charge?"[109] Garden's letters were published together with Whitefield's response to the first letter, wherein he did not directly address any of Garden's charges, denied that there were any inconsistencies, and called him "angry overmuch."[110] The publication of this collection of letters brought the two men's quarrels into the court of public opinion, a court in which Whitefield believed that he was to be victorious: "If there be any Thing contrary to sound Doctrine, or the Articles of the

Church of England, be pleased to let the Publick know it from the Press. And then let the World judge, whether you or my Brethren the Clergy have been rashly slandered."[111]

It should also be noted that Whitefield's derisive comment, comparing the orders of Garden not to preach in the colonies to a "Pope's bull," reflected his own anti-Catholicism.[112] The imperial rivalry between Anglican Great Britain and Catholic Spain and, on a local level, between the colonies of South Carolina and Spanish Florida, made Whitefield's insult all the more calculated and politically reckless, especially since it came just months after the failure of an expedition against Spain had dampened morale in the colony.[113] The unceremonious ejection of Whitefield from the commissary's home that followed his antipapist slur was not surprising. In his responses, the commissary invoked the character of the Pharisee in his charges against Whitefield, suggesting that Whitefield felt that he was above God, a response to the biblical imagery Whitefield interwove into his image.[114] In one of a series of public letters that Garden wrote to Whitefield, he asserted, "For sure I am, that Paul may plant, and Apollos may water, but God alone can give the Encrease. Man may teach true Christianity, but no Man can MAKE a true Christian."[115] Both the quality of the two men's characters and the purity of their brand of faith figured prominently in the battle. Garden sought to undermine Whitefield's public portrayal of himself as a humble messenger and, instead, to show him to be ignorant, arrogant, and overzealous.

Garden's letters drew in part on what he witnessed as well as what he learned from others about Whitefield's missionary activities through the press and his network of gossip in the colonies, including information about Whitefield's recent visit to Philadelphia. He described Whitefield as a divisive and subversive character who arrogantly represented himself as the carrier of the church's true message. In another letter to the bishop of London, Garden called Whitefield an "imposter," "pretending himself a Church of England minister."[116] He mocked Whitefield's claims that he was ordained by the bishop of London, telling the bishop that he, Garden, informed him of Whitefield's activities "lest he should apply to your Lordship for orders."[117] Garden's aim was not merely to destroy Whitefield's public image, but also his reputation within the Church of England's hierarchy.

Given Whitefield's popularity at this point, it is doubtful that any refusal of Anglican orders would have irretrievably damaged his ability to minister in the colonies. Such an act would have been portrayed by Whitefield in his journal and other places as evidence of bigotry by the established church, increasing his support among those who saw him as an icon of religious liberty. Nonetheless, Garden hoped that attacking his character would hamper at least some of Whitefield's activities, such as his ability to raise funds. Most of Garden's letters to the bishop detailed what he was doing to quash Whitefield's missionary work, including his activities in support of the Bethesda Orphan House.[118] In one letter, Garden complained of "the effects of Whitefield's licentious example," wherein itinerant followers were "pretending themselves in the Church of England Orders" while preaching in the colonies.[119] The letter also reiterated Garden's plans for prosecuting Whitefield but expressed frustration at what he saw as the bishop of London's inaction. Since the time had lapsed for Whitefield to appeal Garden's actions, there was nothing to stop Garden from proceeding against Whitefield.[120] Garden continued to discuss his proceedings against Whitefield but also complained that he received not "the least Direction from your Lordship about it."[121] He repeatedly appealed to the bishop to take action against Whitefield, who, however, appeared to evade all efforts by Garden and his allies to quash Whitefield's "subversive" activities.[122]

Garden followed Whitefield's example by airing his criticisms in newspapers. He published a sermon in which he scrutinized Whitefield's journals, demonstrating that Garden understood just how vital these journals were to Whitefield's image. Whitefield, in Garden's mind, was an icon of revivalism, a danger to religious life that needed to be stopped. He noted that "the reader will easily observe, that the plain and professed Scope of the censured Part of the Discourse was, to call my Hearers to their Guard, against that Bane of true Religion, Enthusiasm."[123] He continued by "pointing out, and cautioning Anglicans against the first Causes, Springs, and beginnings of it."[124] He also called Whitefield an "upstart Enthusiast, just entered on the Race" and full of "wild and fanatic Notions and run into someone wicked and immoral," bent on Disturbance of the Church's Peace, Disobedience to Superiors, Slander and Abuse."[125] He repeatedly accused Whitefield of "censuring" their "discourse," including that exchange which resulted in Whitefield's unceremonious ejection from the commissary's home.[126] Garden's campaign against Whitefield provoked a range of responses, which also appeared in publication, though much of it came from other members of the clergy. One newspaper advertisement, appearing in the *Boston Evening-Post* on June 21, 1742, referenced a string of exchanges between Garden and A. Groton, who identified himself only as "of New England."[127] The newspaper announcement advertised Groton's response to Garden's response to Groton's initial response to Garden's three public letters castigating Whitefield's character.[128]

Garden's zealous campaign lasted for more than a decade. Ten years into that campaign, even after he was no longer commissary of South Carolina, Garden was writing to the bishop claiming that it remained his duty to suppress "Methodists" and "Irregulars" on "Plantations in the Americas."[129] Garden's letter writing was so effective that, after only a short span of time, Whitefield felt compelled to respond to the criticisms leveled against him in his own letter-writing campaign to the bishop to try to preserve his relationship with the Church of England. In one of the letters, written as he sailed from Charles Town to Boston in September 1740, he cast aspersions on the commissary's motives. He avowed his loyalty to the bishop and asked him to confirm, in writing, whether the commissary had authority over clergy outside of his jurisdiction.[130] In other letters, he cast doubts on the character and motives of both missionaries in the colonies and those in Great Britain who had brought charges against him. In one letter, written in June 1741, Whitefield claimed that he firmly supported the mission of the SPG and told Bishop Gibson that he was "misinformed of some particulars."[131] Whitefield told the bishop that because he had been "lately been in America," he was "better able to judge of some things than those who live in England."[132]

In a second letter to the bishop of London, about a week after the first, he questioned the character of the "missionaries in America" but asked the bishop to keep his letters a private matter between them.[133] He wrote out of "concern for the welfare of his [the bishop's] Church," asserting that his desire was "not to Expose but Reform."[134] Nonetheless, events during his second missionary tour in the colonies would make preserving his ties with the Anglican Church an increasingly unreachable goal. In 1742, a letter from W. Sharpe of the Council Office to the bishop discussed Whitefield's contact with him regarding confusion over some pending complaints against Whitefield, in which Whitefield appeared ready to appeal directly to the archbishop of Canterbury.[135] As the spiritual head of the Church of England, the archbishop would have final say on any matters concerning the censure of clergy. That Whitefield was considering taking his battle to the archbishop is indicative both of just how much Whitefield valued his affiliation with the Anglican Church and of his confidence that the archbishop would side with him. Success in attaining the archbishop's favor would sanction Whitefield's actions and ultimately make it much more difficult for Garden and other clergymen to continue their public campaigns against him. However, for Whitefield, there is no evidence that the archbishop ever considered intervening on his behalf.

As Garden's litany of complaints suggests, Whitefield continued to preach at dissenting congregations in South Carolina in the days following his dispute with the commissary. Nevertheless, criticism of Whitefield came from many quarters in addition to Garden. Arminins, an ardent and anonymous critic of Whitefield's, frequently wrote derisive letters about Whitefield to the *South Carolina Gazette*.[136] He described Whitefield's followers as regarding him as divine.[137] This was an obvious jab at Whitefield's tendency to legitimize his activities by projecting himself in Christ's image.[138] Rallying against Whitefield as a representation of revivalism, Arminins wanted to undercut Whitefield's deified public self-image and, instead, rebrand him as a flawed cleric who did not fully understand the doctrine he preached.

Ariminins also accused Whitefield of "enthusiasm," associating it with human "Weakness, Ignorance and Rashness."[139] While the true identity of Arminins is unknown, his pen name was an obvious reference to the Latinized name of sixteenth-century Dutch Reform theologian Jacobus Arminius, born Jakob Hermanszoon in Utrecht in 1560. More importantly for Whitefield's time, Arminius was a reference to the Arminian-Calvinist schism that developed within the Methodist movement over the nature of salvation. Calvinists believed that God's sovereignty was absolute. Those followers who were to achieve salvation were preselected by Him. Followers of Arminianism did not believe in predestination. Achievement of salvation, instead, came through an individual's decision to seek faith and atone for his sins. Indeed, 1740 also marks the year in which Whitefield and John Wesley parted ways over this very theological issue, though his schism with the Wesleys did nothing to curtail his detractors' tendencies to associate him with the Methodists.

On March 21, 1740, Whitefield boarded a ship in Charles Town to return to Georgia, where he went straight back to his Bethesda Orphan House. He remained there for three weeks, overseeing its construction. In mid-April he returned to the Middle Colonies. He preached several times at Newcastle, Delaware, where Gilbert Tennent brought a large portion of his congregation to hear Whitefield. His return trip to Pennsylvania was largely uneventful, although the commissary of Pennsylvania could no longer permit Whitefield to borrow his pulpit, saying that Whitefield "had not treated the Bishop of London well" in his answer to his Pastoral Letter and because "he had misquoted and misrepresented Archbishop Tillotson in a letter published in the previous week's *Gazette*."[140] On March 23, 1740, a letter appeared in the *Pennsylvania Gazette* wherein Whitefield informed a friend in London that the archbishop "knew no more of true Christianity than Mahomet [Muhammad]."[141] Whitefield was unrepentant and asked the commissary to demonstrate that he had wronged the archbishop, but the commissary replied that the "printers would not publish anything for them," implying that Whitefield had prejudiced the local printers against representatives of the Church of England, which Whitefield sharply denied.[142]

In March 1741, Whitefield boarded the ship *Minerva* to return to England. His journal ended after this departure, as his publishing efforts transitioned towards publishing his sermons, but it is a fitting metaphor for the solidification of his transformation into a symbol of religious liberty. His friend and traveling companion,

Gilbert Tennent, summed it up most aptly in his 1743 pamphlet, *The Examiner Examined*, which was largely a defense of Whitefield against a litany of charges brought against him by the Congregationalist New England clergy. In it, Tennent railed about "Tyranny" and the "abuse of Christian Liberty" and the "enslavement of High Church bigots."[143] Tennent imitated Whitefield's confrontational behavior and borrowed from Whitefield's language. He castigated ministers who "pretend disorders in Conduct, and Errors in Principle." He then asked, "If so, why don't they exert their Zeal against such Evil, as well as Impieties of the grossest Kind, which are flagrant in the Practice of some of their Brethren? No, such Things, because of the Relation subsisting between them, are past over with silence and negligence."[144] He called opposition against Whitefield "unfounded" and blamed "contempt among the Ungodly," a taunt directed at the clergy who had leveled charges against Whitefield.[145] There were ebbs and flows in the level of controversy that Whitefield generated, as well as his clashes with various colonial Anglican officials, though few of them had the ferocity or staying power of Whitefield's quarrel with Alexander Garden.

CHAPTER THREE

That Province, Under God, Will Flourish

*T*he next phase of Whitefield's transformation to iconic status came through his defense of slavery. It was a process that was tied to the greater discourse in the British Atlantic World over the tensions between Christianity and slavery. More broadly, it was also part of his growing reputation as a polemic itinerant and of the competition for moral authority between orthodox Anglicanism and revivalists.[1] Given his past criticisms of slavery and of the excesses of slaveholding society, Whitefield became a symbol of the hypocrisies that his opponents saw in revivalism, and Whitefield particularly. It is especially significant, given the frequency with which Whitefield accused his opponents of hypocrisy. Ironically, while Whitefield publically defended slavery, his image was co-opted by antislavery activists who sought to abolish slavery on ecumenical, Christian grounds.

Prior to more modern understandings of race, which originated in the late eighteenth century, scriptural language was frequently used as a means to define the "other."[2] Moreover, excluding the other (Africans and Native Americans) from religious rituals, like baptism, that humanized the participants, was a means to enforcing this understanding of race.[3] Eighteenth-century Britons saw religious difference (especially Christianity versus pagan faiths) as even more critical justification than skin color for European domination.[4] That Whitefield advocated ministering to nonwhite souls was therefore threatening to the social order of planters and other Anglicans, even if he did not share their fear that baptism made slaves political equals.

Whitefield's defense of slavery emerged as he became increasingly involved in the socioeconomic development of Georgia. He inserted himself into the campaign to legalize slavery in Georgia, where it had been banned. In doing so, he invoked many of the arguments used by settlers for years beforehand to try to convince the trustees of the colony to overturn their prohibition. And, in fact, African slavery was legalized in early January 1751, just over two years after Whitefield's involvement.

Although Whitefield believed in certain mitigations of slavery, these positions were not entirely radical, even if there were some places where he diverged from the Church of England's views. A number of the Anglican clergy thought, along with Whitefield, that slaveholders should provide religious instruction for their slaves, while slaveholders typically preferred that clergy not interfere.[5] By 1738, there was an uneasy peace between the two parties, with Anglican clergy recognizing that they had little choice but to assent to the interests of the slaveholders. After all, their work was largely dependent on the beneficence and forbearance of colonial authorities, most of whom were slaveholders. Because the Anglican clergy limited their proselytizing among the slaves, slaveholders generally did not see their activities as a threat.[6] By the time of Whitefield's missionary voyages in the colonies, the SPG and the hierarchy of the Church of England in London were encouraging the conversion of slaves, but they still balanced this goal with their desire not to alienate planters.

Whitefield's emphatic pursuit of the catechism of slaves, as well as his harsh public criticisms of slaveholders for their treatment of their slaves, violated this unspoken agreement between Anglican missionaries and colonial slaveholders. In particular, it added fuel to the flames of his dispute with Alexander Garden and Garden's many allies in Charles Town's wealthy southern planter society.[7] Even though Whitefield had always encouraged obedience of slaves to their masters, his defense of slavery in the late 1740s did little to rehabilitate his image in Anglican society.

Whitefield's criticisms of slavery and his encouragement of converting slaves had historical precedent among a very small group of Anglican missionaries.[8] Missionaries like Morgan Godwyn, who supported catechizing slaves, did so in part because they (rightfully) believed that the church's neglect of slaves would lead others to challenge their commitment to their faith.⁹ Godwyn, an ordained Anglican minister from a family of clergymen, staunchly advocated the conversion of slaves and Native Americans. He produced four influential, albeit controversial, tracts advocating church membership for African slaves, Native Americans, and other "infidels" in the 1680s. The two most influential were *The Negros and Indians Advocate, Suing for Their Admission into the Church* (1680) and *A Supplement to the Negros and Indians Advocate* (1681).¹⁰ In listing the reasons why converting slaves was in the slaveholders' best interests, Godwyn instead produced what became a prevailing proslavery argument.¹¹ He noted that Anglican instruction "would make enslaved men and women more efficient and less insubordinate: 'So that this Authority of the Master is so far from being hereby diminished,' he insisted, 'that it is rather confirmed, and a stricter observance for that cause charged upon the Servants Conscience.'"¹² Indeed, Godwyn did little or nothing to challenge the master-slave relationship. After running afoul of colonial slaveholders in Virginia for attempting to catechize slaves, he adjusted his message and tried to engage with slaveholders on their own plane.¹³ As a result, his colonial British American audience ignored the tone of Godwyn's critiques, and so they were not interpreted as a threat.¹⁴ Godwyn exemplified "antislavery without abolition," with religion as a de facto form of social control for slaves (and others).¹⁵ It was a mentality that evangelical proponents of slavery would capitalize upon in the furthering of their spiritual mission, their economic gains, or both. Scriptural validations of slavery were also proffered along with the economic justifications.¹⁶

Initially, Whitefield was conflicted about slavery and publicly raised questions about the treatment of slaves. Later, these instances were used by Whitefield's antirevivalist opponents to demonstrate inconsistencies in his position. His initial view on slavery differed notably from that of many of his fellow Anglican missionaries, who tended to defend it, but he was not alone in his concerns over the treatment of slaves or the circumstances under which slaves were attained.¹⁷ It was his criticisms of planters that played a pivotal role in alienating Alexander Garden and much of Charles Town's elite

Anglican planter society. Whitefield's shift to a defense of slavery was one way he could become more palatable to Anglicans, even as other actions made it more difficult for him to win acknowledgment as an Anglican from his fellow clergymen. This glimmer of respectability ultimately failed when his catechism of slaves led several of them to embrace abolitionism, much as Anglican plantation masters feared it would. Olaudah Equiano and several slaves who admired Whitefield's teachings became staunch supporters and prolific writers in the antislavery movement that swept the Atlantic World in the last decades of the eighteenth century. This came as an effort among antislavery Christians to correct something that they saw as both immoral and economically unsound.[18]

When Whitefield began to openly embrace slavery, he did so on both paternalistic and economic grounds. As will be demonstrated, his shift to a proslavery stance late in the 1740s can be attributed to his experiences in Georgia and South Carolina. In 1747 his proslavery convictions had become so strong that he actively campaigned for the legalization of slavery in the colony of Georgia.

The proslavery paternalism espoused by Whitefield was a central ideology in slaveholding society, though it was, of course, not a paternalism from which the slaves themselves benefited.[19] Rather, it grew from a sense on the part of some slave owners and defenders of the institution that there were inherent problems—legally and otherwise—with slavery as it was practiced. Masters with this mentality acknowledged and embraced the economic benefits of slavery but raised some criticisms about the way the African slave trade was conducted and the way slaves were treated.[20] Usually, though, paternalists rejected freeing their own slaves or calling for abolition. Instead, they sought laws and modeled slave-owning practices that were more "safe" and "humane."[21] They also emphasized their own humane treatment of their slaves. Whitefield definitely fits this mode of paternalism. Other slaveholders of the period, including Henry Laurens of South Carolina, embraced this mentality as well. For Laurens particularly, this mindset was exemplary of an ambiguity of eighteenth-century slavery: slaves merited humane treatment but were not to be fully trusted.[22]

A shift in moral consciousness in the eighteenth century made it increasingly difficult to accommodate either humanitarianism or Christianity into master-slave relationships or to the political, legal, and theological mechanisms that were used to justify the buying, selling, and owning of slaves.[23] Whitefield died before the humanist element of this shift began in earnest. Even so, his switch to a defense of slavery can still be understood as his own process of accommodation to slavery.[24] He believed that slaves were human but subordinate "Creatures."[25] This stance confirmed, or accommodated, slavery's Aristotelian philosophical roots: "From the hour of their birth, some men are marked out for subjection, others for rule."[26]

Whitefield's tendency toward paternalism predated his pro-slavery stance and was not exclusive to slaves. It factored into Whitefield's conscious efforts to project himself in Christ's image in his autobiography as part of his iconic image. Also paternalistic were his references to congregants as sheep, who "will not follow" strangers.[27] Playing on common biblical themes of Christ as the Shepherd and his followers as sheep, or lambs, the children of God. In Mark 6:34, Jesus is described as having compassion toward "sheep without a shepherd."[28] In Hebrews: 13:20, Jesus is described as "that great shepherd of the sheep."[29] Shepherds also frequently appear in the Bible as a positive moral influence. Abel, the good brother, was a shepherd, while his murderous brother, Cain, tilled the ground.[30] In several places in the Book of Genesis, Abel and Abraham, both loyal followers of God, herd sheep.[31]

In another example, in 1739 Whitefield intervened in the case of Joseph Periam, a young man who was hospitalized for being "methodically mad."[32] Periam's behaviors paralleled much of what Whitefield had experienced during his own awakening. Whitefield clearly saw Periam as a kindred spirit, persecuted for his beliefs. He intervened to convince the young man's parents and doctors to release him and took him under his spiritual care, eventually bringing him to the colonies.

A third example is Whitefield's purchase of a tract of five thousand acres of land in Pennsylvania, on the forks of the Delaware River, to build houses for some of the colony's growing population of free persons of African descent. Whitefield frequently sought to take care of those who, he felt, were incapable of providing for themselves.

Paternalism toward a congregation or audience by a preacher is hardly unique to Whitefield, the British American colonies, or even to the eighteenth century. In many ways, a preacher's relationship to his flock was necessarily paternal. Aside from embracing slavery as a key to Georgia's economic success, he also modeled the benign, humane master, asserting his own humane treatment of his prospective slaves as well as his ability to look after their spiritual well-being.

Whitefield's experiences in Georgia and Carolina were central to his embrace of slavery. Carolina was first established as an English colony by a proprietary government, which imagined the colony as a commercial endeavor.[33] The first permanent settlers were largely planters from Barbados, who brought their slaves with them. White European indentured servants were also part of the colony's early labor force.[34] Even before the colony was settled in 1670, the proprietors and white Barbadian planters with interests in Carolina saw the importation of African slaves as an economic necessity. On September 29, 1666, John Yeamans Jr., the third governor of Carolina and a Barbadian planter, wrote that "these Setlements have beene made and upheld by Negroes and without constant supplies of them cannot subsist."[35] Carolina's Fundamental Constitutions of 1669 outlined the social and political hierarchy of the colony and confirmed the legality of slavery.[36] It granted religious toleration to slaves but made clear that Christian conversion would not lead to manumission. The latter provision aided Whitefield in his missionary efforts by reducing planter opposition to those efforts.

Charles Town became the largest port of entry for slaves in British North America as well as the funnel for news from England into the rest of the colony.[37] Charles Town's population in 1720 comprised 1,390 black slaves and 1,415 whites. By that time, direct imports from Africa were increasing. Twelve percent of the low country black population lived in town.[38] The Stono Rebellion of 1739 was blamed on the "barbarous and savage disposition of recent African imports," and an act was passed in 1740 to reduce the number of slaves imported into the colony to "better insure the safety of the colony's white inhabitants."[39] This led to a temporary slowing of the importation of slaves.

That Province, Under God, Will Flourish

By the time Whitefield arrived in South Carolina, the colony had transitioned from proprietary to royal government. The Carolina backcountry remained a desolate place, but South Carolina was among the wealthiest settlements in the British North American colonies.[40] In the 1730s, an increase in cash crops like indigo, rice, and sugar, as well as timber and fur, led to growing refinement.[41] South Carolina was "one of the fastest-growing regional economies in British North America."[42] Perhaps no one exemplified this more than John Guerard, an eminent planter, merchant, and slave trader of French Huguenot descent whose holdings at the time of his death included several Charles Town properties and sixteen thousand rural acres.[43] He was also the patriarch of the family into which South Carolina commissary Alexander Garden married.

Whitefield was disturbed by what he saw as gratuitous displays of wealth by the planters. He was also troubled by the way the planters treated their slaves. In an open letter to the planters of South Carolina, Virginia, and Maryland, published in 1740, Whitefield castigated the planters for their treatment of their slaves: "I think God has a Quarrel with you for your Abuse of and Cruelty to the poor Negroes," he wrote.[44] He also wondered at the "Numbers have been given up to the inhumane Usage of cruel Task-Masters, who by their unrelenting Scourges have ploughed upon their Backs, and made long Furrows, and at length bro-t them even to Death itself."[45] While Whitefield saw the treatment and abuse of slaves as horrific, he was even more concerned with the failure of many planters to properly catechize and convert their slaves.[46] When Whitefield later came to embrace and defend slavery, these early critiques of slave masters and of the failure of SPG clergy to catechize slaves came back to haunt him and frustrated his desires to be accepted as a member of clergy of the Church of England.

In a sharp contrast to its northern neighbor, Georgia initially prohibited African slavery. Prior to the settlement, the enslavement of Native Americans of one group by another Native group—including Upper and Lower Creek, Choctaw, Yamasee, Chickasaw, and Choctaw—was a regular occurrence. The Creeks, who were well supplied with English weapons and resented the Spanish-backed Apalachees' trade demands, were particularly active in raids that frequently produced slaves. The Upper Creek also raided against the Choctaws' settlements, resulting in the regular appearance of Choctaws on the auction blocks of the Charles Town slave market.[47]

The prohibition on African slaves was not due to an opposition to slave owning. Rather, Oglethorpe and Georgia's trustees firmly believed that forbidding slavery would foster a good work ethic among the poorest colonists, who came to the colony as charity cases.[48] Its trustees saw the inclusion of slaves in the colony's population as a potential danger to both Georgia and South Carolina. This fear gained more ground in 1738, when the governor of Spanish Florida issued an edict that guaranteed freedom to English slaves who escaped to St. Augustine and accepted Catholicism.[49] The Stono Rebellion, twenty miles from Charles Town in 1739, further reinforced British fears about Spanish militancy inciting disorder among the slaves. British settlers throughout the colonies blamed the rebellion on Spanish instigators.

By the time of Whitefield's arrival thirty-two years later, aboriginal slavery was discouraged as undermining trade relations with local bands and inviting raids on settlements.[50] The raids that procured Native American slaves (typically women and children) frequently resulted in retaliatory attacks. Resentment on the part of the Yamasees at having their populations so depleted by raids, along with other resentments over trade practices, led to the outbreak of the Yamasee War in 1715. Spurred on by the French, the Lower Creek, who also harbored resentment at English trading practices, joined the Yamasee against the British. Within a year, the Creek and English concluded that it was in their mutual best interests to conclude their fighting, and a peace was negotiated late in 1717. The end of the war reopened Carolina-Creek trade but also spelled the official end of the Native American slave trade.

Even while African slavery was officially prohibited in Georgia, African slaves were used on occasion for specific projects. Early in the colony's founding, Benjamin Martyn, the secretary of the trustees, wrote to Governor Robert Johnson of South Carolina, requesting to borrow twenty "Negro Labourers" to help clear the new settlement.[51] Occasions like these, where slaves were brought in on a temporary basis from South Carolina, came prior to the arrival of any significant, viable European workforce. Because there was no significant settlement as yet, because only small numbers of slaves were used on a temporary basis, and because this activity primarily occurred years before the Stono Rebellion or the governor of Florida's 1738 edict guaranteeing freedom to English slaves, the risk of slaves escaping to Florida was considered minimal.[52]

Whitefield was certainly not the first to broach the subject of legalizing African slavery in Georgia. Georgia remained a poor colony struggling to thrive, its settlers frustrated by sandy and barren soil, an unfavorable climate, and an insufficient workforce.[53] Early in the colony's founding, several settlers wrote to its trustees to demand that slavery be legalized but were rebuffed by the trustees. On one occasion, Georgia's trustees noted their preference for German servants rather than African slaves. Trustee Benjamin Martyn characterized Germans as "a sober, strong, laborious People," with the implication that African slaves were not.[54] Martyn also noted fiscal advantages to using European servants instead of slaves. It cost "at least £20 sterling" for "the worst Negro labouring Man," and "£5 pays the passage of a White Man."[55] That was a better investment in the long run, because one who had the "wherewithal to pay the passage of White Men" could hire more indentured servants than he could purchase slaves.[56] Finally, Martyn suggested that, because they had the prospects of becoming free and contributing members of society once their period of indenture ended, German servants were more virtuous than slaves.[57]

The recipient of this letter was Samuel Eveleigh of Charles Town, another critic of the trustees' decision to bar slavery in Georgia. Eveleigh's argument echoed a common one from advocates of slavery: that the population of white laborers was insufficient to tend to crops, and that whites were ill suited to handle the summer heat. Slaves, he argued, were much more suited to the climate, which was similar to that he had experienced in Jamaica, where slaves tended to the crops.[58] Like many other proslavery settlers, Eveleigh saw white indentured servants as too small in number and, in many cases, too physically weak to handle the demands of clearing wilderness or cultivating crops in Georgia, an argument that Whitefield identified with.[59]

Despite these protests, James Oglethorpe and the trustees clung firmly to their belief that slavery was unnecessary, if not detrimental, to the colony's development. Oglethorpe characterized the setters' clamors to legalize slavery as "petulancy" and lobbied the settlement to support the law barring slavery. In the spring of 1733, he wrote to the trustees that his campaign to persuade settlers to give up their desire for slaves was successful. He characterized the complaints about the barring of slaves and rum as characteristic of people "impatient of Labour and Discipline."[60] His confidence that he had turned around public opinion, however, was premature, and the demands for slaves continued.

In response to the increasing clamors from the colonists and, in some cases, the outright defiance of the law, the trustees became even more assertive about barring slavery as a permanent settlement formed. In September 1735, the Common Council of the trustees ordered the constables of the Town of Savannah to seize of "all and every Black or Negro which shall at any time be found in said Province of Georgia." The Order emphasized that settlers were required to cooperate with the constables, and any violation of the law would cause the offender to "answer the contrary at their Perils."[61] The order did not mention free blacks, implying that any black found in the Province was presumed an illicit slave.

The legalization of slavery came only as Georgia turned from under the stewardship of trustees to a royal colony, in 1752, in no small part due to Whitefield's involvement. His experiences in Georgia and his exposure to its many challenges played an important role in his decision to defend slavery, though it was a decision that had fermented for several years. The first evidence of Whitefield's wavering views came in December 1737, even before he arrived in the colonies. Whitefield saw Georgia's prohibition of slaves as well intended but impossible to enforce. He also believed that the restrictions hampered Georgia economically, yet he still had reservations about the slave trade and the way slaves were treated. His views were in line with those of his friend, James Habersham, who had shared Whitefield's reservations about the lawfulness of slavery prior to his arrival in Georgia.[62]

In 1743 an anonymous slavery-apologist pamphlet appeared. It addressed recently Christianized slaves, a topic central to the discourse on religion and race in the Early Modern British Atlantic.[63] The pamphlet has been attributed to Whitefield.[64] In it, Whitefield praised the fact that converted slaves became "Fellow-Citizens with the Saints, and of the Household of God."[65] Whitefield had long supported the conversion of slaves, believing in equality before God, even if not in political or legal equality for slaves. That he championed the notion of an equal relationship with God is entirely consistent with his previous writings.

Whitefield also reinforced the notion that slaves should be obedient to their masters: "Oh, watch against Disobedience, against Sin, that abominable thing which God hates."[66] He continued, "Sin will dishonour God, and provoke his fatherly Anger."[67] He encouraged slaves to be "good Soldiers of Jesus Christ" and to "live soberly, righteously, and godly in this present World."[68] In essence, a slave who accepted his condition without complaint during his life could expect to be rewarded after death. Whitefield also appealed to the slaves to help disprove the still-common fear among planters that conversion would spoil the slaves:

> The Love of Christ will make it so easy, that it will not hurt your necks; and by your cheerful and constant obedience, put to Silence the Ignorance of foolish Men, of your nominal Christian Masters ... That if you, their poor Slaves, were brought to Christianity, you would be no more servants to them.[69]

These instructions to slaves supported both his paternalistic attitude toward them and his promotion of Protestant Christianity as a means of social control. Calling into question their "nominal" Christianity also illustrated his contemptuous attitude toward planters who rejected religious instruction for their slaves, a group that included South Carolina commissary Garden and many members of elite southern planter society. In his 1740 *Letter to the Inhabitants of Maryland, Virginia, North and South Carolina*, his language was similar.[70] He wrote, "Blacks are just as much, and no more, conceived and born into Sin, as White men are. Both, if born and bred up here, I am persuaded, are naturally capable of the same Improvement."[71] "Most of you are without any teaching Priests," he continued, "And whatever Quantity of Rum there may be, yet I fear but very few Bibles are annually imported into your different Provinces. — God has already begun to visit for this as well as other wicket Things."⁷² Whitefield blamed recent disasters, such as the Stono Rebellion, on the planters' refusal to permit the conversion of their slaves to Christianity and to their mistreatment of slaves. Whitefield's choice of words concerning "blacks" who were "born and bred up here" denotes a qualification that instruction was more suited to slaves born in the Americas than to those newly transported from Africa.⁷³ Nonetheless, in writing of the existence of rum in inverse proportion to importations of Bibles, he challenged the Christianity of these plantation masters, in contrast with himself. This passage also spoke to his attitude toward commerce, wherein commerce most rightfully existed within a religious paradigm, as modeled by his own use of branding and commerce to propagate revivalism.⁷⁴

This pamphlet is one of numerous examples where Whitefield advocated obedience and loyalty of slaves toward their masters even as he struggled with the legality of the institution. In one instance, he sent a slave woman, who appealed to accompany him on his missionary exploits, back to her master.⁷⁵ This marked a departure from Joseph Periam's case, when Whitefield supported his request to be freed from committal by his parents to follow Whitefield to the New World.

Whitefield remained consistent in his views that slaves were not equals, even if he recognized their humanity and was convinced that they possessed immortal souls and believed them capable of receiving religious instruction. His beliefs were in line with evangelical Methodists, who believed that slaves had the capacity for salvation.⁷⁶ The idea of spiritual freedom in the afterlife was solace for those for whom physical freedom was impossible.⁷⁷

Whitefield, in short, was most definitely a believer in deference to the social and political hierarchy of the colony when it came to the slaves.⁷⁸ Slaves out from the immediate control of masters made Whitefield anxious. An incident that occurred during his travels in the colonies, not long after the Stono Rebellion, serves as a clear example. As Whitefield's party traveled southward through Carolina, toward Georgia, it encountered a hut with some slaves. When the slaves were unable to tell Whitefield's two traveling companions anything about the gentleman's house to which they were headed, his friend "inferr'd, that these Negroes might be some of those who lately had made an Insurrection in the Providence, and were run away from their Masters."[79] Whitefield continued that when his friend "return'd we were all of his Mind and therefore thought it best to mend our Pace."[80] The travelers encountered another large fire and observed some slaves "dancing around the fire" under the moon.[81] Frightened, they took great pains to go around these encampments, expecting that they were "in great Perils of (their) lives" at every turn.[82] Finally, they reached a plantation, where they took "great comfort" in learning from its master, who told them to whom the slaves belonged and what they were celebrating out along the road.[83]

Whitefield was not immune from the fears about slave conspiracies held by many colonists. Within the safe confines of the dress balls of Charles Town, or when paid as entertainment for their white masters, dancing and music among slaves was welcome.[84] Outside of these controlled circumstances, it was another story. The fear evident in his depiction of slaves dancing around a fire, away from immediate supervision of their master, helps to illustrate the convoluted nature of his views on race.[85] These slaves appeared to Whitefield and his party to be out from under the control of their master just after a major slave rebellion, when the black population of South Carolina was growing more rapidly than the white.[86] Fears of revolts were intensified by the edict of the royal governor of Spanish Florida guaranteeing freedom to English slaves who escaped to St. Augustine.[87] South Carolina trader Robert Pringle wrote to a business associate, "I hope our Government will order Effectual methods for the taking of St. Augustine from the Spaniards which is now become a great Detriment to this Province by the Encouragement & Protection given by them to our Negroes that Run away there."[88] Johann Martin Boltzius reported in late September that "the Negroes or Moorish slaves are not yet pacified but are roaming around in gangs in the Carolina forests."[89]

The civil authorities in many colonies, including those in the Carolinas, responded by enacting legislation designed to better regulate, or "order," slaves. South Carolina's Slave Code of 1740 reinforced the rights of owners over their slaves, and it clearly laid the burden of proof on the plaintiff in cases where slaves attempted to use the courts to challenge their enslaved status. It also established stiff penalties for harboring or enabling runaways.[90]

The dance Whitefield and his companions observed might have been only social in nature, but the image of slaves dancing around a fire under the moon also suggests African or syncretic religious practices or rituals. Without knowing where these slaves came from, it is not possible to identify precisely the rituals the slaves may have been enacting.[91] Since many slaves in the Carolinas were imported from the British West Indies, it is possible that Whitefield witnessed an Obeah ritual. In any case, given Whitefield's preoccupation with the propagation of Christianity and his fearfulness, he and his companions clearly interpreted the dance they observed as denoting something more sinister than social.

Whitefield's racial attitudes, as well as his motivations for converting slaves, were similar to those of other members of the clergy, even if he was more enthusiastic than some about converting slaves. For many devout British colonists in this period, Christianity was a civilizing influence for slaves.[92] Slaves who practiced traditional religious rituals were seen as undermining not only civil control, but also an important form of nonsecular control. One of Whitefield's justifications for owning slaves was to catechize them, bringing them under his legal, social, and moral control. This encounter, then, serves as another example of how Whitefield's paternalistic attitude pre-dated his proslavery writings. The ideological underpinnings for his change of heart were there, even if that change did not come for another eight years.

In becoming directly involved with the campaign to legalize slavery in Georgia, Whitefield followed precedent set by previous Anglican missionaries. His first clear involvement in the campaign to legalize slavery in Georgia came in a letter to a friend on October 25, 1747. He related that "all is well there, and at my new plantation," writing his letter from a South Carolina property that he had acquired in that colony in 1746.[93] Though a critic of southern plantation owners, he himself had become one, even if he was never really accepted into their ranks. It is, therefore, not surprising that he also soon joined the clamor for slaves.

Whitefield's appeal to the trustees of Georgia in London and his support for the legalization of slavery echoed the appeals Anglican missionaries in the colonies had made in the 1720s, when the controversy over baptism was hampering their efforts. The Yorke-Talbot Opinion, written in 1729 by then-Attorney General Sir Philip Yorke and then-Solicitor General Charles Talbot, largely settled the matter. Yorke and Talbot asserted that "baptism doth not bestow freedom" upon slaves.[94] While the Yorke-Talbot Opinion was merely an advisory opinion, rather than an act of law, Whitefield too sought a change in policy that would prove beneficial to both his spiritual mission and his economic goals for Georgia.

By 1747 Whitefield had consistently tied Georgia's low economic state to the lack of slaves. He wrote later that year to an acquaintance in Charles Town that "it is true the constitution of that colony [Georgia] is very bad, and it is impossible for the inhabitants to subsist themselves without the use of slaves."[95] At about the same time, he publicly joined the campaign to legalize slavery in Georgia, writing to the trustees and other influential figures.

A letter to the trustees on December 6, 1748, laid out his arguments. He claimed that he wrote, not out of his own self-interest, but out of concern about the state of the colony. "I need not inform you, honoured gentlemen, how the colony of Georgia has been declining for these many years last past, and at what great disadvantages I have maintained a large family in that wilderness," he wrote.[96] He echoed the comments of Thomas Stephens on socioeconomic conditions in the colony: "Upwards of five thousand pounds have been expended . . . yet, very little proficiency made in the cultivation of my tract of land, and that entirely owing the necessity I lay under of making use of white hands."[97] He went on to discuss how "these considerations" led him, two years prior, "to purchase a plantation in South-Carolina, where negroes are allowed."[98] Whitefield marveled at the productivity of that plantation in comparison to his ventures in Georgia, informing the trustees that his experience "confirms me in the opinion . . . that Georgia never can or will be a flourishing province without negroes."[99] While promising the trustees that he would not bring any of his slaves into the colony illegally, he also made it quite clear that he would continue to campaign to legalize slavery. "I am as willing as ever to do all I can for Georgia and the Orphan-house, if either a limited use of negroes is approved of, or some more indented servants sent over," he informed them.[100] He concluded by prophesying a failure of his ventures in Georgia without the use of slaves. Given his plantation in South Carolina and the fact that settlers had, for years, been abandoning Georgia for its wealthier neighbor, this comment served as a veiled threat that Whitefield, too, might depart if he did not get his way.

He regularly reported his progress to various acquaintances and allies. In 1748 he wrote to his patron, the Countess of Huntingdon, reporting that the campaign seemed to at last be having some impact. He told her "news also was brought me last night, that the negroes are allowed by the trustees for Georgia. If so, that province, under God, will flourish. Blessed be god, I am more hearty than I have been for a long season."[101] Whitefield saw the legalization of slavery as part personal victory and part divine will.[102] It was God's will for Georgia to prosper. As well, it seemed apparent that God also approved slavery. For most of his adult life, Whitefield interpreted events that were favorable to him as occurring by divine will.

When slavery did come to Georgia in 1751, the trustees determined that they were satisfied that slavery was "consistent with the 'safety' of Georgia," and that slavery would "conduce to the [colony's] Prosperity."[103] The legalization of slavery came with some stipulations, although these were not inconsistent with those proposed by Georgians.[104] These included an imposed maximum ratio between "adult male slaves and white men between sixteen and sixty-five of four to one" and a stipulation that the majority of slaves be restricted to plantation work outside the city limits of Savannah.[105] Even with the incorporation of a census mechanism into the trustees' slave code, enforcement was no simple matter.[106] Of particular significance to Whitefield, the trustees' slave code forbade blacks from working on Sundays and required their owners to provide religious instruction. The Code emphasized the responsibility of planters to catechize their slaves, which was fully consistent with Whitefield's vision of the benevolent Christian master.[107]

Whitefield was elated, though his previous comments, critical of slavery, came back to haunt him. He sought to reconcile his newfound embrace of slavery with the moral ambiguities regarding

Christianity and slavery. In 1751 he still disagreed with the manner in which slaves were brought from Africa, but his experiences in the colonies had eroded his reservations toward slavery. Responding to Mr. B. Bristol, an acquaintance in London, he wrote, "Had Mr. Henry been in America, I believe he would have seen the lawfulness and necessity of having negroes" in America.[108] His assertions in 1751 that he "had no doubt of the lawfulness of slavery" marked a distinct change from his position eleven years earlier, where he wrote "whether it be lawful for christians to buy slaves, and thereby encourage the nations from whence they are brought to be at perpetual war with each other, I shall not take upon me to determine."[109]

Another letter from 1751 suggested that he believed he might curry God's favor by "purchasing slaves, making them comfortable and raising a foundation for breeding up their posterity in the nurture and admonition of the Lord."[110] Thus, he positioned himself as a paternal guardian of their spiritual welfare. For his part, Alexander Garden saw Whitefield, with his power over his public, as undermining social order. During their contentious exchange in 1740, Garden compared Whitefield to religious sects considered dangerous threats to order.[111] For Garden, Whitefield's embrace of slavery and his role in the campaign to legalize slavery in Georgia might expand his influence further still, and in a way that might encourage slaves' disobedience toward their masters.

Whitefield's advocacy of slavery was, of course self-interested, something not lost on his critics. Slaves worked in several of Whitefield's ventures, including improvements on the land where he built Bethesda Orphan House. Since Whitefield saw Bethesda as a charitable operation, he would have indignantly rejected any suggestion that he stood to benefit economically from slavery. Nonetheless, his frequent criticisms of material excess as a distraction from true religion made him the target of criticisms for holding slaves.[112] Whitefield once asked, "Is it not the highest ingratitude, as well as cruelty, not to let your poor slaves enjoy some fruits of their labour? When passing along . . . I have viewed your plantations cleared and cultivated, many spacious houses built, and the owners of them faring sumptuously."[113] These words were flung back at him as he began to utilize slaves in his own endeavors. As historian

Fred Witzig demonstrates, Whitefield's critics, and Commissary Alexander Garden particularly, challenged the spiritual and economic integrity of Bethesda and scorned the idea that Whitefield did not benefit economically from the project.[114] One anonymous critic made this observation in the *South Carolina Gazette*: "Did not [Whitefield] appear as much like a Prigg as a Parson as any ever did," wearing "the best Purnelle and finest Hollands with Wiggs [Whigs] of Five Guineas a Piece?"[115] Whitefield responded to these criticisms with an aggressive public relations campaign throughout the British colonial newspaper and magazine networks.[116] The publishing of Bethesda Orphan House's account books in various colonial newspapers comprised one of Whitefield's responses, to refute claims that he was being hypocritical in his reproaches of the lavish lifestyles of southern planters.[117] Similarly, in 1741 Whitefield placed a chronicle of the children's daily lives at the Orphan House in Philadelphia's *General Magazine*. Not surprisingly, this overview of daily life put heavy emphasis on frequent church attendance and religious instruction by Whitefield.

Whitefield's purpose in placing a public schedule in a well-read publication was threefold. The public airing of his activities was calculated, first, to combat any sense that he was profiting from the families that he took in. Here, he was working to protect the public image he had built of himself as a humble figure, opposed to material excesses.[118] Second, the schedule served to demonstrate Whitefield's personal investment in and involvement in Georgia. One of the tactics his critics took was to paint him as an outsider, which in many senses he was. A positive demonstration of his involvement was crucial if he wanted to appear part of the community, rather than as an outsider who occasionally visited. Third, Whitefield obviously hoped to impress the public with the Orphan House's religious mission. In essence, he was trying to counter antirevivalist critics like Commissary Garden and to paint himself as a pious and charitable figure.[119]

Ultimately, Whitefield's public relations campaigns, both to make public his Orphan House activities and, more generally, to paint himself as a respectable member of the community, failed. Overall, if Whitefield's defense of slavery appeared to bring him into line with the Anglican Church, it was wholly insufficient to overcome his lengthy record of castigating polite Anglican society and policy in the colonies.[120] It also could not make up for his frequent criticisms of the Church of England for its failure to convert slaves in the southern colonies.

There is no evidence that Whitefield consciously thought that his proslavery campaign would help him recapture his Anglican identity within the Anglican Church. By this time, his public image had evolved so far past its Anglican roots that an act so completely in line with colonial Anglican culture became, rather, a source of skepticism and derision for his detractors. The political damage from Whitefield's earlier scathing criticisms of slaveholders, along with his criticisms of Anglican clergymen for not doing enough to convert slaves, was insurmountable. Instead, Alexander Garden and his group of transatlantic Anglicans tried to counter Whitefield's influence, in part by setting up a Charles Town school designed to catechize slaves, which was overseen by Garden and funded by the SPG.[121] It was the Anglican counterpart to Whitefield's revivalist Bethesda Orphan House.

As a highly visible icon of revivalism, Whitefield was, in some ways, a convenient target for Anglicans who saw revivalism as a danger and hoped to establish Anglicanism as the true religion. Garden's school was one of a number of efforts undertaken by the transatlantic Anglican Church to counter revivalism, and particularly the influence of Whitefield and his fellow revivalists among the enslaved.[122] Revivalism had a remarkable impact in the conversion of African slaves to Christianity.[123] It provided the means for a reconfiguration of their (religious) cultural heritages.[124] Many times these expressions of faith were held in secret.[125] Whitefield's follower Hugh Bryan and his brother Jonathan were among the evangelicals—at Whitefield's urging—who held gatherings to provide religious instruction not only to their own slaves, but also to those from other plantations. These assemblies resulted in a 1742 indictment against the brothers for "Pretence of religious Worship" and "enthusiastick Prophecies."[126] As many masters feared, evangelical Protestantism's ideas of spiritual equality and universal fellowship undermined the master-slave relationship and suggested that equality might exist on other planes.[127] The more mobility a slave had, the less likely he or she was to convert.[128] In other acts of "defiance," some newly converted slave women invoked religion against rape.[129] Ultimately, in any case, both the Anglican "ethnic theological exegesis" and Whitefield's ultimately provided intellectual support to slavery.[130]

The complex and convoluted nature of Whitefield's attitudes toward slavery meant that after his death, both proslavery and antislavery evangelical Christians would come to invoke Whitefield's memory as they continued to debate slavery's compatibility with professed Christianity. Some of Whitefield's closest friends—including James Habersham and Selina, Countess of Huntingdon—continued to embrace slavery on the same grounds as Whitefield had. Other white evangelicals, including his mentor, John Wesley, Granville Sharpe, and Anthony Benezet roundly rejected it as immoral. After Whitefield's death, Benezet even attempted to use Whitefield's one-time criticisms of southern planters to persuade the Countess of Huntingdon, in her role as Whitefield's executrix, to support an end to slavery.

As many white planters feared, a number of black evangelicals who converted to Christianity under Whitefield's influence did come to note the incompatibilities between "freedom in the eyes of God" and slavery. Beginning in the early 1770s, Phillis Wheatley, Olaudah Equiano, John Marrant, and other black evangelicals published influential antislavery literature that celebrated their religious conversions, invoking Whitefield specifically.[131] These writings also refuted claims made by Immanuel Kant, David Hume, and others in their attempts to define blackness, that those of African heritage were incapable of creativity or intellectual depth.[132] And ultimately, together with Whitefield's criticisms of southern planters, these writings also served as a means to invoke his memory in challenging slavery.

CHAPTER FOUR

In the Footsteps of the Pilgrims

*W*hitefield's first visit to New England occurred during his third missionary tour, in 1740. Most of his visits to the region took place during a period when New England's religious culture was deeply divided.[1] It is, therefore, hardly surprising that the fiery and emotional sermons from revivalist preachers met with mixed reception from New England clergy. Much about revivalism undermined the established character of New England, and Whitefield was, in many ways, a lightning rod for those concerned with revivalism's impact on New England religious life.[2] This trip was the first of several visits that Whitefield would make to New England, each of which disrupted the fragile consensus in the highly fragmented regional religious landscape.

Whitefield visited each of the New England colonies, but most of his time in New England was spent in Massachusetts, with a few days here and there spent in the region's other colonies. He was quite keen to see the home of the Puritan forefathers and particularly excited to travel to Boston, even if Puritanism had lost its grip on New England by then. Ultimately, Whitefield was entombed in Massachusetts. Therefore, Whitefield's activities there will be the primary geographic focus of this chapter.

New England's settlers were a people with definitive (if not unified) ideas about religion. They were particularly concerned with anything that smacked of "popery."[3] The religious topography of New England included Christians of various denominations, including French Catholics, Dutch Reformed, Quakers, Anglicans, and Congregationalists, but Congregationalism dominated.[4]

In 1740 New England was still largely composed of dissenters, although the Church of England had made inroads into the region. And while the churches were frequently still the center of many New England communities, the theological focus of a number of the more influential clergy underwent a change, beginning early in the eighteenth century. Eminent Boston Congregationalist preacher Cotton Mather set the "precedent for new understandings of providence."[5] His writing marked a departure from Puritan writers like his father, Increase, in that he "de-emphasized extraordinary events."[6] Instead, Mather's fascination with Isaac Newton, Dutch mathematician Christiaan Huygens, and Dutch scientist Antonie van Leeuwenhoek led him to focus on "natural wonders" rather than the supernatural.[7] During New England's smallpox outbreak in the early 1720s, this interest in science and "natural wonders" also led him to support the inoculation of New Englanders.[8] Benjamin Colman's writings similarly emphasized natural laws as explanations for events like earthquakes and comets.[9] Revivalism's emotional preaching and rabid emphasis on the threat of sin and hell were very much the antithesis of this new natural religion of post-Puritan New England and its rational, educated, and well-read clergy.[10]

Many of the prominent and influential clergy in this period, including Nathaniel and Cotton Mather, were the Harvard-educated scions of illustrious ministerial families.[11] This "third generation" of clergy, and New England in general, was increasingly more connected to a growing, commercialized Anglo-American world than its seventeenth-century counterparts had been. Nonetheless, their position in New England society and their relationships with their congregants remained largely unchanged. In spite of New England's growing, more Atlantic tenor, its clergy expected more deference than elsewhere in the British Atlantic.[12] After Whitefield visited, challenges to the authority of the clergy were frequently blamed on his influence.

Whitefield's brash, outspoken style of engagement, as well as his fiery extemporaneous manner of preaching, were in many ways the antithesis of John Cotton's *New England Way*, wherein he had once called Arminianism and Enthusiasm (of which Whitefield was commonly accused) "grosse and damnable," arguing that "the countenance God is upon his people when they feare him, not when they presume of their owne strength."[13] New England had long experienced sometimes intense, but manageable, civil and religious conflicts. George Whitefield was a catalyst that ultimately destabilized New England's already fragile and fractious religious landscape.[14]

Even after Puritanism declined, New England was so much identified with its Puritan roots that revivalists who wrote about New England life in the eighteenth century and into the nineteenth tended to discuss the region's religious identity in idealistic terms. "What did our fathers come into this wilderness for?," asked nineteenth-century revivalist Joseph Belcher.[15] "Not to gain estates as men do now, but for religion, and that they might have their children in a hopeful way of being truly religious," he continued.[16] Belcher referred to a sense of religious decay that was felt by ministers across the denominations in colonial British America.[17] The decline of the authority of the clergy, and particularly of Congregationalism, was part of this transition.[18] The new experimental forms of religion spoke to the spirit of individualism that was a common thread among all the facets of the transition from Puritan to Yankee.[19]

As Puritans became Yankees, individuals (especially men) were more willing to oppose the old clerical order.[20] This social shift had social, economic, and religious ramifications. There were greater economic and trade opportunities.[21] In short, New England became a more open society, where the needs of the individual prevailed over those of the community.[22] These changes eroded the Puritan emphasis on authority, including responsiveness to the Puritan church. The reduction of the community's hold on the individual created an ideal climate for cultivating revivalism, with its emphasis on individuals rather than the good of the community as a whole.

Even before the start of the eighteenth century, Puritanism had started to lose its grip on New England, due to growing wealth and an increased emphasis on self and also in part due to the introduction of competing churches. In the first decades of the eighteenth century, the Church of England tried to make inroads into the region but faced considerable resistance from local dissenting clergy. Timothy Cutler, a Boston-born Anglican minister, who was also rector of Yale College, repeatedly wrote to the bishop of London, complaining of resistance from local authorities. On February 4, 1730, he wrote to report fears about what Jonathan Belcher's appointment as governor of Massachusetts would mean for the Church of England. Belcher was a staunch dissenter who reportedly refused to allow his daughter to marry a young suitor unless he renounced the established church.[23]

Revivalism was yet another factor in the dismantling of Puritanism. It was a renewed popular form of piety that retained vestiges of Puritan culture but was no longer under the Puritan canopy.[24] It replaced the Puritans' old Augustinian strain of piety in favor of a more popular, eighteenth-century form that was less scholastic.[25] It ran counter to the reasoned, natural religion preached by prominent and erudite New England clergymen like Cotton Mather and Benjamin Colman.[26] Revivalism's tendency to emphasize the conversion experience as important above all else for the effectiveness of a minister was among the many aspects of the Great Awakening that chaffed at the schooled members of the old New England religious order.

Jonathan Edwards was one of the most important revivalist figures to help undermine Puritanism. Even before Whitefield's arrival, Edwards challenged such ideas as covenant privileges as well as the whole notion of New England as a covenanted people.[27] Edwards remained Puritan in the sense that he believed in the interconnectedness of God, self, church, and society.[28] Even so, invoking the language of dissent, Edwards's critics accused him of collusion with the Church of England to undermine the civil and religious liberties of New England.[29]

In many ways, revivalism was more threatening to those who desired to preserve the old religious order in New England than the incursion of the Church of England.[30] Revivalism's popularity meant that revivalist churches, which were also dissenting, rather than establishment, had a far greater chance of success in New England than the Church of England. This meant that Whitefield faced a double-edged sword. On the one hand, he might face hostility as an Anglican clergyman, even if perceptions of him as an Anglican were greatly diminished by the time he first visited New

England. On the other hand, he also carried the taint of revivalism, which made him unpalatable to a number of dissenter clergy. Most of his critics from among the New England clergy responded to his revivalism rather than his status as an ordained Anglican minister.

The decision to invite Whitefield to New England was a difficult one for its clergy. A number of clergymen disliked the emphasis on the New Birth by Whitefield, Edwards, and other revivalists. They also feared enthusiasm as well as the tendency of revivalists to blame the ministers themselves for spiritual apathy.[31] And ultimately, the revivalists' insistence, and Whitefield's particularly, on the necessity that ministers be converted had the potential to undermine the credibility of ministers with their congregants and even challenge their legitimacy as Christians.

While some of the clergy welcomed the renewed interest revivalism brought to religious life, the potential repercussions of revivalism for New England clergy made it a complex and tremendously divisive issue. This was despite the revivalist tendency to idealize the Puritan past. Some New England ministers recognized revivalists like Whitefield as kindred spirits, in that they shared with him their historic goals for religious toleration. Jonathan Edwards, for instance, saw Whitefield as a symbol of hope, an Anglican minister with whom those of dissenting Protestant sects could work toward a common goal of religious toleration.[32] This hope speaks to the idea of Whitefield both as an icon of revivalism and his being seen as a "shadow of good things to come."[33]

Some New England clergy took a pragmatic view of revivalists like Whitefield, even if they did not always agree with Whitefield's doctrinal interpretations. They recognized that his flamboyant style helped to renew interest in a spiritual life, as many denominations faced challenges raised by a growing refinement in material life as well as the rationality of the Enlightenment.[34] Although in a more limited sense than in Jonathan Edwards's view, Whitefield remained a potential symbol of hope for a renewal of providential life.[35] Among these ministers taking a pragmatic attitude toward Whitefield was Benjamin Colman, minister of the Brattle Street Church in Boston. Colman advocated a separation between Anglicans and Congregationalists, but nonetheless "maintained a sympathetic and mutually supportive relationship with the Church of

England."³⁶ An Anglican revivalist like Whitefield, therefore, would have had a particular appeal to him.

Colman corresponded with a number of revivalists, including Jonathan Edwards. In responding to a letter from Colman, Edwards referred to the mutual concern the two ministers had about the state of religion in New England. He wrote that he had a "particular concern at Deerfield," more than at Northampton, and that "something of it seems to be beginning in some other of the neighboring towns."³⁷ Edwards did not elaborate more specifically about what this concern was, but the letter's overall tenor suggests that he was especially concerned with the decline of religious life in Connecticut and that the two clergymen had discussed places where they had seen evidence of religious apathy. Whether the letters were between Colman and Edwards or Colman and Whitefield, or others, they also demonstrate that in spite of doctrinal differences and the "cautious optimism" that frequently characterized the attitude of the more convivial nonrevivalist dissenting ministers toward revivalists, there was clearly a dialogue between the two camps about the state of religion in the region.

As a fellow Protestant, Whitefield was, for some dissenter clergymen like Colman, a counterpoint to "Popish Darkness, Superstition and Idolatry."³⁸ Colman, in fact, reinforced Whitefield's own view of himself as emulating the divine, once writing that "God would cause him always to triumph in Christ."³⁹ Whitefield was, in Colman's estimation, an "Instrument to bring back many wandering Sheep to the Shepherd and Bishop of their Souls."⁴⁰ The rise in church attendance that followed Whitefield's visits to the British American colonies supports Colman's theory that revivalism could help boost religion. In 1729, there were approximately thirty-five thousand Congregationalists and Presbyterians in the British American colonies. By 1745, seven years into Whitefield's missionary work, there were at least seventy-five thousand.⁴¹

Not all New England clergymen shared Colman's optimism that revivalism could reverse religious apathy. Some felt that revivalism was damaging to religious life and Christian unity. This was particularly true of the more authoritarian clergymen, who had little sympathy for anything that challenged their own theological beliefs and social authority. To these eighteenth-century

In the Footsteps of the Pilgrims

Parrawankaw [and] Dr. Squintum. [London: Publish'd by A. Hamilton Junr. Fleet Street, 1769] Library of Congress Prints and Photographs Division, Washington, D.C.

clergymen, revivalism was most certainly a threat to the foundation of Christian religion.

By the time of Whitefield's initial arrival in New England, religious heterogeneity was on the rise and the influence of local clergy over governors and legislatures had shrunk considerably.[42] Revivalism represented yet another force eroding the influence of traditional New England religious life. Whitefield arrived fifteen to twenty years after the start of an active press campaign on the part of New England clergy to counteract anticlericalism.[43] New England churches also turned to voluntary institutions for prayer and pious consultation.[44] The result was that, by the time of Whitefield's missionary tours in the Americas, many churches had to change if they wanted to compete for adherents.[45]

Authoritarian clergymen also took to heart a seventeenth-century New England mentality, once law, which required that the establishment, or gathering, of new churches required the consent of (and deference to) existing churches in the same county.[46] Each town or parish, by law of the General Court, was required to have an "able, learned, and orthodox minister."[47] Whitefield was certainly "learned," but many of his actions were inconsistent with this decree, and he was far from deferential to New England clergy with whom he disagreed. That Whitefield also stirred up passions among the populace and encouraged them to challenge their clergy, rather than deferring to their wisdom, was unacceptable to these clergymen. He was seen as a negative and corrupting influence with the potential to undermine their moral society.

As in other colonies, Whitefield and his fellow revivalists also reached out to slaves, free blacks, and other outsiders. Their controversial visits to Yale inspired David Brainerd and his brother, John, a pair of Presbyterian missionaries who ministered among Native Americans throughout the colonies. Though David Brainerd was gravely ill at the time Whitefield visited Connecticut in 1740, he wrote in his memoir that "my soul was refreshed and seemed knit to him."[48] His friend, Jonathan Edwards, who helped Brainerd write his memoir, attempted to edit this line out of the memoir. Edwards hoped to create an alliance that was calculated to quash the influence of Arminianism in New England.[49] Since Whitefield's visit to Yale stirred up considerable controversy, Edwards was afraid that Brainerd's expression of admiration for the Grand Itinerant, along with Brainerd's own reputation for zeal, might prove problematic for Edwards's plan to use Brainerd to help convince New Englanders to eschew Arminianism.[50]

Revivalism also inspired Connecticut-born Mohegan preacher, Samson Occom. Occom studied for his ministry at the Connecticut Indian Charity School of Yale-educated Eleazar Wheelock.[51] Wheelock, a Congregationalist and staunch supporter of the liberty of conscience, later founded Dartmouth College with the principle goal of educating Native Americans.[52] Along with fellow evangelist missionaries, the Reverends James Davenport, Jonathan Parsons, and Benjamin Pomeroy, Wheelock encouraged Whitefield to visit their Native American students when he came through Connecticut in 1745.[53] Whitefield's influence on Occom will be explored later in this chapter, but his catechism across racial lines and his conviction that all races had equal propensity for sin and salvation in the eyes of God left a mark on Occom's own ministry. Whitefield also supported Occom early in his career.

Whitefield was also influential among the slaves in New England.[54] He most famously influenced Phillis Wheatley, a prolific African American writer and early contributor to antislavery literature. Wheatley's mistress, Susanna Wheatley, was a devout follower of Whitefield who brought her slave to hear him speak during his sixth tour of America. Wheatley was among several African Americans who attained the Countess of Huntingdon's patronage through Whitefield, and Christianity, in turn, became a subtle and effective way to resist slavery.[55]

Whitefield's first visit to New England was much anticipated and, as in colonies to the south, was preceded by considerable attention in the newspapers to his activities in Great Britain and elsewhere in the colonies and by the publication of Whitefield's journals and other writings.[56] An excerpt of his journal, recounting his exchange with the bishop of Gloucester, in which the bishop advised Whitefield "to preach only in the Congregation in which he was lawfully appointed," appeared in the *Boston Evening Post* in November 1739.[57] This excerpt included Whitefield's impetuous reply, in which he informed the bishop that he "equally offended" when he preached "outside of [his] own diocese."[58] The publication of the excerpt was clearly intended to legitimize Whitefield's itinerancy and refute attempts to paint him as unorthodox in a period where his traveling and his preaching were coming under fire throughout Great Britain and its dominions.[59]

News of Whitefield's activities in other colonies also reached New England. In 1740 the *New England Weekly Journal* republished his "infamous" letter rebuking southern planters for their treatment of their slaves and their failure to catechize them. Although Whitefield clearly intended the letter's original publication and frequently sought out publication of his letters and other writings in newspapers, it is less clear whether he was also behind the reprints. By 1740 Whitefield was generating enough interest that he received plenty of attention in the press without having to solicit it. The reprint of this letter appeared in the *New England Weekly Journal* just four-and-a-half months ahead of his first visit to New England.

Whitefield's visit to New England was also preceded by a flurry of publications warning frantically of impending religious strife from those who were apprehensive about the impact of his visit on the region along with the impact of revivalism as a whole. Alarmists characterized his meetings as "unlawful," capable of inciting "riots, perpetual Quarrels among Friends, and Neighbours, continual Insults and Bullying."[60] Another writer feared that Whitefield would further the "disorders . . . already too visible among us."[61] The actions of individuals who engaged in itinerancy were considered "threatening" and "disruptive."[62] Those who disliked itinerant preaching also tended to conflate ordained revivalists like Whitefield with the unschooled itinerant preachers that he helped to inspire.

For his part, Whitefield eagerly "entreated to visit the descendants of the Pilgrim Fathers."[63] He arrived in Newport, Rhode Island, on Sunday, September 14, 1740. Shortly after Whitefield's appearance, he received an invitation to stay in the home of Mr. Clap, a dissenting minister. Whitefield wrote that Clap "looked like a good old Puritan, and gave me an idea of what stamp those men were who first settled New England.[64] Later that evening, he went with Rev. Clap to visit the Reverend Honeyman, Newport's Anglican minister, to request the use of his pulpit. Whitefield reported that Honeyman at first "seemed a little unwilling" and was particularly suspicious of Whitefield's desire to preach on weekdays, calling it "disorderly."[65] Honeyman eventually consented, allegedly telling Whitefield that "if [his] preaching would promote the glory of God, and the good of souls," he was "welcome to his church."[66]

When Whitefield reported that his words were mostly well received in Newport by large audiences, which he described as consisting of a "very plain people in general" who were "sadly divided amongst themselves as to outward things."[67] He wrote that there were no fewer than "four different congregations of Baptists, two of the Independents, and one of them Quakers."[68] Whitefield also reported that the "Established Church is in excellent order as to externals; but many of the chief members were bigots."[69] He noted that the Anglican clergy in particular "seemed very fearful lest I should preach in Mr. Clap's meeting-house," though Whitefield denied that the "bigotry" amongst the Anglican clergy was worse than "those of other communions."[70]

On the morning of September 18, 1740, he went on to Boston. Despite an alarmist response to his impending visit to that city, Whitefield reported being well received upon his arrival by a number of the local clergy, including Benjamin Colman.[71] Colman initially believed that bringing Whitefield to New England was the right action. In a letter written shortly after Whitefield's first tour, Colman noted that Whitefield was a clergyman of the Church of England, but he nonetheless felt that his popularity overcame his association with the church and that Whitefield was received with much "affection."[72]

During Whitefield's visit, Colman spent considerable time squiring Whitefield around to see various local clergymen. At one sermon, attended by over five thousand, Colman recounted that there was such a clamor to hear Whitefield speak that the pews broke underneath the crushing audience, leaving some in the congregation with "greatly bruised arms, thighs and body black and blue."[73] He also wrote of his surprise that Whitefield initially refused his invitation to preach from Colman's pulpit until after he had heard Colman preach.[74] This surprise was, no doubt, based on the not infrequent reports concerning Whitefield's lack of humility and deference towards other members of the clergy.

In addition to Benjamin Colman, Whitefield enjoyed considerable support from other local clergy, including Thomas Prince, Robert Abercrombie, William Hobby, and Thomas Foxcroft.[75] Even Governor Belcher and the commissary reportedly received Whitefield politely on several occasions. The only church or meetinghouse he found consistently closed to him was King's Chapel, then an Anglican church.[76] Once Whitefield preached, some of the things he said did displease his hosts among the New England clergymen. Colman was reportedly offended by some of Whitefield's more abrasive comments, although he did not withdraw his support.[77]

The next day, a group of five Anglican clergymen condemned Whitefield and particularly castigated him for his friendship with the Tennents. These ministers, who included SPG missionary Timothy Cutler, were hostile to the New Lights and criticized Whitefield "for calling that Tennent and his brethren faithful ministers of Jesus Christ."[78] For his part, Whitefield continued to insist that, indeed, they were faithful ministers. The Anglican ministers continued to berate Whitefield and "questioned the validity of Presbyterian ordination," using words from Whitefield's own journal against him.[79] They also questioned him about Wesley's sentiments, noting that when Wesley was in Boston, "he was very strenuous for the Church, and rigorous against all other forms of government when he was at Boston."[80] Whitefield replied, "He was then a great bigot, but God has since enlarged his heart, and I believe he was now like-minded with me in this particular."[81] Though it is doubtful that he realized it, Whitefield failed what was intended by these Anglican clergymen as a litmus test to gauge his loyalty to the church and its scripture. The queries continued into doctrinal matters, with no progress on either side. Whitefield eventually grew tired of their line of questioning and departed.[82]

An anonymous critic also wrote a scathing letter to Whitefield, published in the *Boston Evening Post* in July 1745. He referred to a letter in support of the College Testimony against Whitefield and told him that it "is beyond Dispute, that you have sown the pernicious Seeds of Separation, Contention, and Disorder among us."[83] The writer also took Whitefield to task for undermining the authority of New England's clergy. "Your injurious Insinuations respecting Ministers as unacquainted with Christ," he wrote, have "greatly impeded the Success of the Gospel, and struck boldly, not only at the Peace and good Order, but at the very Being of these Churches."[84]

The letter's writer exemplified a "speaking aristocracy," attempts by more traditional Old Light ministers to channel the increase in New England piety.[85] His letter painted Whitefield as an outsider and a troublemaker and also delivered a snide remark on Whitefield's itinerancy. He remarked that he thought that Whitefield and the New England clergy had an agreement that Whitefield "would not preach in any Pulpit without the settled Minister's Consent."[86] The writer called into question Whitefield's honesty and told him to "hasten to your own Charge, if you any you have."[87] The message was clear. Whitefield was not (or no longer) a welcome reviver of religious piety to the region; rather, he was a dangerous interloper and destructive force (as they saw revivalism).

Whitefield was not unaware of the hostilities directed at him. He was obviously less aware of the complexities of New England religious life and its contentious history. After a sermon he delivered in Salem, he noted that "the inhabitants had been sadly divided about their ministers."[88] Whitefield reported it as though this were a relatively new development, although religious fissures had existed in New England for over a century. He does not appear to have realized how his visits only increased those divisions.[89]

Whitefield knew that the fractious nature of New England's religious landscape meant that there would be ebbs and flows in his reception. He reported that one night, after he dined with the governor and "most of the ministers" in town, he honored a request from the governor to pray for all who were in attendance and then "went in the Governor's coach to the end of town."[90] While Whitefield did not report the specifics, it is clear that something must have occurred after these prayers. During that ride, Whitefield noted that he felt "such a sense of my vileness upon my soul, that I wondered people did not stone me."[91] This sense of foreboding, or "damp" as Whitefield described it, lasted for much of the day, which suggests that there were unpleasant elements of this visit that Whitefield elected not to share with those who would eventually read his (consciously public) journal.

In spite of the misgivings of a number of Boston clergy, many ministers were quick to support Whitefield. William Hobby, pastor at the Old South Church in Reading, even wrote a pamphlet defending Whitefield's preaching and particularly his itinerancy. Hobby was a Boston-born Congregationalist minister with sympathies toward New Light preaching. He served in the Council that in 1755 dismissed Jonathan Edwards from Northampton, Massachusetts, but supported Edwards and protested against the majority.[92]

Richard Pateshall, a Harvard-trained minister from Boston, roundly criticized Hobby for his defense of Whitefield.[93] Pateshall was particularly incensed at "that haughty Air which manifestly runs thro' the whole of it; and your supercilious and scurrilous Way of treating Gentlemen, of much greater Figure and Character of yourself."[94] Pateshall castigated Hobby for writing a letter "in Vindication of the grand itinerant" with "the most unmannerly Reflections on Gentlemen of superior Note and Merit."[95] In his zest to defend Whitefield, Hobby had modeled the grand itinerant's lack of deference to senior figures of authority. His zealous defense of Whitefield, along with his criticism of Whitefield's opponents, irked more traditionally minded preachers like Pateshall. They expected younger ministers such as Hobby, who did not come from ministerial families, to defer to the older order. Elders, in the Puritan tradition, maintained order over the church.[96]

Whitefield's dramatic, extemporaneous preaching was in marked contrast to the solemn, deeply hierarchal Puritan church experience that was predicated on prayer and nonexplicative and nonemotive preaching by the minister.[97] In Pateshall's criticisms of Whitefield that followed his scolding of William Hobby, he charged Whitefield with enthusiasm and ridiculed his attempts to model Christ. In particular, Pateshall denounced as "literalist" Whitefield's assertions that some dreams which he recounted in one of his sermons came directly from God."[98] He wrote of Whitefield's tendency to play the divine: "It's the Manner of Enthusiasts to take their crude and extravagant Notions of Things to be the infallible Dictates of the Spirit of God, and in no wise to call them in question."[99] Pateshall continued, "Are not Enthusiasts the Bane of the Christian Church? They ought therefore be crush'd."[100] As one who consciously projected a divine image that was tied to revivalism, Whitefield's public image (icon) was a prime target among antirevivalist New England ministers, much as he was with Alexander Garden. More than just the man, the clergymen were reacting to the image.

News of Whitefield's troubles with the Anglican planter elite, Alexander Garden, and others had preceded him to New England and contributed to criticisms of Whitefield. Thomas Foxcroft was among the members of the New England clergy who defended Whitefield, issuing a pamphlet that proposed to offer "a fair solution of certain Difficulties, objected against some Parts of his publick Conduct."[101] Colman was also initially quick to defend Whitefield against Garden and his other detractors in the South who had challenged the administration of Whitefield's Orphan House at Bethesda. Colman dismissed rumors that Whitefield appropriated the money to his own purposes. He countered that "the order of it was admirable."[102]

This first visit to New England also marked Whitefield's introduction to Jonathan Edwards, who was somewhat of a kindred spirit. Edwards, a Connecticut-born, Yale-trained theologian, was born into a family of clergy. His father, Thomas Edward, was a minister in Connecticut. His mother, Esther Stoddard, was the daughter of the Reverend Solomon Stoddard, an eminent Congregationalist minister from Northampton, Massachusetts. Stoddard's controversial ideas, which included admitting to communion those who were not full members of the church, led critics to dub him the "pope" of Connecticut Valley.[103] His grandson, too, came to evoke controversy.[104]

During his years at Yale, Edwards came under the influence of Enlightenment philosopher John Locke. Most of the younger, educated New Englanders, and particularly clergymen, had at least a passing knowledge of the writings of Locke, Newton, and other Enlightenment thinkers, along with classical philosophers like Aristotle.[105] Locke's endorsement of a "broader, more tolerant, and more 'reasonable' religion" particularly intrigued Edwards, though he was "not strictly, a Lockean."[106] Whitefield was not an intellectual, but he shared Edwards's interest in a broader and more tolerant religion.[107]

Edwards also shared the fears of other dissenting New England clergy in the eighteenth century that the Church of England had "injurious, oppressive designs" against the dissenting congregations. Although Whitefield was an Anglican priest, his reputation as a defier of the structure of the Anglican parish and his ability to appeal to the laity over the Anglican clergy was promising to Edwards.[108] Whitefield, for his part, was excited to meet the grandson of Solomon Stoddard.[109] Both Whitefield and Edwards reported that the visit to Northampton went well. Edwards reportedly wept with joy through Whitefield's sermon.[110] Edwards wrote, "Mr. Whitefield's sermons were suitable to the circumstances of the town; containing just reproofs of our backslidings and in a most moving and effecting manner."[111] Edwards wrote that "the minds of the people in general appeared more engaged in religion, showing a greater forwardness to make it the subject of their conversation."[112]

Whitefield's visit to Northampton was not without its dark aspects. He quarreled with a minister who approached him to assert that "it was not absolutely necessary for a gospel minister, that he should be converted."[113] What the minister meant was that the effective Gospel minister need not be an adherent of the New Birth. Whitefield vehemently disagreed. He took this opportunity to sermonize on the necessity of a minister's conversion to the New Birth and to castigate several of the ministers present, Whitefield asserting that unconverted ministers were "the bane of the Christian Church."[114] Continuing, he said that he "honour[ed] the memory of that great and good man, Mr. Stoddard: but I think he is much to be blamed for endeavouring to prove that unconverted men may be admitted into the ministry."[115] Whitefield saw Gilbert Tennent's sermon, "The Danger of an Unconverted Minister," as "unanswerable."[116] He also claimed that only one of the ministers in the audience was offended and that many thanked him for his directness.[117] Nonetheless, this was an important point of controversy during the visit; it further eroded his relationship with the Church of England and made Whitefield an even more polarizing figure in New England.

His second visit to New England occurred during his third voyage to the Americas. He arrived in York Harbor, then still part of Massachusetts (later Maine), in November 1744, after an arduous eleven-week voyage, and received a hearty welcome from the Reverend Samuel Moody.[118] In spite of Whitefield's still-queasy traveler's stomach, he was persuaded by Moody to put aside his nausea and preach a sermon.[119] Still nauseated, Whitefield continued on to Boston on November 24, 1744. A number of Bostonians reportedly still held some ill will against him, but an acquaintance of Whitefield's reported that "the prejudices of most that set themselves against him before his coming, seem to be in great measure abated, and in some, wholly removed."[120]

Despite his poor health, Whitefield maintained a busy schedule of preaching and offering communion to congregants in and around Boston, including at a church in Malden, at the behest of the Reverend Joseph Emerson. Emerson was impressed with Whitefield and wrote, "He comes with the same extraordinary spirit of meekness, sweetness and universal benevolence as before. In opposition to the spirit of separation and bigotry, he is still for holding communion with all Protestant churches."[121] Emerson firmly defended Whitefield against accusations of enthusiasm. He wrote that Whitefield "preaches a close adherence to the Scriptures, the necessity of trying all impressions by them, and of rejecting whatever is not agreeable to them as delusions."[122] Emerson continued that "in opposition to Antinomianism, he preaches up all kinds of relative and religious duties, though to be performed in the strength of Christ; and, in short, the doctrines of the Church of England."[123]

The more contentious nature of Whitefield's second visit can be attributed largely to his outspokenness about unconverted ministers during his previous visit, four years earlier, which had offended many. A considerable exchange of pamphlets and other writings on the subject had followed among the members of the New England clergy. Charles Chauncy, of Boston's First Congregational Church, wrote a pair of pamphlets castigating revivalism in general and Whitefield in particular. The first pamphlet, published in 1742, railed specifically against Whitefield and bemoaned the state of religion in New England. Chauncy blamed Whitefield and the other revivalists for inciting "confusion" and "trouble" over the conversion of ministers. "They [the parishioners] become very turbulent, and disorderly," he wrote.[124] "They give their Minister, if he is not of this new Way, a great deal of Trouble, and form parties to turn him away from his Charge," he continued. "Order, Regularity, Decency, and such Things, are made light of and, in their Opinion, the more confusion there is, the more there is of the spirit of God amongst them," he wrote.[125]

Chauncy blamed Whitefield for inciting further religious division, stating that "the Ministers here are divided, and look upon one another with an evil and jealous Eye."[126] Of the parishioners, he wrote, "Several of them have rambled through the country, after the Pattern of Mr. Whitefield, and without asking leave of the Minister of the Parish, have gathered the People together, and in a riotous manner entered the Meeting-house and preached."[127] Very few Ministers, he continued, "have dared to open their Mouths in favor of Reason, Virtue, Order, or any-thing that is thought to be against this World."[128] Chauncy clearly saw revivalism in general, and Whitefield specifically, as having a profoundly negative impact on New England religious life and as having turned the people against the clergy.

In a second pamphlet against unschooled revivalist itinerant ministers, published in 1743, Chauncy "prevailed" upon the clergy of New England to tend to their "obligations" to "use their

Endeavours" to "suppress the prevailing disorder."[129] Among his many other criticisms of revivalism, Chauncy clearly responded to the arguments of Whitefield, Tennent, and Edwards that a minister's conversion was by far the most important qualification to preach. Chauncy dismissed their teachings as "without any Respect to, or Concurrence with the Word."[130] He also firmly rejected the notion that a man could "evidence his Justification by his Sanctification."[131] "It is a Fundamental and Soul-damning Error, to make Sanctification an Evidence of Justification," he wrote, roundly dismissing the entire notion of justification by faith on which revivalism was predicated.[132]

Chauncy went a step further in 1745, issuing a public letter calling upon Whitefield to "Vindicate his Conduct, or Confess his Faults." In it, Chauncy claimed that, when Whitefield first came into New England, he was "much prejudiced in favour of you, from the accounts I had heard of your abundant labours and success in the Gospel."[133] He also claimed to have heard Whitefield preach several times and that his "preaching as well as conduct were stumbling to me."[134] "And the sad confusions I have since been a mournful spectator of, have fully convinced me you were in a wrong way," he continued.[135] Chauncy's letter echoed Pateshall's criticisms of William Hobby and Whitefield. He outlined the ways in which Whitefield was brash in his interactions with local clergy. He also called into question Whitefield's commitment to the Thirty-Nine Articles of the Church of England. Recognizing Whitefield's assertions that he was an Anglican minister, Chauncy asked, "how [he] can reconcile the 26th of these Articles, with what [he] both preach'd and printed?"[136] The Twenty-Sixth Article of the Church of England specifically addresses the worthiness of clergy, with the implication that they be properly educated and sanctioned by the Church. Chauncy insisted that Whitefield's repeated assertions, in sermon and elsewhere, about the importance of the conversion experience over all, was in violation of this article, which gave critics an opening to challenge the purity, or orthodoxy, of his message.[137]

As Whitefield's experiences with Alexander Garden and South Carolina's planter elite show, Whitefield was often perceived as an outsider to the colonies. For Gardner, Whitefield was a foreigner whose presence would incite the appearance of other foreigners who would then displace ministers who had been voluntarily incorporated into their communities by the community members. Ultimately, the Harvard Corporation and Whitefield's venerable enemy, Rev. Holyoke, were forced to taper their anti-Whitefield rhetoric in 1768 after Whitefield and his supporters donated a large collection of books to replace the collections destroyed by fire.[138] In doing so, Whitefield demonstrated that he could support the good of the community and potentially overcome his status of threatening interloper or imported divinity.[139] Nonetheless, this did not stop the tide of condemnations against him as, by now, an established icon of revivalism.

Other ministers also spoke out against Whitefield. In a letter published in 1745, two associations of ministers from the country addressed the ministers of Boston and Charlestown, Massachusetts, about the "hasty Admission that Whitefield Obtained into some of [their] Pulpits, and is, [they] feared, about to find into others."[140] Its signers included clergy from both Massachusetts and New Hampshire, including Caleb Cushing of Salisbury, Joseph Parsons of Bradford, John Cushing from Boxford, Nathaniel Gookin of North-Hampton, and William Johnson of Newbury.[141] The writers insisted that their design was not to dictate whom their fellow ministers should receive. Rather, they argued that any receipt of Whitefield should be done under less public circumstances.[142] Their concern was that public receipt of Whitefield by reputable members of the clergy might provide undesirable encouragement to "Itinerants of far less name than Whitefield."[143]

Even some of Whitefield's supporters, like Benjamin Colman, expressed concern about Whitefield's imitators among the young, untutored ministers. Colman issued a letter on May 15, 1742, outlining his concerns. He called the itinerant ministers "confused in their Discourses, which are addressed to the Passions of their Hearers without opening their subjects in any proper Method for enlightening their minds."[144] He also described them as "without [Whitefield's] Gift."[145] Clearly, Colman intended to defend Whitefield and counter tendencies to associate him with unschooled itinerants. In his reference to the "Passions of their Hearers," he also conveyed his belief that Whitefield was not a dangerous enthusiast. His denunciations of enthusiasm were both a defense of Whitefield's character and respectability and of Colman's as well. That this letter appeared in extract form in an antirevivalist pamphlet by consummate Whitefield critic Charles Chauncy is an example of how a respectable sermon speaks to revivalism's partial success. Chauncy still detested Whitefield, but he did not contest Colman's ministerial respectability despite Colman's defense of Whitefield.

Colman and the other Whitefield supporters believed that the renewed interest in religion occasioned by Whitefield and the revivalists was worth the drawbacks. Whitefield and the Boston ministry who supported the revivalists launched a campaign to garner support behind the renewed interest in religious life and the spirit of interdenominational cooperation. A convention of ministers, which included the Reverends Sewall and Prince of Boston, the Reverend William Hobby of Reading, and twenty-nine other members of the clergy, met together. The meeting produced a proclamation in which the supporters announced that they thought it their

> indispensible duty—without judging or censuring such of our brethren as cannot at present see things in the same light with us—in this open and conjunct manner to declare . . . that there has been a "happy and remarkable revival of religion in many parts of this land through an uncommon divine influence."[146]

The ministers did not all necessarily support Whitefield's message of the New Birth, but they recognized revivalism as a positive force, both in terms of its promotion of religious toleration—symbolized in Whitefield—and counterpoint to the "long time of decay and deadness" that preceded it.[147]

A total of 114 ministers, including Thomas Foxcroft, Samuel Sewall, and Benjamin Colman "gave attestations, either by their signature or by written attestations."[148] Of these, 96 had earned their bachelor of arts degrees more than ten years earlier, before the revival began.[149] Whitefield's support crossed denominational lines. The fact that many of the more senior members of the clergy lent their backing demonstrates that his message for religious toleration also transcended the traditional bounds of the Great

Awakening in New England. Historians have consistently found that revivalists in New England tended to elude democratic, economic, and geographic categorizations.[150] It is therefore not surprising that Whitefield produced such a response from among a diverse group of clergy. Another "dissenting Protestant" who wrote in support of Whitefield just a few years later took this argument further. He maintained that "the right of private judgment belongs to Christians of every Denomination."[151] The author wrote that churches ought to "have the Power, according to the Directions given in the Word of God, to choose their Own Minister."[152] He believed that the ability of dissenters to elect their own minister was the highest sort of liberty.[153]

Whitefield continued to face opposition, of course. In the winter of 1745, he was denied the use of several pulpits. In a visit to Ipswich, Massachusetts, on February 7, 1745, the Reverend Theophilus Pickering refused Whitefield access to the pulpit of the Second Church. Pickering cited an antirevivalist publication by the bishop of London on "Lukewarmness and Enthusiasm." Whitefield caustically replied, "All ought to be thankful to the pilot who will teach them to steer a safe and middle course."[154] Pickering drolly replied, "But what if the pilot should take the vane for the compass?"[155] While there is no evidence that the bishop was referring directly to Whitefield in the pamphlet, Bishop Gibson had long been concerned with the effect of Whitefield on the British American colonies. The pamphlet was intended to send a message to Anglican clergy that revivalism was not to be tolerated. In doing so, it undermined the Anglican identity of revivalist itinerant preachers like Whitefield. Pickering took this message to heart, snidely implying that Whitefield was ignorant of church doctrine and Anglican law.

Whitefield's third visit to New England took place in 1748. He arrived in Boston from Pennsylvania on October 9. He reported an outpouring of support and tears on his arrival. He also briefly revisited Portsmouth, New Hampshire, continuing down to Rhode Island and then on to Maryland. The details of this voyage are scant, though it is clear that he continued to attract large crowds at his sermons.[156] He returned to Great Britain after only a short time and remained there through 1751. He made three subsequent tours to the American colonies during the last nineteen years of his life.

He also went through a series of changes during this period, facing obstacles to his efforts to establish a college and dealing with the death of his wife on August 9, 1769, following a bout of inflammatory fever.[157] Shortly thereafter, he began to prepare for his seventh and final voyage to the Americas.

Whitefield bid his friends in England farewell in a sermon he delivered in the summer of 1769. He had delivered farewell sermons before other missionary voyages, and this sermon made no mention of any plans to remain in the Americas permanently. He arrived in Georgia for the last time in January 1770. In a letter to his friend Robert Keen of London, he wrote that he enjoyed "a greater share of bodily health than I have known for many years."[158] Whitefield obviously did not expect that he would be dead in just over seven months.[159]

Whitefield's experiences in New England changed both him and the religious landscape of the region dramatically. His experiences with the dissenter culture of New England excited and encouraged him, even if, as was the case in South Carolina, his understanding of the local colonial culture was often incomplete or inaccurate. Like his experiences in the more southern colonies, they also demonstrated just how contentious a figure Whitefield had become within less than five years of the start of his missionary career. Even though each colony had its own character and religious geography, his Anglican respectability in the colonies was all but gone among the Anglican clergy by the early 1740s.

Whitefield had another lasting impact on the subaltern members of the New England community by inspiring others to catechize Native Americans. In September 15, 1763, the *Pennsylvania Gazette* published a report by Presbyterian minister John Brainerd refuting claims that "the Christian Indians in New-Jersey, under my Care, were many of them gone back to join the murdering Indians on the Frontier."[160] The report does not mention Whitefield by name, but Brainerd was a revivalist who was profoundly influenced by Whitefield. His brother, David, matriculated Yale in 1740, just as a division arose over the influence of visiting preachers, including Gilbert Tennent and George Whitefield, as well as a controversial speech by Jonathan Edwards, in inciting religious enthusiasm among the students. The reference to the "murdering

Indians" served as a critique of revivalism's engagement with non-white audiences and also implied that Whitefield (and revivalists, generally) not only was ideologically dangerous, but also inspired physical danger.

David was expelled from Yale in the wake of these visits after he said that his tutor, Chauncey Whittelsey, "has no more grace than a chair" and inquired why Whittelsey "did not drop down dead" for fining students he perceived to be "over-zealous."[161] He was unable to finish his studies, but despite his lack of a college degree, he received a license to preach from the Presbyterian church in Philadelphia. Together with his brother John, he undertook missionary work among the Native Americans throughout the colonies.[162] For antirevivalists, a report of Christianized Native Americans attacking their nonconverted brethren had two implications. The first was that they saw another example of revivalism stirring up religious division. The second was racial, akin to fears that revivalist conversions might induce African slaves to rise up against their masters. In order to continue their work, it was imperative for preachers like the Brainerds to counter accusations that their teachings were an impetus for trouble. This was not unlike Whitefield's public appeal to African slaves to help him prove to opponents of religious instruction for slaves that their conversion would not be a negative influence on them.[163]

Whitefield himself played a significant role in the early career of Mohegan preacher Sansom Occom. When Occom made his preaching debut in 1766, he did so in Whitefield's London Tabernacle. Occom's preaching followed Whitefield's example of focusing on sin rather than race, something that factored into the ideology of antislavery evangelicals who converted under Whitefield.[164] His sermons classified all as sinners.[165]

Although apparently quite supportive of Occom, Whitefield managed to sow some discord between Occom and his mentor, Eleazar Wheelock, before the Mohegan preacher returned to the colonies from Great Britain from his preaching tour. Occom's tour of Great Britain was intended in part to raise money for Dartmouth College, much as Whitefield had once done for Bethel Orphan House. However, Occom grew concerned about the racial composition of the college after Whitefield told Occom that he had been "a fine Tool to get Money for them [Wheelock], but when you get home, they won't Regard you, they'll Set you a Drift."[166] Occom wrote to Wheelock to express doubts about his mentor's intentions. In this letter, he complained about the lack of Indian students at Dartmouth and told Wheelock what Whitefield said to him about being used as a fundraiser, informing Wheelock, "I am ready to believe it now."[167] Occom continued to feel Whitefield's influence through the rest of his life. On April 2, 1786, nearly sixteen years after Whitefield's death, Occom recorded a dream about Whitefield in his journal. In this dream, he envisioned Whitefield preaching to "a great number of Indians and Some White People," as he had so often done in the past.[168] Whitefield saw Occom, took his hand in a fatherly manner, and told him "I am glad that you preach the Excellency of Jesus Chris yet."[169] In this dream, Whitefield continued to praise Occom for his work, which Occom interpreted as a divine approval of sorts for his life's labors.

As noted previously, Whitefield's preaching was also a source of inspiration to Phillis Wheatley, the influential black writer and voice of African American Christians against slavery, and to revivalist preacher John Marrant, who became an evangelical Christian after he heard Whitefield speak, when Marrant was a teen. Marrant's ministry was particularly focused on the catechism of blacks and Native Americans throughout British North America.[170] In 1789 he preached in Boston at the invitation of the African Lodge of the Honorable Society of Free and Accepted Masons, or Prince Hall Masons. This lodge was established by Prince Hall in the 1770s as the first brotherhood for African Americans.[171] Marrant's sermon emphasized "the great duties of Brotherly Love" and reminded its listeners that they were "all members of the body of Christ with the Church."[172] "First the anciency [long existence] of Masonry, that being done, will endeavour to prove all other titles we have a just right as Masons," he said," to claim—namely, honourably, free and accepted."[173] Marrant's words were directly specifically at African Americans, but the brotherhood was, unsurprisingly, quite active in speaking out against slavery and violence against blacks and in championing for other rights for blacks.[174] Marrant's words were another example of Whitefield's influence on antislavery forces in the colonies generally, and in New England particularly, invoking his image in ways that were not consistent with his views in life.

Whitefield's own efforts could never fully shape his image. People's understandings and uses of his public image, in fact, contradicted Whitefield's own image of himself as an orthodox Anglican. Since Whitefield continued to appeal to the bishop of London for permission for various projects of his, at least through 1768, it is clear that he still believed that he was engaged in a dialogue with the church about religious toleration. He seems never to have recognized that he had all but alienated himself from the Anglican Church, even to the end of his life. His funeral and memorialization in the colonies, alleged to have been orchestrated by Whitefield himself, are also intriguing.[175] Whitefield does not appear to have expected to die quite when he did, but by a number of accounts, he did set clear wishes as to how he was to be remembered. This included an entombment within the Old South Presbyterian Church in a colony that was profoundly divided on the subject of religion. It also included sermons by a number of non-Anglican ministers, including John Wesley. Whitefield's will does not detail his funeral wishes, and there are no records that confirm whether these plans were made as he knew he was dying or if he had made them earlier. Nonetheless, his funeral was, in many ways, the ultimate manifestation of his declaration in 1739 that "the World is Now My Parish" as people from across denominational lines paused to mourn and remember him. His tomb became a site of sacred and contested memory for evangelical Christians.[176] Because he was a pluralist Protestant icon in life, it was not always clear what his legacy would be after death. The malleability of his public image meant that as an icon, he was readily co-opted for a variety of purposes.

With Whitefield's death came also a negotiation with the politics of history and memory. The act of memorializing Whitefield (if not always unified) was a social activity that linked individuals to group identities.[177] Whitefield became part of a religious collective memory, and one tied to a cultural phenomenon that continued to evolve and refine itself, much as Whitefield's iconic image continued to evolve.[178] Even in death, and within a religious culture that transcended geography, denominations, race, and other boundaries, he represented what Maurice Halbwachs called "Christian truth(s)" that "can be historical and eternal," with "truth" tied to both debates over the purity of the religious message and ongoing tensions about religious toleration.[179] As such, the fact that the memory of Whitefield was not cohesive, much as the understanding of revivalism was not unified, should be understood as a reflection of the multilayered nature of (a religious) culture.[180] As an icon, Whitefield continued to evolve, though his image was invoked in ways that he likely did not intend.

CHAPTER FIVE

Inventing George Whitefield

George Whitefield's funeral was a veritable spectacle. He was mourned on both sides of the Atlantic. His entombment in the colonial church that he helped to found and the subsequent pilgrimages to his grave solidified his status as an icon of transatlantic religious revivalism. Any chance of Whitefield having a legacy as an Anglican who simply wanted reform of the church came to an end, particularly with his enshrinement in a Presbyterian church. Often accused in life of sowing religious discord, it is with some irony that he was buried in a region where members of the established church felt threatened by the new religious freedom.[1]

To Whitefield's followers, the mourning that followed his death also gave rise to a legacy that was suggestive of sainthood. For his American followers at the outset of the American Revolution, it suggested an image that was part heroic, and entirely filiopietistic, as they sought to construct a new religious identity and tradition in a new republic without a national church. Notably, the American Revolution challenged the status of the old erudite clergy.[2] Upon the death of Gilbert Tennent in 1764, Benjamin Rush remarked that "the Rich and the Poor, Black and White had equally free access to his person."[3] Rush, a statesman and physician, was a revivalist from a mixed Protestant background. His observation about Tennent was also true of Whitefield and many other evangelicals, though none were quite as high profile as was Whitefield. These ministers exemplified the democratization of Christianity. It was a Christianity that Lyman Beecher derisively described as full of ministers who were "generally illiterate men, often not possessed of a good English education, and in some cases, unable to read or write."[4] Debates over ministerial training were not unique to the American Revolution, but in this context, Christianity was democratized because of its accessibility to all, regardless of education, socioeconomic standing (though elites were usually less attracted to revivalism), ethnicity, or race.[5]

With the ratification of the U.S. Constitution in 1788, the religious freedoms it promised offered what must have seemed like limitless hope and potential to religious Americans, if that freedom was not absolute in practice.[6] The new framework for religion also set off a clash over American self-identity and values.[7] Disagreements over religious truth that were a key feature in seventeenth- and eighteenth-century debates over toleration in a pluralistic British Atlantic Empire entered into a new landscape. For Christianity, religious truth is both eternal *and* historical.[8] Much as the young country could not fully divest itself of its cultural, political, and economic ties to the Atlantic community, it remained inexorably linked to a transatlantic providential network as well. Nonetheless, some American revolutionaries, including Benjamin Rush, saw the Revolution as an "epochal step toward the millennial day," whether that meant the "literal return of Christ," or (more commonly) an "age of perfect peace in which Christ's spirit would inform every act and thought."[9] As an icon who fashioned himself as an Imitatio Christi of sorts and who was perceived as such by his followers, the memorialized Whitefield represented the ideal.

Whitefield died in 1770, but his memory was still fresh a few years later in the minds of those who were directly involved in Revolutionary politics. His followers simultaneously sought both to defend his iconic image and to reinterpret it in ways that made sense within the evolving American religious landscape and the greater British Atlantic World, making societies their own historians.[10]

Though historians have disagreed about the extent to which the Revolution was directly influenced by religion, the co-option of Whitefield into Revolutionary politics localized memories. "The memory of the same fact," Halbwachs wrote, "can be placed within many frameworks, which result from distinct collective memories."[11] The process of memory changes the historical narrative, a problem that Americans were wholly aware of by the early nineteenth century. As early as 1811, John Adams wrote to his friend, Benjamin Rush, begging him to write on "the causes of the corruption of history."[12] "For I myself do believe that both tradition and history are already corrupted in America as much as they were in the four or five first centuries of Christianity," Adams continued.[13] What concerned Adams—a concern with which Rush readily concurred—was that not thirty years after the American Revolution, the men perceived that the narrative of the Revolution, and the reputation of its leaders, were already being changed, or "warped."[14]

What is evident is that the first phases of memorialization came as the First Great Awakening gave way to the second, a religious cultural shift that was marked by postmillennialism, which stressed moral preparation for Christ's return to earth. That Whitefield made every effort to channel God in building his own iconic image, therefore, became all the more significant.[15] Because of Whitefield's lack of permanent ties to any specific formal institution—church or nation—his legacy was incredibly fragmented. He left behind an enormous body of religious literature in which he consistently reaffirmed his ties to the Church of England but often contradicted church doctrine. Other writings about him either spoke of his transdenominational appeal or occasionally tied him with the Methodist Church, which formally split with the Church of England in 1790, twenty years after his death. As an extension of his public image, his writings—to say nothing of the distinctive (and accessible) religious print culture and tradition he created—were also posthumously used by others, and in ways that Whitefield likely never intended.[16] This use was akin to what Adams and Rush perceived as a corruption of tradition.[17]

Because of ambiguities in his writings on slavery, and in much of the scriptural debates over involuntary servitude, Whitefield's memory was very quickly invoked in the growing divide over that institution.[18] For example, Anthony Benezet's (mostly unsuccessful) attempt to reframe Whitefield's image, vis-à-vis Whitefield's early criticisms of slavery, into the abolitionist narrative serves as one example.[19] These religion-based objections to slavery matured into part of the reform cosmology that included a distinctive abolitionist movement in the decades leading up to the American Civil War.[20] In this context, slavery was a specific evil that needed to be eradicated as a Hydra sin, a violation of all Biblical principles, though not unique to the United States.[21] Even at the moment of reproducing the past, our imagination remains under the influence of the present social milieu.[22] It would, therefore, make sense for those who opposed slavery on religious grounds and those who favored it, to identify with the aspects of Whitefield's wavering position on slavery that seemed to best support their cause.

Most posthumous accounts of Whitefield recognized that he was a transnational figure. His tomb drew pilgrims from around the Anglo-American world. After his death, memorials and other literature appeared in periodicals both in Great Britain and, after the War for Independence, the United States. At the outbreak of the American Revolution and thereafter, American evangelicals seeking to carve out a national religious culture began to invoke Whitefield's image as a symbol of their own. It was a popular, accessible religious culture whose leadership frequently transcended denominational lines in order to increase its membership.[23] What drew it all together was a divine figure that could help the group to achieve a sense of immutability (or serve as a point of clarification to negotiate potential conflicts) in the face of massive social and political change.[24] Yet owing to the problem of religious pluralism, enough ambiguity was necessary for that divine figure to make sense across different, and sometimes conflicting, narratives.

As Whitefield himself constructed a public self-image through print, some of his followers worked to reconstruct that image into the national narrative of the young United States, recreating Whitefield as a heroic founding father. Historian Benedict Anderson notes of the early religious print market that "Protestantism was always fundamentally on the offensive."[25] Anderson's point was directed at the proliferation of print culture during the Reformation, but it is relevant here nonetheless. Whitefield's evangelical followers harnessed the image that he carefully constructed through this religious print market in imagining a post-Revolutionary Protestant American society, a phenomenon that Anderson identifies as an old language used within a new model.[26] "Print-languages," Anderson observes, "laid the basis for national consciousness."[27] In this case, it was a national conscious specific to evangelical Americans, rather than Americans as a whole. That national consciousness—on political and religious levels—embodied a struggle over power and authority.[28] It was a struggle that Whitefield exemplified. The reprint of Whitefield's past writings at his death, along with the publication of new writings, accentuated Whitefield as, simultaneously, an icon of religious freedom, a model for pious life, and the biblical debate over the morality of slavery. These layers all congealed to form the basis of Whitefield's image—an iconic befitting the religious climate of the Second Great Awakening—that was accessible to an increasingly interconnected providential world.

Whitefield's preaching was contemporary with the transition from toleration to religious liberty in the colonies, but the American brand of religious liberty that these Christian writers have attributed to him did not solidify until after the American Revolution, becoming enshrined in the First Amendment of the Constitution, seventeen years after Whitefield's death. And while his preaching did inspire antislavery resistance, his influence in religious culture was still felt throughout the Anglo-American world rather than restricted to a young United States. This was because evangelicalism was, by definition, a transatlantic cultural movement.

Publications critical of Whitefield and his doctrine continued to appear throughout Great Britain and its dominions during the last years of his life. In 1764 English astronomer James Harman twice published his observations on Whitefield's character. He attempted to use astronomical calculations to discredit Whitefield's frequent assertions that his success was assured by divine will, a function of Whitefield the icon. Harman argued that, rather, it was the result of a "mere Fatality, evident in the fatal Catastrophe of his unhappy, gloomy, and misguided Followers."[29] The publication included a note, acknowledging that some of Harman's readers "may . . . take him for a Conjurer."[30] The anonymous writer or editor gleefully described Harman as "a comical, out of the way sort of a Genius, who has contrived to plague the Methodists, and their great Leader, in the style of an Almanac-maker, and with all the antiquated jargon of Astrology."[31] Bemusement aside, while the article is not, on the whole, particularly pro-Whitefield, it does suggest that Whitefield's popularity was sufficient so that there were some who saw attempts to discredit Whitefield the icon as futile.

Other criticisms included a published letter to Whitefield from the Reverend Dr. Durell, vice chancellor of Oxford, which appeared one year before Whitefield died. It blamed Methodism, and also Whitefield (as an influence on Methodism), for the "Neglect of the Parochial Clergy."[32] It also asserted Durell's belief in the necessity of "Episcopal ordination, Episcopal baptism, and Episcopal communion" as "essentials of the Christian religion."[33] The implication, of course, was that in his insistence on the conversion experience as tantamount both to the trueness of faith and qualification to serve as a minister, Whitefield was neither a proper Anglican, nor a true Christian. As with Alexander Garden, Durell's efforts to discredit the purity of Whitefield's religious message were a means to undermine him as an icon, and they serve as another example of anti-Whitefield iconoclasm. The description of Durell's letter in *The Monthly Review*'s catalog exhibited some Whitefieldian sympathies and described Durell as "a zealous stickler for the established church, and of course, an utter enemy to all dissenters, as such."[34] In doing so, the article rejected efforts to undermine Whitefield as an icon by means of attacking his orthodoxy.

None of this divisiveness derailed Whitefield's popularity, of course. News of George Whitefield's travels throughout the colonies and Great Britain continued to appear in newspapers throughout his career, with numerous accounts of his arrivals, preaching, and departures in various localities around the Anglo-American world.[35] These newspaper accounts frequently reported Whitefield's activities in other vicinities. A Boston newspaper, for instance, reported Whitefield's visit to Charles Town in January 1765, along with his plans to return to Georgia to tend to some legal matters concerning his goal of turning Bethel Orphan House into a college.[36] The *Pennsylvania Gazette* reported Whitefield's arrival in London in August 1763 in a "poor State of Health."[37] Two additional colonial papers reported Whitefield's preaching activities in Scotland and England, respectively.[38]

There is continued evidence of Whitefield's own hand in the press that he received in the newspapers, even if he could not control everything that appeared in print about him. The extract of one of Whitefield's letters to an acquaintance, concerning his plans to voyage from Scotland to Boston aboard the *Jenny*, and some

Old South Presbyterian Church, Newburyport, MA.
Photograph © 2014 by J. Thomas Parr. Used by permission.

comments about his ill health, appeared in the *New York Gazette* on July 25, 1763.[39] Other newspaper articles also mentioned the itinerant's health; in one instance, an article denoted a rather frail Whitefield as he struggled in "not more than two feet [of] water" as he went "to cool himself" after preaching on a hot summer day.[40] The personal details suggest that Whitefield contributed to these reports; the appearance of extracts of letters is entirely in line with his long-standing practice of slipping snippets of his letters and journals to the media.

Whitefield's association with Presbyterians—namely the Tennents—cost him a great deal in terms of his reputation with the Church of England. As noted previously, his public support of

Gilbert Tennent's sermon asserting the necessity of the conversion experience drew fire from Church of England commissary, Alexander Garden, and Charles Town's Anglican planter elite, as well as from New England dissenters who were concerned both with preserving Christian unity; respect for erudite, orthodox clergy; and resistance to dangerous symbols. By the 1750s, newspapers began to note specifically when Whitefield preached at a Presbyterian church; for example, news of his 1754 visit to Philadelphia noted that he "preach'd almost every Evening in the New Presbyterian Church."[41] In 1764 a Boston newspaper reported that Whitefield "preached twice in the Presbyterian Church. . . . We hear he is to preach To Morrow at the Same Place" during a visit to New York City.[42] A similar report appeared in the *Boston Evening-Post* in 1764 regarding a visit that Whitefield made to Boston in July of that year.[43] A fourth example appeared in the *Newport Mercury* two months later, noting Whitefield's sermon at "the new Presbyterian church" in Fort Cumberland, Maryland, along with his plans to preach at St. Paul's Church on the morning of September 3, 1764.[44] While newspaper reports of his sermons were not uncommon, and these reports occasionally mentioned the church by name, it was far less common to note the denomination.

Whitefield's association with Gilbert and William Tennent, and his 1740 visit to New England that inspired the Presbyterian church in which he was eventually interred, brought about the special attention to his activities in Presbyterian churches. Old South Presbyterian Church was founded in Newburyport, Massachusetts, in 1742, as a small, unaffiliated house of worship of about one hundred members.[45] By the time of the church's founding, Presbyterianism already had a long, contested existence in New England's religious landscape. Scottish missionary George Keith, a then-Quaker minister born into a Presbyterian family, wrote a lengthy pamphlet in 1689, attacking the church.[46] He declared that these "independent visible churches" were "no true church of Christ" and urged their followers to "repent."[47] Keith's attitude toward the Presbyterian church was relatively typical of the reaction in much of the British Atlantic World toward Presbyterians, even into the eighteenth century.

Many of the Old South Church's original members came from the First Religious Society of New England, a Congregational parish founded in 1725. After its early members decided to withdraw from the First Religious Society, they called Jonathan Parsons of Lyme, Connecticut, to serve as pastor.⁴⁸ Parsons was a Yale-trained Congregationalist minister who was mentored by Jonathan Edwards and became strongly influenced by revivalism.

The founding of the Old South Church came on the heels of Whitefield's first missionary tour of New England. In part on the advice of Whitefield, the church's brethren voted to unite with the Presbyterian Church on September 15, 1748.⁴⁹ Whitefield's influence is evident in the church's founding documents, which construed the church as a "society of Believers . . . shewing their faith by an holy life and an heavenly conversation, being professed, subjected to Christ in the Faith and Order of the Gospel and by mutual consent."⁵⁰ The church's founding members declared that they were to "maintain the worship and ordinances of God" but were "not necessarily bounded by the lines of Civil Society but may be made of many such societies, provided it be most for Edification."⁵¹ The emphasis on the Gospel and mutual consent and the rejections of civil authority are particularly Whitefieldian. The church quickly outgrew its small meetinghouse, and in 1756, a new church building was constructed on its present-day location, on the corner of Federal and School Streets in Newburyport.⁵² At Whitefield's death, this church took center stage for the memorialization of him as a major figure of the Great Awakening. Whitefield had never rejected his Anglican orders, even if the Anglican hierarchy largely no longer recognized or accepted him as an Anglican minister. Old South also became the site of a contested memory, wherein various fractions claimed Whitefield and sought to preserve his legacy and mold it in accordance with their own agendas.

George Whitefield died in the parsonage of the Old South Presbyterian Church at around six o'clock in the morning on September 30, 1770, at the age of fifty-five. He had suffered from ill health and had experienced several serious bouts of wheezing in the last two to three days of his life. At around four o'clock on that Sunday morning, he awoke and said, "My asthma, my asthma is coming on."⁵³ He expressed concerns not only that he would be unable to meet his upcoming preaching commitments, but that he might be dying.[54] Whitefield's deathbed pronouncement was characteristic of eighteenth-century rituals of death in which the individual "prepared to die—preferably with resignation to God's will," which Whitefield certainly did.[55] The widow of fellow evangelical preacher Jonathan Edwards expressed similar premonitions shortly before her own death, the year before Whitefield's.[56] A local doctor was called to the parsonage to tend to Whitefield, but he confirmed Whitefield's suspicions that his asthma attack was to be fatal.[57] His death came just under an hour after the doctor arrived.[58] It attracted an unusual amount of attention across the British Empire.

Shortly after Whitefield's death, the Reverend Parsons, the pastor of the Old South Church, summoned Captain Fetcomb and several of Rev. Parsons's church elders and deacons to begin the preparations for Whitefield's funeral.[59] As was typically the case in the eighteenth century, these preparations occurred quickly, and the rituals that surrounded death were a group event, to "insure that neither the dying nor survivors faced this momentous passage alone."[60] Such rituals usually included the decedent's family, but Whitefield's wife had predeceased him two years beforehand, and their only child had died in infancy. A collection of clergymen and friends of Whitefield's stood in their stead. The Reverend Sherburne of Portsmouth sent several representatives to ask that Whitefield be interred at his church. Sherburne offered to have Whitefield's body interred in Sherburne's new tomb at his own expense. Parsons denied these requests, owing to a repeatedly expressed wish by Whitefield that if he died at Newburyport, he wished "to be buried before Mr. Parson's pulpit."[61]

On the afternoon of Whitefield's funeral, all the bells in Newburyport tolled for thirty-minute intervals at three separate times, first at one o'clock, then a second time at two in the afternoon, then again at three, signifying the start of the funeral.[62] A similar spectacle announced the beginning of the Grand Federal Procession to a rainy Philadelphia morning almost eighteenth years later, on July 4, 1788.[63] The ringing of bells from church steeples reflected the changing tide of religious architecture in post-Puritan society, where Boston-area churches built after 1700 typically had bells, even if Bostonians were not always "quite clear what to do with them."[64] Churches and meetinghouses in the colonies had traditionally been without steeples, which were considered ostentatious and suggestive of either Roman Catholic churches or of Anglican parishes, but the architecture of many colonial churches changed to make the parishes and worship experiences of dissenting churches more competitive with the influx of Anglican churches.[65] It is therefore unsurprising that some observers complained about the pandemonium and excesses surrounding Whitefield's funeral.[66]

The tolling bells were not the only signifiers of change. The emotional responses of his followers to Whitefield's death were another. "Vicarious emotion" and the "persistent centrality of the sentimental in American life" emerged during the eighteenth century.[67] Whitefield's funeral was marked by profound sentimentality. As Nicole Eustace observes, expressions of grief could have multiple interpretations, ranging from signs of respect to signs of rebellion. In many ways, outpourings of emotion that surrounded death were not that different from enthusiasm in their potential to be construed as seditious, especially within the context of the challenges that revivalism posed to the authority of clergy. In the context of the eighteenth century, grief was never inconsequential, as it could be construed as a challenge to authority.[68]

The sentimentality that surrounded Whitefield's death is reflective of both respect and a bit of rebellion. The respect and admiration of his followers was quite evident in the outpouring of grief. This outpouring served as a challenge to anyone who might denigrate the late minister after his death and to elevate his standing and respectability posthumously. Whitefield's death most certainly transformed him, and his status as an international religious figure solidified his status as a transdenominational revivalist icon. He remained as such even as denominational boundaries became much more important in the subsequent Great Awakenings.

For revivalists particularly, the tension between eighteenth-century sentimentality and fears of false hopes of salvation ran deep around funerals. Those who believed in predestination balanced a need to issue reassurance as part of the funeral while not appearing presumptuous about the achievement of salvation.[69] The general fear against an excess in emotion surrounding a funeral was that, unable to restrain themselves, survivors might succumb to hypocrisy by being more emotional than considered appropriate for what was traditionally a more dignified occasion.[70]

For the funeral of an icon of revivalism, the problem was twofold. First, followers knew that they were memorializing a man who was a central figure of revivalism; if his salvation was ever in doubt, then so was that of his many converts and followers. Whitefield himself had wrestled with the problem of predestination in a letter to a friend six years prior to his death, ultimately reaching a hopeful conclusion:

> Tho' they pass through the fire, yet it does not consume, tho' through deep, yes very deep waters, it does not overwhelm so as to destroy them—And all these are only earnests of good things to come—so many assurances that we shall at least be carried through the Jordan of Death, and ... landed in the Canaan of everlasting rest.[71]

It is therefore fitting that in death, Whitefield became a symbol of hope in a religious landscape that was profoundly concerned with preparing for the Second Coming—the ultimate hope for devout, evangelical Christians.

A second problem was that his followers knew that Whitefield and his memory would come under fire from his critics. His elegies and enshrinement therefore became an exercise in claiming, shaping, and protecting his legacy on the part of his supporters. Their actions were, in no small way, an extension and preservation of the iconic image that Whitefield had so carefully constructed for himself.

There was also a question of what was appropriate for the funeral of someone who embraced Calvinism (as did his followers). Whitefield had carefully planned his own funeral, and the rites he chose were not those of the more simplistic funerary traditions of Calvinists and orthodox Puritans. His funeral seemingly went against his own public sentiments about the corrupting nature of the excesses of wealth. It also went against the prevalent seventeenth- and eighteenth-century attitudes that the wealth of the departed should not be wasted on extravagant funerals, but spent on the living.[72]

Inventing George Whitefield

Christians in general were suspicious of wealth, and many ministers across denominations, including Whitefield, expressed alarm over the "effects of wealth and luxury as manifest in growing contentiousness in many areas of public life."[73] As noted, during his life, Whitefield called out the southern planters for their gratuitous displays and, in turn, had been called a hypocrite by his detractors for his own spending habits and manner of dress.[74] Thus, his funeral served as yet another example of the tension between long-held values and the promise of improvements in mobility and in the material lives of many in the eighteenth century.[75]

Whitefield's funeral expenses, which included construction of his tomb, were estimated at around fifty pounds sterling.[76] Since the second half of the seventeenth century, on both sides of the Atlantic World, funerals had tended to be simple occasions that largely avoid "ceremony."[77] Whitefield's funeral was very much a departure from this character and more reflective of the great social changes in New England society in the eighteenth century.[78] That is part of the reason some observers raised objections to the pomp that surrounded it.

An assemblage of Whitefield's supporters from the New England clergy carefully tended to his funeral arrangements. Rev. Dr. Haven of Portsmouth, New Hampshire, the Reverend Rodgers of Exeter, New Hampshire, the Reverends Jewett and Chandler of Rowley, Massachusetts, the Reverend Moses Parsons of Newbury, Massachusetts, and the Reverend Bass of Newburyport, Massachusetts, all served as pallbearers. The procession was a mile long, reduced to just under half the planned length because the day of the funeral was raw and rainy. Because of the weather, the crowd of 104 couples that followed the coffin was also greatly reduced from what it would have been.[79]

When the cortege reached the end of its route, Whitefield's coffin was carried into Old South Presbyterian Church and placed near the vault at the foot of the church's altar. Attendance at the funeral was estimated at around five thousand people.[80] Attendees included ministers from around the New England colonies. The turnout did not rival the largest audiences of Whitefield's sermons, but it was still a sizeable number of attendees for an eighteenth-century funeral. Each of the clergymen who helped carry

Whitefield's Tomb in the crypt of the Old South Presbyterian Church, Newburyport, MA. Photograph © 2014 J. Thomas Parr. Used by permission.

Whitefield's coffin took a turn memorializing him. Following his offering of prayers, the Reverend Daniel Rodgers declared that he owed his conversion to Whitefield. According to Richard Smith, he then cried out, "O my father, my father!' then stopped and wept as though his heart would break."[81] The remainder of the funeral service consisted of additional prayers, weeping, and some singing. In his address, Rev. Jewett urged the congregation to "follow his [Whitefield's] blessed example."[82] For someone to be a true icon, they have to be seen as an example, and that example must have a recognizable legacy that surpasses the life of the individual from whom the iconic image evolved. This memorialization of Whitefield during his funeral therefore served as an important point of transition.

After his funeral, Whitefield was entombed in the crypt of the Old South Church in accordance with his wishes.[83] The existence of church crypts goes back to medieval Europe, but as the previous discussion of funerary rituals suggests, their presence was unusual in the colonies, and particularly in Massachusetts. These places of memorialization became sacred spaces for the followers of the departed. Rev. Smith, who regularly attended to Whitefield, said, "When I visited the place where he is entombed,

Newburyport, I could not help saying, 'The memory of the just is blessed.' Few are there like George Whitefield however zealous, they do not possess the masterly power, and those who do, too often turn it to a purpose that does not glorify God."[84] Smith's words were intended to convey the Truth of what Whitefield represented, in contrast to others. In doing so, he defended the purity of the icon.

Numerous other sermons and eulogies of Whitefield were offered in churches and appeared in the popular press throughout the British Atlantic World in the weeks and months following his funeral. Some of these eulogies were of those who admired Whitefield's work in reinvigorating an interest in religious life. Many of them spoke to his preaching, his moral character, and the success of his labors. Others, like Phillis Wheatley and Selina, the Countess of Huntingdon, were devout followers. Some of the eulogies, including that of William Cowper, elevated Whitefield to a proverbial level of sainthood. Some of the eulogists were considered "respectable" clergy of dissenting sects; others were not.[85]

Among the most famous of the memorials was Phillis Wheatley's elegiac poem, published shortly after Whitefield's death, in 1770. Wheatley extolled Whitefield's virtues, including his commitment to Christian charity through the Bethel Orphan House.[86] Like others, she captured Whitefield in near-messianic terms, writing "Hail happy Saint on thy immortal throne," but expressed concerns about the posthumous fate of his message:

We hear no more the music of thy tongue,
Thy wonted auditories cease to throng
Thy lessons in equal'd accents flow'd!

Unhappy we the setting sun deplore!
Which once was splendid, but it shines no more.[87]

Another of Whitefield's eulogists was John Wesley, his one-time mentor with whom he had fallen out after Whitefield challenged Wesley over his preaching in favor of free grace. In August 9, 1740, in response to comments of Whitefield about Wesley's sermon, Wesley wrote to Whitefield that "there are bigots both for predestination and against it," implying that Whitefield himself was a bigot.[88] These words must have struck a painful cord with Whitefield, who frequently accused those of challenging his preaching and doctrinal interpretation of bigotry. Whitefield's reply to Wesley, which he wrote on Christmas Eve of 1740, was abrasive and lengthy. The caustic letter concluded, "I cannot but blame you for censuring the clergy of our church for not keeping to their articles."[89] Although they did reconcile before Whitefield's death, the great friendship between the two men was thereafter never quite the same.[90]

Still, Wesley eulogized his onetime friend twice in London on November 18, 1770, approximately seven weeks after Whitefield's death. The sermon was delivered at the behest of Whitefield's executors, who reiterated that it had been Whitefield's wish for Wesley to deliver a eulogy.[91] Wesley spoke once at the chapel at Tottenham Court Road, again at the tabernacle near Moorfields. Wesley recalled Whitefield's commitment to righteousness, the history of his missionary work, and his ability to draw crowds of thousands to religious life. In contrast to his private comments of thirty years before, warning Whitefield against bigotry, Wesley wrote in his eulogy that Whitefield was "endued with the most nice and unblemished modesty."[92] He also remarked upon how Whitefield's personal style altered the way individuals responded to clergy: "He feared not the faces of men," but "used great plainness of speech" to persons of every rank and condition, high and low, rich and poor; endeavoring only "by manifestation of the truth to commend himself to every man's conscience in the sight of God."[93] He continued, "You are not ignorant that these are the fundamental doctrines which he everywhere insisted on . . . the new birth, and justification by faith? . . . These let us insist upon with all boldness, at all times, and in all places."[94] In doing so, Wesley acknowledged the way in which Whitefield's ministry had changed the relationship between minister and congregant and encouraged his audience to carry on in the example that Whitefield he had set.

His brother, Charles Wesley, also wrote elegiac verse about his late friend. He spoke of Whitefield's ability to elicit conversion from "hardened sinners."[95] He also wrote of Whitefield's labors in the colonies, as well as his championing of "redemption from above."[96] He also expressed regret that Whitefield was buried in the colonies rather than back in Great Britain:

> Shall I a momentary loss deplore,
> Lamenting after him that weeps no more?
> What though, forbid by Atlantic wave,
> I cannot share my old companion's grave,
> Yet, at the trumpet's call, my dust shall rise,
> With his fly up to Jesus in the skies,
> And live with him the life that never dies.[97]

Charles Wesley's elegy is romantic in tone, in that it also suggests that he will share Whitefield's afterlife. The idea of living a godly life with the promise of salvation, of course, had been rather central to Whitefield's work during his life. Invoking it in the elegy and encouraging Whitefield's followers to continue to live these messages gave Whitefield a means to live beyond his death.

On another related point, Andrew Burstein's analysis of romantic verse elegies describes how late-eighteenth-century elegiacs sought to immortalize and enshrine figures, like George Washington, who "required a metaphorical foundation that would withstand internal conflict."[98] The eulogies of Benjamin Franklin, Washington, and others extolled the virtues of the deceased and ascended their subjects to a "supernatural guardianship."[99] Burstein's analysis speaks specifically to Founding Fathers, which Whitefield was not. Nonetheless, Whitefield certainly was a figure whose followers, like those who defended the Founders' immortality, knew that Whitefield's legacy would need to be shored up against critics. Like the elegies of the Founding Fathers, those of Whitefield were also designed to help shape Whitefield's memory and, in his case, offer a dialogue about the character and future of the Great Awakening.[100]

In the colonies, an article that appeared in the *Pennsylvania Journal* on October 1, 1770, reported the "melancholy" news of Whitefield's death. The testimonial called him a "truly pious and very extraordinary personage" as well as a "prodigy of eloquence and devotion."[101] Another report attributed to Whitefield the conversion to "serious religion" of the Reverend Dr. Cooper of Brattle-Street, Boston, "called an enthusiast by none."[102] Cooper himself eulogized Whitefield, favoring his "holy and successful activity in the cause of vital and practical religion through the English dominions."[103] Sermons such as these solidified Whitefield's legacy as one who succeeded in reaching across denominational lines in the colonies and elsewhere.

Whitefield was the subject of intense memorialization in Georgia, where, prior to his death, he arguably put down the most roots of anywhere in the British American colonies. Georgians bought out black fabric in the stores, and the pulpit, desk, and organ loft of the church in Savannah were draped in black bunting. So, too, were the pews of the governor and council, who convened at the State House and processed in the church. A lengthy memorial service followed. Georgia's legislature honored Whitefield with high eulogies in admiration of the preacher and unanimously appropriated a sum of money for having Whitefield's remains disinterred and removed to Georgia. The proposed move was met with fierce opposition by the residents of Newburyport and was eventually dropped.[104] Whitefield's tomb became a place where his followers came to honor his memory. His remains became a tool of rhetoric; they became the subject of a cultural form of adoration.[105] From 1775 onward, ministers and laypeople alike procured permission to visit Whitefield's crypt and view his remains, especially in the wake of reports in Christian magazines that his corpse showed no signs of decay. In 1790 a Mr. Brown, an Englishman, wrote of his visit that Whitefield's body remained "'perfect' aside from its discolored flesh," and further reported that "the skin immediately rose after I touched it."[106] The alleged lack of decomposition had obvious religious connotations, though a Newburyport resident reported in 1796 that the "flesh was totally consumed."[107]

The veneration of the remains combined with the veneration of Whitefield through print culture continued to shape his legacy in the decades (and beyond) after his death. Memory is never static. From his funeral onward, Whitefield's significance to religious culture evolved into what might be characterized as a narrative within a narrative: one American, one more Atlantic in scope. They were narratives that sometimes ran parallel to each other, and as the next chapter demonstrates, sometimes clashed even beyond the divide between proponents of revivalism and those who saw all that he represented as a danger. In that sense, it can be argued that all sides were concerned with the "corruption" of Whitefield. His opponents toiled in futility against his transition into a posthumous symbol of religious truth. His supporters worked tirelessly to promote him as the quintessential model of piety.

More ironically, for someone who was rather virulently anti-Catholic, much about Whitefield's memorialization came to echo the veneration of Roman Catholic saints. His crypt was repeatedly entered, and the corpse's apparent lack of decay was often a point of observation. The theft of artifacts and bones from Whitefield's coffin mimicked the fate of saintly relics—the removal and display of fingers, skulls, arm bones, tongues, and even foreskins of saints (even if many are of dubious authenticity), an enduring occurrence in the history of Christianity, and especially Catholicism. While religious pilgrimages are hardly an exclusive domain of Catholics, or even Christians, the particular way in which the veneration occurred did suggest some conventions ordinarily identified with the Roman Catholic Church.

CHAPTER SIX

A Transnational Icon

An article that appeared in 1781, following the burning of New London, Connecticut, by General Benedict Arnold and his band of British troops, claimed that the image of Whitefield "frightened them into a burnt offering of all their finery," on threat of damnation.[1] This referenced Whitefield's 1740 sermon, delivered in New London, in which he encouraged listeners to hand over their finery—silks, damasks, emeralds—all constructs of a corrupt life of excesses, to be burned on the common in a bonfire.[2] General Arnold, now a British officer, had by this time visited Whitefield's tomb along with fellow members of the Continental troops. That a onetime American officer and turncoat who visited the tomb was "haunted" into burning his [British] finery is significant, particularly for an icon that was so identified with a particular type of (religious) consumerism of his own.[3] As T. H. Breen observed, "eighteenth-century Americans communicated perceptions of status and politics to other people through items of everyday material culture."[4] Boycotts of certain goods, akin to those that Arnold and his troops burned, were in some cases a response to political grievances or political principles.[5] The depiction in the public prints of Arnold and his troops being frightened into burning their clothes by the ghost of Whitefield was highly political in nature, and it suggested one of several ways in which his image became politicized by Revolutionary evangelicals. It is from this environment that Whitefield the American religious icon emerged; an icon that strove to claim the United States as a "holy nation."[6]

The emergences of Whitefield the American religious icon and Whitefield the antislavery icon were essentially complications

A Transnational Icon

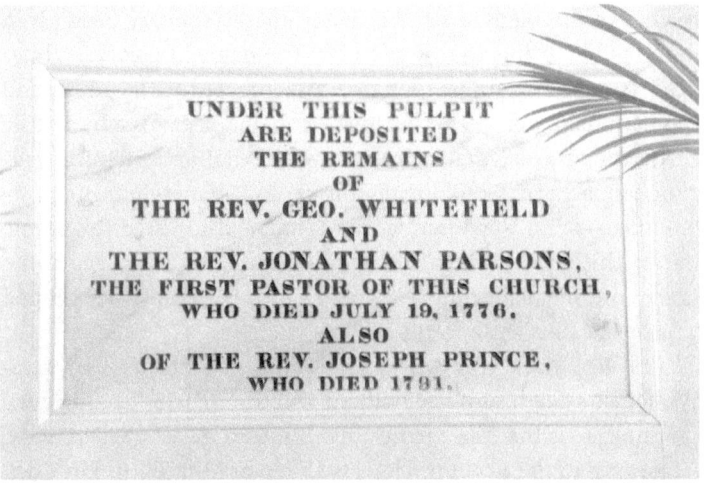

Whitefield memorial next to the altar of the Old South Presbyterian Church. Newburyport, MA. Photograph © 2014 J. Thomas Parr. Used by permission.

of the religious pluralism that characterized the British Atlantic World before the American Revolution. They represent some metamorphoses, with the new "interpretations" of Whitefield running alongside, and sometimes these versions of Whitefield intersected with each other. That Whitefield was no longer able to influence his own image after 1770 afforded more malleability to how he was interpreted and understood.

Whitefield's death was also a catalyst for the widespread reprinting of his many writings, including additional translations thereof. A number of his sermons, for example, were translated into Welsh at the beginning of his missionary career.[7] Additional translations, or at least reprints of these translations, appeared in print in the 1770s.[8]

New Whitefield memoirs also appeared as news circulated about his demise. Barely a month after his death, the *London Magazine* circulated an abbreviated memoir of Whitefield's life, which included extensive quotes from Whitefield himself. Not surprisingly, the *Memoir* mimicked the tone of his earlier autobiographies, which emphasized the centrality of his conversion experience in his turn to religious life.[9] It concluded with an insistence upon Whitefield as "universally esteemed the principal teacher of the Methodists, that many characters have been given in the public prints to this effect."[10] "The name of George Whitefield," it proclaimed, "will long be remembered with esteem and veneration not only by his personal acquaintance ... but by all true christians of every denomination, while vital and practical religion hath a place in the British dominions."[11] Veneration as a posthumous symbol was essential for Whitefield to reach full iconic status. This article, which also appeared in *Scots Magazine* at the same time, melded Whitefield's own words with those who hoped to propagate his legacy in print.[12]

The *New-Jersey Magazine* followed suit sixteen years after Whitefield's death, as it had with his will. The article's heading was, "Memoires of the Life of the Rev. Mr. George Whitefield, A.M. According to the Account He Has Given of Himself in His Own Journals, Desired to be Inserted in the Present Magazine."[13] Since Whitefield unquestionably desired the publication of his journals, his supporters were certainly doing what he would have wanted. It was not a mere matter of a magazine posthumously following a Whitefield directive. What it demonstrates is that Whitefield's followers were actively perpetuating the legacy he constructed for himself in the public prints.[14]

Almost two years later, this effort was still ongoing. In March 1772, the English Baptist minister Rev. Andrew Gifford published a new volume, containing eighteen of Whitefield's sermons. Advertisements appeared in both the *Monthly Review* and *Scots Magazine*.[15] The following July, Whitefield's patroness, the Countess of Huntingdon, released *The Works of the Reverend George Whitefield*, a seven-volume publication that contained Whitefield's sermons, journals, and other writings.[16]

Whitefield's *Last Will and Testament*, which was probated in a Georgia court, was also reproduced in periodicals around Great Britain and its dominion. It appeared both in the *London Magazine* and *Scots Magazine* during the winter following Whitefield's death. *Scots Magazine* published it in January 1771, and the *London Magazine* followed a month later.[17] The will was reproduced yet again in the *New-Jersey Magazine and Monthly Advertiser* sixteen years after Whitefield's death, in December 1786.[18] The appearance of memoirs and the legal documents of his state internationally all demonstrate the staying power of the transnational nature of Whitefield's character and image. He was not one whose influence was confined to a particular locality, and this was not lost on his followers.

The remembrance by Selina, the Countess of Huntingdon was another poignant attempt at protecting and enshrining Whitefield's memory. The lengthy memoir she commissioned was written by John Gillies, a minister of the Church of Scotland, and published two years after Whitefield's death.[19] The memoir detailed Whitefield's entire life, beginning with his birth, his education at Pembroke College, his conversion, and his missionary work in the Americas. It also included an assessment of Whitefield's character as a minister and excerpts of select elegies, including Jonathan Parsons's, delivered during Whitefield's funeral service. Parsons's funeral sermon emphasized Whitefield's Oxford (i.e., English) roots and refuted common criticisms of Whitefield and the tendency of his opponents to conflate him with untutored itinerants.[20] Another minister, Boston's Rev. Pemberton, wrote that "he was no contracted bigot, but embraced Christians of every denomination in the arms of his charity, and acknowledged them to be children of the same father, servants of the same masters, heirs of the same undefiled inheritance."[21] Every one of these eulogies spoke to Whitefield's character and countered criticisms of him, including those of persons who had characterized him as a force destructive of Christian unity.[22] The volume concludes with an assortment of Whitefield's published sermons.

The Gillies memoir served as a literary monument to Whitefield's life, but as the conception of a revivalist minister and Whitefield's dear benefactress, friend, and executrix, it was also a conscious endeavor to shape Whitefield as an icon. The repeated references to Whitefield's education and sanctioned ordination are particularly important, given revivalism's and itinerancy's increasing association with unschooled preachers. As previously noted, Whitefield was criticized by several New England ministers for what they saw as a failure on his part to differentiate himself from the unschooled itinerants.[23] His followers clearly wanted to distinguish Whitefield from the "less reputable" sorts and to protect his memory from his critics.

Significantly, the Gillies memoir was also published during a period of inter-evangelical warfare between Wesleyan Methodists and Calvinists, in which Lady Huntingdon was a key figure.[24] The doctrinal feud began before Whitefield's death but raged on for at least a decade afterward. The countess sent some students to Bethesda Orphanage, by then being converted to a college, to oversee religious instruction there and expand Calvinist Methodism into the British American colonies in 1772. The students boasted that they were going to "drive all the [Wesleyan] Meth[odist] preachers from the American continent."[25] The timing of the publication of the memoir therefore can be understood as an effort by Huntingdon to harness Whitefield in her ambitions to expand the influence of Calvinist Methodism.

Other devotees of the late minister also proactively sought to shape Whitefield's legacy. William Cowper, an evangelical Christian and an English poet and hymnodist, never personally knew Whitefield but greatly admired him and eulogized him in a verse. "Hope" somewhat martyrized Whitefield, recounting the criticisms that he faced over the course of his ministry. Cowper placed Whitefield upon a proverbial pedestal, calling him "pilloried on infamy's high stage" and "the butt of slander."[26] The poem also compares Whitefield to the Apostle Paul, recounting how he, too, "cross'd cheerfully tempestuous seas" and bore the "shame" of ridicule "where'er he went."[27] In the final verse, Cowper reframes Whitefield's legacy in near-messianic terms:

> Blush, Calumny; and write upon his tomb
> If honest eulogy can spare thee room
> They deep repentance of a thousand lies
> Which aim'd at him, have pierced the offending skies
> And say, Blot out my sin, confess'd deplored
> Against Thine image in Thine Saint, O Lord![28]

Cowper's deeply romanticized remembrance of a man he never knew was not unlike that of Charles Wesley, even if Wesley made no comparisons between Paul and Whitefield. Cowper elevated Whitefield to sainthood and suggested his tomb as a site of pilgrimage for the faithful; the tomb did indeed become such a site, and Whitefield's skull became a relic of sorts.[29]

Those of Whitefield's followers who knew him when he was alive remained loyal for decades after his death. The Reverend Archibald Alexander, a prominent Presbyterian theologian, visited the Old South Presbyterian Church in 1800. He reported seeing an elderly woman of between eighty to ninety years of age who had belonged to the Old South Presbyterian Church since Whitefield had helped to found it. She still attended the weekly prayer meeting.[30]

Whitefield's tomb became the sight of macabre visits that continued long after his death. Two visits of note occurred in the eighteenth century. The first, in 1775, was by a Revolutionary chaplain and a group of officers that included Benedict Arnold. When the visitors viewed Whitefield's body, they removed his clerical collar and wristbands as souvenirs to pass among their soldiers.[31] The second visit, by a trio of evangelical ministers, was more characteristic of visits to Whitefield's tomb. Jesse Lee and two Methodist ministers entered the tomb in 1789 to view Whitefield's body. They lifted the lid of his coffin and peered inside, with Lee remarking, "How quiet the repose, how changed the features."[32]

The nineteenth century saw a number of visits to Whitefield's tomb. Methodist minister Abel Stevens visited sometime in the 1820s. He picked up the skull and examined it "with great interest."[33] Stevens was to become one of many to report handling the skull and scrutinizing it. Handling the skull became a sort of ritual that was an accepted and, indeed, expected part of the pilgrimage to Whitefield's tomb. The tomb and the rituals surrounding its visitation became a cult of the skull of sorts, the term Margaret Stratton coined to characterize the Neapolitan devotion to the dead and care for skulls and corpses.[34]

Whitefield's followers' actions at his tomb differed from those of the Neapolitans in that the Neapolitans cared for the remains mainly in hopes of receiving material assistance.[35] Whitefield's followers were more concerned with their spiritual well-being, and Whitefield became an immortal messenger of the Great Awakening.[36] The visitations were part of a long tradition of looking

A Transnational Icon

for the "wisdom that comes to Christians from above."[37] Visitors looked to Whitefield's memory for wisdom and inspiration. These visitations had a touch of the supernatural, with Whitefield's skull and remains taking on a role where, in death, Whitefield could serve as a potential aid to followers. They were a deeply spiritual experience for Whitefield's admirers, who craved a direct contact with the man. As such, his tomb became a sacred space. His tomb, combined with the "growing sentimentalization of religious culture," communicated a desire for optimism about salvation, much as Jesus's ascension had also suggested the promise of an afterlife.[38]

Two additional visits to Whitefield's tomb occurred in 1834. One was by Freewill Baptist minister David Marks, who remarked on the bones and on how the skull was "detached from the rest and turned over," no doubt from the penchant of visitors for handling it. The other visit was by Congregationalist ministers Andrew Reed of London and James Matheson of Durham, England. With the blessing of the pastor of the Old South Presbyterian Church, the two men entered Whitefield's tomb, where his coffin lay between those of his friends, the Reverends Prince and Parsons. They slipped the lid of Whitefield's unsealed coffin aside, and in a Shakespearian gesture, Reed picked up Whitefield's skull. He recalled being able to say little as he held the skull. Back in the chapel of the church, Reed, Matheson, and the pastor held a special memorialization of Whitefield. The men "collected over the grave of the eloquent, the devoted and seraphic man, and gave expression to the sentiments that possessed us, by solemn psalmody and fervent prayer. It was not an ordinary service to any of us."[39]

In Christian tradition, dating from the Middle Ages, a seraphim is the highest of the nine orders of angels. They are also the most removed from reflecting the human image. In Christian theology, seraphims regulate the heavens. To describe Whitefield in such terms was really to elevate him to otherworldly status. Given the fears predestination posed concerning salvation for Whitefield followers, these images should be understood as hopeful: a promise of what Gold would bring about.[40]

The visitation ritual was repeated a year later by another delegation from Great Britain and Ireland. The delegates included the Reverend F. A. Cox of London and the Reverend James Hoby of

Birmingham. They made a thirty-nine-mile detour from Boston specifically to visit Whitefield's grave. Like Reed and Matheson, they descended into the vault and sat on either side of the coffin. By this time, the upper part of the lid of Whitefield's coffin had been removed for easier access to his remains. The two men handled the grand itinerant's skull, whispering their adorations back and forth to each other.[41] These visits continued well into the nineteenth century.

The Reverend William B. Tappan wrote a verse about Whitefield in September 1837. His opening lines read,

> And this was Whitefield! — this, the dust now blending.
> With kindred dust, that wrapt his soul of fire —
> Which, from the mantle freed, is still ascending.
> Through regions of far glory, holier and higher.[42]

Tappan's verse clearly refers to the power and veneration surrounding Whitefield's remains.

Whitefield continued to appear in the popular press long after his death. An 1845 article in one of London's daily papers detailed Whitefield's life, with considerable attention also paid to his death, funeral, and tomb. The writer recounted his experiences discussing Whitefield with an unnamed person in Ipswich, Massachusetts, where Whitefield had once met with widespread refusals by local ministers to use their pulpits. The by that time quite elderly man had heard Whitefield preach in Ipswich during his childhood. The writer mentioned his plans to travel to Newburyport the next day. The old man replied, "I suppose, sir, you'll be going to see his bones? He was buried at Newburyport, and you can see 'em if you like."[43] The writer resolved to visit Whitefield's crypt. When he was in Newburyport, he visited the room in which Whitefield died and then walked the short distance to the Church. The sexton of the Old South Presbyterian Church escorted the writer to the basement. He lifted the coffin's lid, adjusted the lamp, and told the writer, "Here, look in.... THAT'S THE MAN."[44] The writer held Whitefield's skull like the others before him, then put it back into the coffin.[45]

Since Whitefield died of natural causes; he cannot be construed as a true martyr. Still, Whitefield's skull was a connection to a fallen symbol, and his message transcended his death. The practice was suggestive of the "cult of relics" that existed during the Middle Ages, the relics regarded as "sacred objects that have been in touch with the body."[46] In Whitefield's case, there were obvious biblical connotations to the handling of his remains. There was a long-standing practice by which the relics of purported saints were kept in churches for veneration by the faithful. No miracles have been attributed to Whitefield, nor was any care to preserve the remains taken, as with the bodies of saints that were preserved as relics. Nonetheless, his remains were still housed in a place where pilgrims could visit them and, in a manner of speaking, connect to the living man.[47] The distribution of "parts" among the faithful symbolically transferred a share of sanctification from Whitefield.[48]

The rituals surrounding veneration of Whitefield's skull also assumed a posthumous existence vis-à-vis a holy necromancy.[49] This was not the occult art ritual of necromancy that was feared as a challenge to religious orthodoxy and outlawed in many of the British American colonies by the beginning of the eighteenth century, in which practitioners believed that they could truly resurrect the dead.[50] Whitefield's followers who visited his tomb did not expect to actually raise the dead. Rather, the rituals surrounding the visitation of his grave and the rituals around the handling of his remains did serve to rejuvenate the messenger. The visitations that involved handling the remains continued until 1932, when the town of Newburyport ordered that the crypt be sealed for sanitary reasons.

The veneration of Whitefield's remains by an interdenominational and transnational band of followers marked the fruition of a goal he set as a young minister. In 1739, back near the beginning of his missionary work in the colonies, Whitefield echoed his mentor, John Wesley, when writing to a friend that "the whole world is now my parish."[51] "Wherever my Master calls me I am ready to go and preach his everlasting gospel," he continued.[52] Whitefield resigned himself to, and even embraced, the idea that he would never be a settled minister. Nonetheless, this itinerant life was also incompatible with his desire to be seen as an Anglican reformer. With what Whitefield came to mean for religious liberty in the colonies, with the failure of his defense of slavery to align him with the Anglican planter elite in the colonies, and with his death and enshrinement in the colonies, Whitefield failed in his desire to be seen as a respectable Anglican clergyman. Even after his death, he remained a central figure of the pluralist Great Awakening and a hero to evangelicals on both sides of the Atlantic. In spite of his virulent quarrel with John Wesley and the fact that he died twenty-one years before the official split of the Methodist Church from Anglicanism, he became recognized as a central figure in Methodism's founding. However, much to Whitefield's consternation, Wesley's Arminian brand of Methodism was more influential in the colonies than Whitefield's Calvinism.[53] In any case, Whitefield's influence expanded well beyond that of any settled minister, but it alienated him from the Church of England even as it transformed him into an icon. Whitefield continued to be frustrated with this conundrum through much of his life, though he appeared to accept the fact that his success at conversion came with a price.

Whitefield's pluralism also suggests another problem regarding the complexity of his legacy. The territorialness over Whitefield's body, and the fact that he was eulogized on both sides of the Atlantic, demonstrate that he was a figure of the Anglo-American religious world. Conversely, his entombment in the colonies, and particularly the well-known elegy by Phillis Wheatley, claimed George Whitefield as a heroic American figure. As a result, determining whose hero Whitefield was proves challenging, as multiple factions sought to claim him.

Many contemporary American evangelicals still claim him as a hero of American religious life, and even as a Founding Father figure. His entombment in Massachusetts effectively created a "body politic" of sorts. The bones of soldiers were venerated as a means to "continue to cultivate memory, nationalism, patriotism, and the particular political agendas of memorializers."[54] Whitefield was not truly a national figure like the patriot-martyrs whose bones received reverential treatment after the American Revolution, but his body did serve as a holy object, intended to keep alive the spirit and momentum of revivalism after the death of one of the movement's vital figures.[55] His tomb most certainly helped to cultivate the memory of Whitefield and revivalism as well as of revivalism's advancement and expansion. Whitefield's tomb effectively became a symbol of the movement, just as the bones of the patriot-martyrs served as powerful symbols to a young country also involved in a process of self-determination.

Whitefield was neither particularly engaged in the discourse of republicanism nor did he share the commitments to civic humanism embraced by the Founding Fathers. He admired Penn's liberty of conscience, but the liberty of conscience is a construct of the English Civil War that cannot be conflated with the Revolutionary rhetoric that led to the American Revolution. Moreover, while the liberty of conscience had some religious connotations, it was not exclusively a religious construct. Claiming it as such is a gross oversimplification.

In contrast with Whitefield, some colonial religious leaders did, on occasion, discuss political matters from the pulpit. In the years leading up to the Revolution, Jonathan Mayhew, for instance, occasionally delivered highly charged politicized sermons that are suggestive of the growing rift between Great Britain and the American colonists. For example, many Loyalists blamed one sermon of his for "inciting the riot" that "destroyed Lieutenant Governor Thomas Hutchinson's mansion the next day."[56] Other clergy, like Samuel Cooper, were much better at walking a line that "muted the troubles of the day with a reassuring, warm spirituality," an ability appreciated by Whigs and Tories alike.[57] In short, there were certainly "patriot preachers," but Whitefield was not among them. In fact, careful attention to sermons of the eighteenth century reveal that, although dissenting clergy occasionally spoke of the "tyranny" of Charles I and II against nonconformists, for most, it was a limited sort of engagement with politics that did not really cross into Revolutionary rhetoric, even if religion and politics were commonly intertwined in the eighteenth century.

As the previous discussion of the erosion of Whitefield's Anglican identity suggests, many of his contemporaries made connections between Whitefield and dissenter politics. These connections, however, drew on historical memory rather than contemporary events.

For example, a farcical script for a play that was reproduced in the *Newport Mercury* suggests that Whitefield's contemporaries recognized his oratorical skills but saw him as a troublemaker who stirred up old religious passions.[58] This script depicts an exchange between a "Mr. Jack Wilkes" and a "Lord Mercurio." Wilkes, a staunchly anti-Catholic English politician and satirist who was seen as an "imprudent demagogue," was in his apartment reading Milton's *Paradise Lost* when Mercurio dropped by.[59] The two began to discuss Wilkes's creation of a dictionary, wherein Wilkes suggested the inclusion of some subheadings under the term *minister*. Wilkes suggested that the subheadings include "insolent minister, all-grasping minister . . . Hungry harpies of the minister, Ministerial zeal; Ministerial effronter . . . Dregs of ministerial power."[60] All of this is suggestive of Wilkes's frequent scathing criticisms of the appointment of Lord Bute, a Scottish "favorite" of George III.[61] Mercurio cut Wilkes off, "Enough, enough — The dictionary is a real treasure; and every word in it, when transplanted into *The North Briton* [Wilkes's weekly newspaper], should be printed in Italics, that the readers may pronounce them with a proper [derisive] emphasis."[62] Wilkes continued, suggesting other terms: "English Whig; Tools of corruption and despotism; Despotic principles; Highland chiefs; Tyranny of a Stuart."[63] He was once again cut off by Mercurio: "Stop, Jack; stop — My very ears are stunn'd. One half of those dreadful words properly applied, is enough to throw half the people of England into a panic, as effectually as George Whitefield does his auditory, by thundering out the devil, hell, and damnation to them."[64]

This exchange recognized the power of particular words, even one hundred years after the English Civil War, to incite strong feelings in those who read them. Mercurio also acknowledged the ability of Whitefield to stir up people's passions, as well as the potential for religious speech to contribute to revolution. Nonetheless, the character's primary concern in invoking Whitefield is his distaste for Whitefield's revivalist theology, rather than identifying him as revolutionary character. And, certainly, the play concerned British religious toleration rhetoric rather than the American religious liberty that Whitefield's followers tried to associate with him.

This play was published in 1764, after tensions between Great Britain and the colonies had already begun. It followed enactment of the Royal Line of Proclamation in 1763. The play was also published four months after the Sugar Act was passed. Whitefield's preaching definitely broke rules and probably influenced the republican Christianity that came later. In challenging the authority of the orthodox clergy, he was a discernable symbol of changing attitudes about hierarchy.[65] Yet his preaching really was focused on eternal matters rather than the politics of the growing imperial crisis.[66] Absent is any evidence that the writers made a connection between Whitefield during his life and the contemporary politics of the 1760s. That Whitefield was such a visible symbol of challenge to authority makes him an excellent candidate for the corruption of history and tradition articulated by Benjamin Rush and John Adams.[67]

Given the article's obvious distain for dissenter politics and the speed with which Whitefield's opponents jumped on any instance of him stirring up dissent, any displays of revolutionary politics on his part would have almost certainly provoked comment. And indeed, with perhaps one exception, reports of his activities that appeared in colonial newspapers during this period contain only benign announcements of his travels—when and where he preached, how many times he preached in a location, and occasional reports of his health.[68] These reports appeared sporadically alongside other news items concerning the Seven Years War, but there are no reports of his preaching politics.

There were, on the other hand, some connections made between Great Britain's renewed interest in its American colonies after the Seven Years War and the inroads made by the Church of England and by dissenters in the colonies. By the 1760s, according to Frank Lambert, there was already a concern in the colonies about the appointment of a residential Anglican bishop.[69] "It was not a new threat," Lambert notes, "but in the broader context of Britain's new imperial policies of the 1760s and 1770s, it took on a much more sinister character."[70] Whitefield received an enormous amount of attention in the press, and many colonies chafed as Great Britain ended decades of salutary neglect of its American colonies. Therefore, had his preaching turned patriotic, this change would have appeared in the news. Collectively, all of this casts considerable doubt on Whitefield as a figure of revolution and on the belief that his preaching was intertwined with contemporary statecraft or politics. Rather, this connection was made by some of the evangelicals who co-opted him after his death.

Whitefield was certainly a figure in the shift from toleration to religious liberty that had begun by the middle of the eighteenth century. Nonetheless, he was still irretrievably tied to the greater discussion about toleration and religious freedom throughout the British Atlantic World, and specifically to the colonies. He was, as one contemporary observer in the Americas wrote, "an 'imported Divinity,'" likening Whitefield and the revival he sparked to the latest London fashions.[71]

Whitefield frequently invoked the threat of "tyranny," but it is also very important to differentiate between the politics of toleration that inspired Whitefield and the politics behind the American Revolution, over one hundred years later. Whitefield shared the anti-Catholic and social reform ideologies commonly attributed to English Whigs, but there is no evidence either that he self-identified as one or that anyone in the colonies identified him as a Whig. And as Mark Noll demonstrates, revivalism was not always compatible with the Whig ideology that fueled the American Revolution. Jonathan Edwards was castigated by those who used the language of Whiggism to challenge any religious preaching they saw as suggestive of the influence of the Church of England.[72] Even though he intermingled considerably with dissenters and on many occasions was critical of the behaviors of a number of Church of England clergy, Whitefield identified very strongly with the Church of England. This makes him an unlikely Whig.

Whitefield's politics, instead, were more anti-Catholic than revolutionary.[73] Antirevivalist and staunch Whitefield critic that Charles Chauncy was, in contrast to Whitefield, he was much more inclined to employ Real Whig ideology from the pulpit than was Whitefield. Yet Chauncy, too, was still predominantly concerned with inflating anti-Catholic sentiments throughout the colonies, "'referring to the pope as the 'Anti-Christ' and the 'Man of sin'" as colonists celebrated British defeats over Catholic France following the siege of Louisbourg.[74] Even if this can be argued as patriotism, in the context of the Seven Years War, it is still British patriotism rather than American. There were occasional references to America and Americans among the colonists by the 1750s, but the Seven Years War was, nonetheless, an imperial war and had no revolutionary underpinnings.

Arguably the most "political" of Whitefield's sermons from the middle of the eighteenth-century was a 1746 sermon titled *British Mercies*, a response to the Jacobite Rebellion of 1745–1746. This rebellion was the second of the eighteenth-century Jacobite Risings, in which the Scottish prince Charles Edward Stuart (Bonnie Prince Charlie) raised an army of Highland clansmen in an unsuccessful attempt to restore the Catholic Stuart house to the British throne. This uprising took place during the Austrian War of Succession, when a substantial part of the British Army was occupied in combat on the European continent. It was ultimately quashed on April 16, 1746, with British success at the Battle of Culloden and the enactment of a pair of laws, one stripping Scottish lords of their heritable jurisdictions (Heritable Jurisdictions Act of 1746) and the other outlawing traditional Highland dress (Act of Proscription of 1746).

Whitefield's sermon, *British Mercies*, preached in Philadelphia, was a response to this rebellion, which he called "unnatural," but its concerns are almost entirely focused on what victory meant as far as preserving Great Britain as a Protestant state. The sermon opens with a brief mention of the "remarkable Deliverances wrought out for the Kingdoms of Great-Britain and Ireland, from the Infant State of William the Conqueror."[75] In light of the Jacobite uprising's effort to restore a Catholic monarch (Charles Edward Stuart), the invocation of a historic Norman king should be understood to reflect Whitefield's fears of the infiltration of a foreign, Catholic threat.[76]

His sermon also reminded its listeners of the "many unspeakable Blessings which we have for a Course of Years enjoy'd, during the Right of His present Majesty [George II]," and called him "one of the best of Kings."[77] "It is now above Nineteen years since he began to reign over us," Whitefield remarked, as he invoked Samuel's address to the Israelites. Samuel's followers told him, Whitefield observed, "Thou hast not defrauded us, nor oppressed us."[78] To Whitefield, and most revivalists and dissenters, the victory of a Catholic nation or army over the British throne would most certainly have been a threat to English civil liberties. Whitefield called the Jacobite Rebellion a plot "hatched in Hell, and afterwards nourished at Rome, having taken Place, supposing, I say, that the old Pretender (Charles Edward Stuart's father, James III) should have exchanged his Cardinal's Cap for a Triple Crown, and have transferred his pretend Title to his Eldest son."⁷⁹ Following in his Catholic sympathizer's footsteps, "The Young Pretender," Whitefield asserted, might "keep the three Kingdoms of England, Scotland and Ireland, in greater Vassalage to the See of Rome."⁸⁰ Whitefield continued to speculate of a Great Britain and its dominion with a "Popish Pretender" on the throne, "instead of being represented by a free Parliament, and governed by Laws made by their Consent, as we now are."⁸¹ His use of this particular language was all the more significant because he delivered this sermon in Philadelphia, a locality with considerable Quaker, Presbyterian, and other dissenter populations. It harkened back to the violence of the English Civil War and the Glorious Revolution and the struggle for religious toleration faced by dissenters in Great Britain. Nonetheless, these politics were old British politics and this sermon reinforces what his contemporaries saw of Whitefield—not a man of rebellion, but a man who certainly could stir old dissenting British feelings and fears concerning religious persecution.

American Revolutionaries did raise concerns about representation. Indeed, the British concept of "virtual representation" was one of their many grievances against Great Britain. Whitefield raised the question of what a "popish victory" over the British throne might mean for the American colonies.⁸² Nonetheless, the concerns that Whitefield raised in this sermon were entirely steeped in anti-Catholicism and a British political rhetoric and history that were reflective of the Protestant Reformation and British questions about toleration, rather than questions about religious liberties in an American context. The "Young Pretender," according to Whitefield, was

> descended from a Father (the deposed James II), who, when Duke of York, put all Scotland into Confusion; and afterwards when crowned King of England, for his arbitrary and tyrannical Government, both in Church and State, was justly obliged to abdicate the Throne, by the Assertors of British Liberty.⁸³

His point about "British Liberty" references the politics of the English Civil War and the struggle over toleration rather than the notion of religious liberty as it evolved later in the eighteenth century. In short, this sermon is not substantively different from the anti-French, anti-Catholic utterances that were occasionally offered from other pulpits during the eighteenth-century by dissenter clergy.

Sometimes, Whitefield's sermons emphasized the notion of God as the ultimate sovereign. For example, his 1737 sermon, *The Benefits of Early Piety*, imparted to his audience the importance of an early commitment to piety when "we are then best qualified to endure Hardness as good Soldiers of Jesus Christ."[84] Christianity—and particularly adherence to the true Christianity, as prescribed by Whitefield—was a concern that defied national boundaries. Whitefield discussed "freedom" in this sermon, but to him, service to God "is perfect Freedom."[85] It was a spiritual freedom, akin to the one he ascribed for all souls, including slaves, rather than a political freedom that Christian writers and scholars have sometimes ascribed to him.[86] This sermon is reflective, once again, of Whitefield's primary concern with eternal matters.

Other sermons of Whitefield's contained warnings about religious oppression, though they either referenced the persecutions faced by primitive Christians in the early days of Christianity or contained further references to seventeenth-century politics that emphasized the importance of religious toleration. His sermon *The Burning Bush*, which invoked Old Testament biblical images of God appearing to Moses, also referenced primitive Christianity and suggested Whitefield as a more recent messenger of God.[87] In the sermon, Whitefield asked, "Now what must the Christian burn with? With tribulation and persecution."[88] In this sermon, he certainly warned his audience to be on guard against religious persecution. Even so, it still exemplified fears common among English dissenters from the second half of the seventeenth century onward about civil and religious leaders from other denominations impeding their ability to determine their own religious paths. It was not particularly revolutionary or radical.

Whitefield's 1739 sermon, *The Almost Christian*, referenced "Princes and Rulers of the Earth" who were "too happy to be disturbed by unwelcomed truths."[89] It also referenced those "set out with false Notions of Religion; and though they live in a Christian

Country, yet know not what Christianity is."⁹⁰ Religious leaders preached toleration, but had definitive and different ideas of what true religion was and were determined to promote their own visions.⁹¹

The idea of a consent-based, republican style of church government did make nonconformist colonists sympathetic to civil republicanism.⁹² They also tended to be deeply suspicious of church and civil hierarchies and therefore more inclined to side with the Revolutionaries.⁹³ Whitefield was alive for and influential in some of the early "cultural terrain" in which "republican Christianity would later flourish," and he was "familiar with the newer language of liberty."⁹⁴ Nonetheless, he tended to employ the language of liberty for limited purposes.⁹⁵ He criticized monarchs for "arbitrary and tyrannical government, both in church and state," but his "religious language" was mostly "innocent of political connotations."⁹⁶ Although his words were taken out of context, it is easy to see why those concerned with religious freedom might have drawn inspiration from him.

In the soon-to-be United States, his image became co-opted first for patriotic purposes, and later by American evangelicals seeking to make sense of the place of religion in early American culture and politics. It was part of what Lambert calls an "American Revolution of Religion."⁹⁷ It evolved from a struggle to determine how eighteenth-century ideas of religious liberty would play out in the new Republic. Lambert envisions this revolution of religion as a social movement that had some roots in the American Revolution but was not entirely intertwined with it.

The majority of Americans feared religious tyranny and supported at least some degree of separation between church and state. It was up to the individual to decide matters of faith.⁹⁸ This belief was partly the result of the Great Awakening and partly of the Enlightenment.⁹⁹ Religious freedom was to be assured by virtuous individuals who could limit the authority of the court and church, and both American dissenters and Radical Whigs saw religious liberty as a facet of civil liberties.¹⁰⁰ Whitefield was certainly seen as virtuous by his followers, so he was an ideal symbol on which to draw inspiration for those who were concerned about religious freedom from the American Revolution into the nineteenth century, and especially for those who desired a more democratic and accessible religious experience.[101] A number of itinerants in particular drew inspiration from Whitefield, modeling their writing after his.[102]

The struggle for religious freedom was not a simple matter of accommodating a broad view of Christianity.[103] The bitter divides that existed between Catholics and Protestants, and between different Protestant sects, still remained.[104] The Early Republic complicated religious life by sending foreign religious authorities into retreat.[105] The result was a First Amendment that protected religious freedom and a Constitution that did not establish a national church. Beginning in 1776, almost a full six years after Whitefield's death, the delegates of the Continental Congress began the process of drafting an instrument of government to safeguard American liberties.[106] Much debate ensued over whether the new Republic should embrace toleration or the more radical religious freedom.[107] As arguably the most visible icon of the Great Awakening, which had helped to foment eighteenth-century discourse about religious liberty, Whitefield provided a powerful symbol for those who sought to enshrine religious liberty in the cultural and political structures of the fledgling Republic. It was a posthumous extension of the heroic self-image that he carefully constructed for himself through the transatlantic print networks through his life, though with a more localized, national context.[108]

Phillis Wheatley was arguably the first person to claim an "American" image for Whitefield in her 1770 elegiac poem.[109] Her poem depicted Whitefield as a spiritual savior of the colonies. The second and third verses of her elegy are devoted almost in their entirety to describing what he meant for religious life in the colonies:

When his AMERICANS were burden'd sore,
When streets were crimson'd with their guiltless gore!
Unrival'd friendship in his breast now strove;
The fruit thereof was charity and love.

Towards *America*—couldst thou do more
Than leave thy native home, the *British* shore,

A Transnational Icon

To cross the great Atlantic's wat'ry road,
To see *America's* distress'd abode?"[110]

Her poem specifically addresses his entombment in Massachusetts:

Great COUNTESS! we *Americans* revere
Thy name, and thus condole thy grief sincere:
We mourn with thee, that TOMB obscurely plac'd,
In which thy Chaplain undisturb'd doth rest.
New-England sure, doth feel the ORPHAN's smart;
Reveals the true sensations of his heart.[111]

While this poem reveres Whitefield as a force in providential life in the colonies, it did not necessarily preclude his Englishness the way a true claim of Whitefield as a Founding Father would suggest. Wheatley saw herself as "American, but, like many colonists in 1770, it did not automatically preclude her loyalty to King George III. In 1768 she even wrote a poem in which she praised King George: "May George, belov'd by all the nations round, Live with heav'ns choicest constant blessings crown'd!"[112] Even some of Whitefield's ardent supporters—including Phillis Wheatley, Selina Hastings, and James Habersham—did not turn Revolutionary at the outbreak of war.

Wheatley acknowledged Whitefield's British home, a shared grief with his patroness, the Countess of Huntingdon, and "his lonely [Moorfields] *Tabernacle*, [in London] sees no more ... A WHITEFIELD landing on the *British* shore."[113] Even as she mourned what his death meant for the future of religious life in the colonies, she did not lose sight of his status as an international figure. And while Wheatley self-identified as an American in a period where the strain between Great Britain and its British North American colonies grew, her discourse is limited to religious life and offers no suggestion of Whitefield having a role in Revolutionary politics.

As the previous image of the ghost of Whitefield suggests, the mingling of Whitefield's discourses of politics and religion was the product of his disciples, beginning shortly after Whitefield's death, rather than by Whitefield himself. In his elegy of Whitefield,

Presbyterian Nathaniel Whitaker began the process of reformulating Whitefield into a revolutionary. Walker's elegy reshaped Whitefield's language from a tour of Great Britain to argue that Whitefield "was a patriot, not in shew, but reality, and an enemy to tyranny."[114] Whitefield's language had, in fact, been used in an entirely different context, concerning religious toleration.[115] Whitaker inserted Whitefield's concerns for spiritual liberty into the discourse for "liberation from terrestrial tyranny."[116]

During the American Revolution, Whitefield's American supporters also invoked him in the context of victories. This can be ascribed to what Bernard Bailyn describes as a facet of Revolutionary culture that tended to emphasize the heroic quality of dominant characters, which Whitefield certainly was for the religious community.[117] This ascribed heroism elevated victories to a higher level, making them a moral victory.[118] Such is the case of treatments of Whitefield in the Revolutionary period by evangelical Christians and Whitefield followers who sought to assign meaning for Whitefield not only after his death, but also in the religious culture of an emerging country. The construction of a heroic and patriotic image for Whitefield is entirely consistent with the reverence and deification surrounding him, which also had the potential to signify sedition.[119] In remembering Whitefield, his evangelical American followers transformed him into a figure of rebellion.

Whitefield the icon was also invoked in other areas of resistance and reform. Thomas Clarkson, Granville Sharpe, William Wilberforce, and other evangelicals headed the Clapham Sect, a group of prominent Anglican British abolitionists who opposed slavery on religious grounds, though most of their antislavery activities occurred after Whitefield's death. The members of the Clapham Sect, as well as evangelicals of other Protestant denominations, like John Wesley, saw slavery as incompatible with Christian principles.

Whitefield's preaching had a powerful impact on several key antislavery figures, and this influence became part of his legacy. A number of them, including John Wesley, studied the slave trade and, following the Somerset Case of 1772, decided that "no material considerations" could "justify the injustice and cruelty of the slave-system."[120] The Somerset Case, arguably the most significant development in Anglo-American slave law since the Yorke-Talbot decision, evolved when James Somerset, a slave, was brought from Virginia to England by his master, Charles Steuart, a merchant and slave trader. Somerset ran away and was recaptured. In response, Steuart decided to sell Somerset in Jamaica. Abolitionist Granville Sharpe, a devout Anglican, learned through his network of ecumenical abolitionists of Somerset's plight. He successfully sought a writ of habeas corpus from Lord Mansfield, chief justice of the Court of King's Bench.[121] The writ argued that Somerset's imprisonment was illegal. While some scholars have argued that Mansfield did not intend to eradicate slavery, his ultimate ruling in Somerset's favor was, nonetheless, a significant legal strike against that institution.[122]

Like Sharpe, the deeply pious Franco-American Quaker abolitionist Anthony Benezet also opposed slavery on religious grounds. Approximately three and a half years after Whitefield's death, Benezet appealed to Whitefield's executrix, Selina, Countess of Huntingdon, to support abolition. In his letter, he invoked Whitefield's *Letter to the Inhabitants of Maryland, Virginia, and North and South Carolina* (1740), which said that
"the encouragement which is thereby given to the nations from whom the Negroes are bought, [causes those nations] to be at perpetual war with each other."[123] He continued,

> I am persuaded if thou art rightly informed of the situation of slaves in ... [Georgia] as well the other South Colonies, thou wilt be engaged to give such direction with respect to their managers there, making any further purchase of slaves, as well as their treatment of those already under their care, as will be agreeable to best wisdom, and thou wilt be willing to grant thy assistance in furthering the good designs of putting an end to this mighty destroyer, "The Slave Trade."[124]

The Countess did not share the humanitarian impulses of Benezet or his fellow evangelical abolitionists. She rebuffed Benezet and wrote to him, "God alone, by His Almighty power, who can and will be His own times bring outward, as well as spiritual deliverance to his afflicted and oppressed creatures."[125] Instead, she acknowledged some problems in slavery but found religious accommodation for it by placing its abolition in God's hands, not of her own. Rather than freeing the slaves, she followed Whitefield's designs for his estate, which included bequeathing his slaves to his friend, James Habersham.[126]

Benezet recognized just how powerful a symbol Whitefield was; that is precisely why he invoked Whitefield in his abolitionist campaign. Unfortunately for Benezet, Whitefield's public defense of slavery on religious grounds frustrated his efforts to harness Whitefield's image. He "chided the late George Whitefield" for embracing a biblical defense of slavery and noted that as long as individuals continued to use Christianity to defend the institution, there was little hope for its end.[127]

Antislavery sentiments were not uncommon in the British Atlantic World by the 1780s, but Whitefield died before the abolition movement began in earnest. Somewhat ironically, given Whitefield's proslavery sentiments in the last decades of his life, his preaching struck a chord with African Americans. To them, the idea of equality in the eyes of God suggested that that freedom should extend to their earthly lives. His flamboyant style of preaching was also likely appealing because it was similar to the energy found in many indigenous African religious practices.[128] While Whitefield was never an abolitionist, he unwittingly helped to inspire a number of black evangelicals who, in turn, used his preaching to refute scriptural arguments for slavery.

Olaudah Equiano, who became a Methodist, was an African abolitionist strongly influenced by Whitefield. Equiano converted to Christianity sometime in 1774, fervently embracing the teachings of the New Birth.[129] In his narrative, he described observing Whitefield preach in Philadelphia eight years earlier.[130] Equiano was awestruck at what he saw: a "church crowded with people; the church-yard was full likewise, and a number of people were even mounted on ladders."[131] Told that Whitefield was preaching, Equiano noted that he "had often heard of this gentleman, and wished to see and hear him" but had "never before had an opportunity."[132] He pushed eagerly into the church and saw "this pious man exhorting people with the greatest fervour and earnestness, and sweating as much as I ever did while in slavery on Monserrat beach."[133] Whitefield's energy resonated with Equiano, who wrote, "I thought it strange I had never seen divines exert themselves in this manner before, and I was no longer at a loss to account for the thin congregations."[134] Christianity, which would come to underscore Equiano's abolitionist convictions, resonated like it had not before.

Phillis Wheatley's antislavery impulses, too, were born of her religious beliefs. Wheatley, a devout Methodist, captured in her elegy to Whitefield both his transdenominational appeal and the emotional appeal of his preaching with words like "Glow'd," "inflamed," and "captivate."[135] Wheatley's elegy catapulted the young writer to a level of fame unprecedented for an African American. Like Equiano would with his 1789 slave narrative, Wheatley helped force eighteenth-century society to confront the humanity of slaves in the midst of an ongoing debate among eighteenth-century philosophers like Francis Bacon, David Hume, and Immanuel Kant about "what kind of creatures Africans truly were."[136] In fact, an effort in 1772 to publish her book in Boston failed because an insufficient number of Bostonians believed that a slave could have written the poem without assistance.[137] Nonetheless, Wheatley continued to rise in fame through her elegy. Ultimately, though, she rejected the role Whitefield suggested for African Americans when he said, "Negroe who prays, 'Lord, keep the door of my lips, that I may not offend with my tongue.'"[138] Instead, her transatlantic fame, eloquence with words, and keen sense of politics transformed her into an important figure in the abolitionist world.

Wheatley, of course, continued to write and to publish. Three years after she wrote her elegy to Whitefield, she published a series of poems and other writings, which included her thoughts on slavery. Appended to the publication's introduction was an attestation signed by Massachusetts governor Thomas Hutchinson, Charles Chauncy, Ed Pemberton, and a host of other influential religious and civil leaders of colonial Massachusetts that Wheatley had, indeed, written these words herself, without help from her mistress or other white person.[139] Her topics included slavery. One poem called it a "mercy brought me from my Pagan land" but advised her readers to "Remember, Christians, Negros, black as Cain, May be refin'd, and join the' angelic train."[140] This passage, which alludes to the Curse of Ham, also illustrates Wheatley's belief in Christianity as an equalizer but also saw converted Africans as higher in status than those who still followed indigenous African spiritual practices. Slaves had their own hierarchies that, in some cases, privileged Christianized slaves who had been brought over some time ago.[141] In his abolitionist narrative, he also echoed this sentiment, comparing himself favorably to a scarified African.[142] Even among Africans, religion was a factor in the determination of race and status.

Wheatley addressed the possibility of freedom in another verse, addressed to the Earl of Dartmouth:

> Fair Freedom rose New-England to adorn...
> Elate with hope her race no longer mourns;
> Each soul expands, each grateful bosom burns.[143]

The poem contains repeated references to "her" race as well as to her "dread" of "the iron chain."[144] She wrote,

> I, young in life, by seeming cruel fate...
> Was snatch'd from Afric's fancy'd happy seat:
> What pangs excruciating must molest,
> What sorrows labour in my parents' breast?
> Steel'd was that soul and by no misery mov'd
> That from a father seiz'd his babe belov'd.[145]

Here she remembers her capture and sale into slavery in 1761 and mourns the separation of families inflicted by slavery. Like her other work, it reminds its readers of the humanity of slaves.

The African American preacher John Marrant, too, was influenced by an early encounter with George Whitefield. According to his narrative, which chronicles his conversion to evangelical Christianity, he was en route to play his French horn for someone in Charles Town at the age of about thirteen when he passed a meetinghouse overflowing with people. When he inquired about what was taking place, he was told that "a crazy man was halloing there."[146] Marrant contended that his conversion experience took place as he first heard Whitefield speak. The preacher appeared to look and point directly at him and utter "Prepare to meet thy God, O Israel."[147] Marrant was overcome and passed out. After hearing of young Marrant's conversion experience after his sermon, Whitefield entered the vestry, where Marrant had been taken to recover. He told Marrant, "Jesus Christ has got thee at last."[148] This episode marked the beginning of Marrant's religious life.[149]

Marrant was not a slave like Wheatley or Equiano, but his narrative was of similar importance because it helped to humanize African Americans. He became, like Whitefield, an itinerant minister who tended to black communities in the Americas and to Native Americans.[150] The publication of his narrative in 1785 coincided with his ordination. Perhaps not coincidentally, it contained a number of themes similar to those in Whitefield's autobiography, such as a lack of support from Marrant's family over his religious conversion.[151] His formal religious training and ordination took place under the tutelage of the Connexion of Whitefield's patron, Selina Hastings, the Countess of Huntingdon. The Connexion was a small society of evangelical Methodist churches that the countess founded in 1783. Marrant's writings had the same message of equality in the eyes of God that inspired ecumenical abolition. In one passage, he observed, "black nations may be white in the blood of the Lamb; that vast multitudes of hard tongues, and of a strange speech, may learn the language of Canaan, and sing the song of Moses."[152] It was this sort of thought that inspired Equiano and other black evangelical abolitionists.

Marrant and Equiano, in turn, inspired other black abolitionist writers and preachers, including Quobna Ottobah Cugoano. Cugoano, a former slave from Ghana and friend of Equiano, authored two important abolitionist works. The first was *Thoughts and Sentiments on the Evil and Wicked Traffic of the Slavery and Commerce of the Human Species* (1787). The second, appearing same year, was a narrative of his enslavement, *NARRATIVE of the Enslavement of OTTOBAH CUGOANO, a Native of Africa; Published by Himself, in the Year 1787.* Cugoano's narrative contains religious themes similar to those of Wheatley and Equiano. Of his eventual release from slavery he wrote, "This Lord of Hosts, in his great providence, and in great mercy to me, made a way for my deliverance from Grenada."[153] He described the inhumane conditions of slaves, "beholding the most dreadful scenes of misery and cruelty, and seeing my miserable companions often cruelly lashed, and, as it were, cut to pieces, for the most trifling faults."[154]

His *Thoughts and Sentiments* contained much more direct ecumenical challenges to slavery. His language was much stronger, but like Whitefield and John Wesley, he raised questions about whether Christian nations ought to be involved in the "insidious piracy of procuring and holding slaves."[155] He also asked, "can the slave-holders think that the Universal Father and Sovereign of Mankind will be well pleased with them, for the brutal transgression of his law, in bowing down the necks of those to the yoke of their cruel bondage?"[156] Cugoano used the language of equality under the eyes of God to assert that slavery was "contrary to all the genuine principles of Christianity.[157] He denounced the use by proslavery writers of the Curse of Ham, a biblical story from the Book of Genesis, wherein Noah's son, Ham, was cursed for witnessing his father's drunkenness.[158] The Curse of Ham was an important piece of rhetoric for Christian proslavery apologists who argued that Africans were Ham's descendants.[159]

Whitefield and the writings of Isaac Watts and Edward Young inspired Lemuel Haynes, a biracial indentured servant, Calvinist evangelical, and Massachusetts Minuteman. Ordained in 1785 into the Congregational Church, the immensely popular preacher served (white) parishes in Connecticut, New Hampshire, Vermont, and New York over his forty-plus-year pastoral career.[160] Haynes was a virulent opponent of slavery, but for the most part he restricted himself to subtle and tangential rather than strong, direct criticism of slavery until around 1801.[161] Haynes then spoke out frequently and forcefully, often using both republican and scriptural language to condemn slavery and remark on the contradictions between the promises of the Revolution and the fate of slaves. In 1801 he wrote, "Is it any distinction that the God of nature hath made in their formation? ... On the whole, does it not appear that a land of liberty is favourable to peace, happiness, virtue and religion, and should be held sacred by mankind?"[162] Slavery was, in Haynes's assessment, politically and morally incompatible with American values.

Some of Haynes's theological critiques of slavery were more understated. In 1805, in Rutland, Vermont, he gave a sermon titled "Universal Salvation." The sermon focuses on the idea of original sin, and that all mankind is equally vulnerable to sin. Salvation is the antithesis to damnation; to fail to grant all access to grace is to allow victory for the devil.[163] Haynes echoes the idea proposed by Whitefield of equality in the eyes of God but asserts it as a long-standing tradition: "Universal Salvation is no newfangled scheme, but can boast of great antiquity."[164] He continued, "It is probable that the doctrine of Universal Salvation will still prevail . . . every effort against him [God] only enrages him more and more, and excites him to new inventions and exertions to build up his cause."[165] Moreover, the comment that universal salvation will likely prevail can be a thinly veiled warning that resisting it (and by extent, the end of slavery) will only make those who oppose slavery more determined to fight.

Whitefield shares credit with many preachers for evangelizing African Americans and for the effect it had on religious African Americans.[166] Evangelical Protestantism had a "powerful integrating ideology and an ethos whose emphasis on spirituality had the potential for creating the first distinctive African values in relation to Protestant Christianity."[167] Its message of universal fellowship undermined notions of racial inferiority.[168]

As with other Whitefield followers, black evangelical Christians were subject to derision by those who opposed revivalism. Some of the derision entailed racist jokes that depicted his black followers as misguided, ignorant, nominal Christians inquiring whether the preacher they heard was "Massa Whitfield."[169] Other discussions, both before and after the American Revolution, depicted the evangelical conversion of Africans and Native Americans as "failed."[170] Race underscored these particular criticisms of Whitefield and revivalism, but they were also part of the greater dialogue over religion and the authority of clergy—especially where evangelicalism spawned a number of itinerant black preachers who went on to propagate the Gospel to other mixed-race audiences.[171]

Where race was a scriptural problem, conversions of any sort raised the possibility that colonized people (whether African or Native American) who became Christian should be recognized as members of the polity.¹⁷² In this context, black Christianity was yet another example of Christianity democratized as well as a powerful impetus for social reform beginning with the end of the eighteenth century.¹⁷³ And thus, Whitefield the American religious icon, Whitefield the British Atlantic icon, and Whitefield the accidental abolitionist were all interconnected.

EPILOGUE

The early nineteenth century marked the rise of the nationalist period in the United States and elsewhere. This Era of Good Feelings produced an interest in the preservation and invention of tradition, shepherded by self-appointed custodians.[1] For the United States particularly, the competing visions of Whitefield as an American icon versus a simultaneous, competing Atlantic religious icon were effectively an exercise in defining the young country's position within the greater global community.[2] The shaping of tradition continued and evolved well after the early national period, with both regions of the United States and Great Britain fighting to claim him. In Whitefield's case, there were many such custodians, not all of whom worked in synchronicity with each other. While Whitefield was a figure in American religious memory, he was not confined to it exclusively.

The Guestbook at Whitefield's Tomb in the crypt of Old South Presbyterian Church, Newburyport, MA. Photograph © 2014 J. Thomas Parr. Used by permission.

Epilogue

Whitefield's Cenotaph, Old South Presbyterian Church, Newburyport, MA. Photograph © 2014 J. Thomas Parr. Used by Permission.

By the 1830s, most if not all of the people who had known Whitefield during his lifetime were gone. Yet his influence did not end with the Second Great Awakening. The evolution of Whitefield's memory and legacy during the First and Second Great Awakenings established guidelines for the understanding of Whitefield by future generations.[3] The Civil War further transformed American history and memory. During and after the War, both sides regularly invoked their own versions of American history and memory in support of their respective causes.

Certain understandings of Whitefield survived with relative consistency through the centuries. Old South Presbyterian Church remained proud and conscious of its role as a site of memory for

Epilogue

the Grand Itinerant: a cenotaph was added to the crypt in 1829, detailing Whitefield's ministry and documenting the efforts undertaken to prepare and preserve the vault. Around that same time, a plan by Old South Presbyterian Church's Rev. Dr. Proudfit to construct a grand "monument temple" to Whitefield was considered, but dropped, absent sufficient political and fiscal support.[4] And in 1869, almost one hundred years after his death, Anglican minister J. C. Ryle wrote in praise of Whitefield's "unrivalled voice, manner, delivery, action, and command of words," though criticisms of his "religious enthusiasm" remained.[5] In many ways, Whitefield became more powerful and in death than in life.

Twenty-first-century evangelicals still understand him as an advocate of the importance of the conversion experience. Also remembered is his lack of adherence to strict denominationalism. As such, even as denominational lines became more important from the Third Great Awakening onward, he remains a figure who is admired by a diverse group of Protestants rather than being strictly in the domain of a particular sect. In 2004, almost 290 years after Whitefield's birth, the Reverend William Larkin gave an address titled *George Whitefield: Hero of Faith* to the First Presbyterian Church in Columbia, South Carolina. During his address, Larkin asked his audience, "How can we begin to get the measure of a man of such prodigious efforts, whom God used so greatly?"[6] Larkin continued, "Who are the George Whitefields today? They are the individuals with a calling grounded in the new birth ... individuals with competence to persuasively appeal to the heart for soul transformation."[7] He concluded, "Will you ask God to make you such a person?"[8]

Whitefield's defense of Presbyterian Gilbert Tennent's sermon "On the Dangers of the Unconverted Ministry" (1739) resonates in Larkin's twenty-first-century address to his congregation. The address also demonstrates that the iconic image that Whitefield created for himself in the eighteenth century as channeling God also persevered to the twenty-first century, no doubt due to the ongoing work of Whitefield's surviving supporters and the generations that followed him.

ACKNOWLEDGMENTS

It is a pleasure to thank all those who have made my completion of this manuscript possible. I would like to thank Lige Gould for his considerable patience and encouragement over the years. Bill Harris challenged and guided my work in ways that made the project much better than it was before he laid hands on it. I am grateful to Funso Afolayan, Jessica Lepler, Funso Afolyan, and Bill Ross. W. Jeffrey Bolster, Kurk Dorsey, Ellen Fitzpatrick, Jan Golinski, Lucy Salyer, and Molly Girard-Dorsey have been generous with their advice on academic and pedagogical matters over the years.

Outside of the University of New Hampshire (UNH), a number of scholars have shared their expertise in ways that made this a better project. I have benefited from conversations with Richard Bailey, Vincent Carretta, Heather Miyano Kopelson, Christopher Cameron, Gretchen Adams, James Brewer Stewart, Margot Minardi, and David Ceri Jones. Paul Finkelman deserves a special mention as one who has tirelessly answered my questions about law and religion in early America. Thank you to editor Craig Gill and to the anonymous reviewers from the University Press of Mississippi. I found the readers' reports genuinely thoughtful. Any oversights or errors are mine, and mine alone.

Several administrators and colleagues at institutions where I have held teaching positions deserve mention. At Granite State College, thanks go to Marilyn McGair and Laurie Quinn. At UNH Manchester, I thank John Cerullo, Dan Reagan, and Jack Resch.

This project has received considerable financial support from a number of sources. A pair of Gunst-Wilcox grants from the History Department of the University of New Hampshire supported some local research. The generosity of David Steelman and Ginny Theo-Steelman, via a Steelman Fellowship from the UNH Department of History, made possible valuable weeks of research in London. The Steelmans have remained enthusiastic supporters of my work,

Acknowledgments

and I am truly grateful. Travel funds from the Graduate School of the University of New Hampshire and an Annette K. Baxter Grant from the American Studies Association enabled me to present work at the annual meetings of the American Studies Association and the Organization of American Historians. Additional support came from a Paul Cuffe Memorial Fellowship from the Munson Institute at Mystic Seaport, the Gilder Lehrman Institute of Early American History, and a George Washington College Fellowship in Early American History from the Boston Athenaeum.

In the course of my research, I was aided by a number of fantastic librarians and archivists. I want to thank Dimond Library's Inter-Library Loan librarian nonpareil, Jan Salas, for securing what must have seemed an unreasonable amount of material from other libraries. I am grateful to the Library's loan desk staff for lugging dusty volumes up from the basement and for not grumbling on the many occasions when I came to the library with a rolling suitcase full of books, either to check out or to return. At the Boston Athenaeum, I am grateful to Mary Warnement and the rest of the welcoming library staff. Thanks also go to Anna Cook-Clutterbeck at the Massachusetts Historical Society, Lynette Stout and the reference staff of the Georgia Historical Society, and the staffs of the American Antiquarian Society, the Fales Library of New York University (especially Lisa Darns), the New-York Historical Society, Lambeth Palace Library (London), the National Archives (UK), the Parliamentary Archives (UK), and the Gloucester County Council Archives (UK).

I was warmly received at the Old South Presbyterian Church in West Newburyport by its current pastor, the Reverend Rob John, Sophia McLin, and church archivist Nancy Stokes. Pastor Aaron James, his wife, and the staff of the First Bryan Baptist Church in Savannah, Georgia, also took time out of their busy schedules to speak with me and allow me to tour the church during a trip to Savannah. Pastor James generously arranged for local historian Jamal Touré to meet me at the church to share his knowledge of the history of the black church in Savannah. I am grateful to Dr. Touré for his time and expertise.

Writing a book can be an isolating process. I am fortunate to have a number of friends, inside and outside of academia, who

Acknowledgments

have supported me in various ways. I am grateful for the friendship of Jordan and Jennifer Fansler, Kang Tchou, Lauren Turner, Molly Gallaher, Deena Parmelee, Mary Fuhrer, the late Angelo Kontarinis, Sonic Woytonik, Rhiannon Dowling, Laura Prieto, Heather Roth, Margeret Sankey, Liz Throop, and Chryssa Sharp. Family friend Johan Bjarneman used his travel industry connections to aid me with my flight arrangements for research trips. I ask forgiveness for anyone whom I might have inadvertently overlooked.

Finally, I wish to thank my family. I am indebted for the unconditional support I received from two women who are no longer with us. The first is the late Claire Dolber, my childhood caregiver. She was a woman of unmatched strength and determination. My daughter, Lily Claire, carries on her name. The second is my paternal grandmother, the late Ruth Gabriel Parr. She was a consummate supporter of my education, from my grammar school years onward. I was completing my master's program at Simmons College when she died. Even after Alzheimer's disease had robbed her of most of her memory, she still inquired about my schooling.

My parents, Tom and Mary Parr, provided both financial support and helped out with child care. My sister, Sasha Corken, and her husband, Ryan, helped care for their precocious niece on a number of occasions so that I could work undistracted. My brother, Brendan Parr, who successfully defended his PhD in chemistry as I finished writing this book, provided both camaraderie and a friendly sibling rivalry. Thank you also to my other sister, Gillian Hermance, and my brother-in-law, Chris. My husband's parents, Domenic and Elaine Cacciapuoti, and sister-in-law, Debra Coveney, also supported this project in a number of ways.

The two people who deserve the biggest thanks of all, are my husband, DJ Cacciapuoti, and our daughter, Lily. At key points in the writing process, DJ took time away from work to keep Lily entertained so that I could write. I would not have gotten through this process without his patience, understanding, love, and support. And while she is still too young to understand, Lily's happy smiles were a considerable source of cheer and encouragement, as well as her reminders (demands?) of the importance to take time to play. I dedicate this book to both of them, with all my love.

NOTES

Introduction

1. Justin Martyr, *Horatory Address to the Greeks 16*, 150 C.E., at http://www.ccel.org/ccel/schaff/anf01.viii.vi.html.
2. Clement of Alexandria, *Exhortation to the Heathen* 4, 190 C.E., at http://www.ccel.org/ccel/schaff/anf02.vi.ii.html.
3. Fulham Papers (hereafter FP), vol. XII: General Correspondence, 1724–1743: Virginia, ff. 55–98; FP, vol. 15: General Correspondence, 1704–1730: Bermuda, ff. 276–277, 280–281, 294–295, Lambeth Palace Library (hereafter LPL).
4. Roxann Wheeler, *The Complexions of Race: Categories of Difference in Eighteenth-Century British Culture* (Philadelphia: University of Pennsylvania Press, 2000); Colin Kidd, *The Forging of Races: Race and Scripture in the Protestant Atlantic World, 1600–2000* (New York: Cambridge University Press, 2006); Clive Webb and David Brown, *Race in the American South: From Slavery to Civil Rights* (Gainesville: University Press of Florida, 2007); Travis Glasson, *Mastering Christianity: Missionary Anglicanism and Slavery in the Atlantic World* (New York: Oxford University Press, 2011); Rebecca Goetz, *The Baptism of Early Virginia: How Christianity Created Race* (Baltimore, MD: Johns Hopkins University Press, 2012).
5. Harry S. Stout, *The Divine Dramatist: George Whitefield and the Rise of Modern Evangelism* (Grand Rapids, MI: Wm. B. Eerdmans, 1991); Frank Lambert, *"Pedlar in Divinity:" George Whitefield and the Transatlantic Revivals, 1737–1770* (Princeton, NJ: Princeton University Press, 2002); Peter Charles Hoffer, *When Benjamin Franklin Met the Reverend Whitefield* (Baltimore: Johns Hopkins Press, 2011); Jerome Dean Mahaffrey, *Preaching Politics: The Religious Rhetoric of George Whitefield and the Founding of a New Nation* (Waco, TX: Baylor University Press, 2007).
6. Mark A. Noll, *America's God: From Jonathan Edwards to Abraham Lincoln* (New York: Oxford, 2005): 75.
7. See Frank Lambert, "'Pedlar in Divinity': George Whitefield and the Great Awakening, 1737—1745," *Journal of American History* 77, no. 3 (December 1990): 812–837, which proposes that he was a salesman for religion, and Harry S. Stout, *The Divine Dramatist: George Whitefield and the Rise of Modern Evangelicalism*

Notes

(Grand Rapids, MI: Wm. B. Eerdmans, 1991), which describes his gift for theatrics.

8. George Whitefield, "A Letter from the Rev. Mr. George Whitefield, to the Inhabitants of Maryland, Virginia, North and South-Carolina," *Pennsylvania Gazette*, April 17, 1740.

9. David T. Morgan, "The Consequences of George Whitefield's Ministry in the Carolinas and Georgia, 1739–1740," *Georgia Historical Quarterly* 55 (1971): 62–82; Stephen J. Stein, "George Whitefield on Slavery: Some New Evidence," *Church History* 42, no. 2 (June 1973): 243–256.

10. Moshe Barasche, *Icon: Studies in the History of an Idea* (New York: New York University Press, 1995): 192.

11. Ibid.

12. Mary H. Allies, trans., *St. John Damascene: On Holy Images*, part 1 (London: Thomas Baker, 1898): 13.

13. With thanks to an email conversation with David Ceri Jones in December 2013.

14. David Ceri Jones, "'So Much Idolized By Some, and Railed at by Others,' Towards Understanding George Whitefield," *Wesley and Methodist Studies* 5, no. 1 (2013): 9; Boyd Stanley Schlenther, "Whitefield, George (1714–1770)," in *Oxford Dictionary of National Biography*, online ed., May 2010, at http://www.oxforddnb.com/view/printable/29281 (accessed November 13, 2013).

15. The word *unschooled* here means that that particular clergyman might have received some training from other ministers but was not university-educated, like most of the traditional clergy.

16. Nathan O. Hatch, *The Democratization of American Christianity* (New Haven, CT: Yale University Press, 1991): 9.

17. Noll, *America's God*: 13.

18. Ibid.: 22. On the religious landscape of the British Atlantic, see especially Carla Gardina Pestana, *Protestant Empire: Religion and the Making of the British Atlantic World* (Philadelphia: University of Pennsylvania Press, 2010).

19. Patricia U. Bonomi, *Under the Cope of Heaven: Religion, Society, and Politics in Colonial America* (New York: Oxford University Press, 2003); Jon Butler, *Awash in a Sea of Faith: Christianizing the American People* (Cambridge, MA: Harvard University Press, 1992); Thomas S. Kidd, *The Great Awakening: The Roots of Evangelical Christianity in Colonial America* (New Haven, CT: Yale University Press, 2009).

20. Jim Forest, *Praying with Icons* (New York: Orbis Books, 1997): 10–11; Barasche, *Icon* (New York: New York University Press, 1995).

21. Chris Beneke, *Beyond Toleration: The Religious Origins of American Pluralism* (New York: Oxford University Press, 2008); Chris Beneke and

Notes

Christopher S. Grenda, eds., *The First Prejudice: Tolerance and Intolerance in Early America* (Philadelphia: University of Pennsylvania Press, 2010); Eric R. Schlereth, *An Age of Infidels: The Politics of Religious Controversy in the Early United States* (Philadelphia: University of Pennsylvania Press, 2013); Gary Remer, *Humanism and the Rhetoric of Toleration* (University Park, PA: Pennsylvania State University Press, 1996).

22. Noll, *America's God*: 76.

23. Nathan Hatch, *The Democratization of American Christianity* (New Haven, CT: Yale University Press, 1991).

24. See especially Charles E. Clark, *The Public Prints: The Newspaper in Anglo-American Culture, 1665–1740* (New York: Oxford University Press, 1994), and Mark Valeri, *Heavenly Merchandize: How Religion Shaped Commerce in Puritan America* (Princeton, NJ: Princeton University Press, 2010).

25. Noll, *America's God*; Butler, *Awash in a Sea*; Bonomi, *Under the Cope of Heaven*; T. S. Kidd, *Great Awakening*; Frank Lambert, *Inventing the "Great Awakening"* (Princeton, NJ: Princeton University Press, 2001); Hatch, *Democratization of American Christianity*. On the historiography of religion and politics in the American Revolutionary and Early Republic eras, see especially Bonomi, *Under the Cope of Heaven*; Frank Lambert, *The Founding Fathers and the Place of Religion in America* (Princeton, NJ: Princeton University Press, 2006); and Saul Cornell, *The Other Founders: Anti-Federalism and the Dissenting Tradition in America, 1788–1828* (Chapel Hill: University of North Carolina Press, 1999).

Chapter One

1. Luke Tyerman, *The Life of the Rev. George Whitefield*, vol. 1 (London: Anson D.F. Randolph, 1876): 606.

2. Ibid.

3. Michael Kammen, *Digging Up the Dead: A History of Notable American Reburials* (Chicago: University Press of Chicago Press): 45.

4. Richard Burridge, *Imitating Jesus: An Inclusive Approach to New Testament Ethics* (Grand Rapids, MI: Wm. B. Eerdmans, 2007): 28

5. Ibid.

6. Ibid.: 19.

7. Ibid.

8. George Whitefield, *An Account of God's Dealings with the Reverend George Whitefield, A.B., Late of Pembroke-College Oxford from His Infancy to His Entering into the Holy Orders* (London, 1740): 8.

9. Ibid.

Notes

10. George Whitefield, "The Pharisee and Publican," in *Fifteen Sermons Preached on Various Important Subjects by George Whitefield, Late of Pembroke College, Oxford*, ed. Joseph Smith (London: Paisley, 1794): 152–160.

11. Ibid.: 16.

12. Ibid.

13. Stout, *Divine Dramatist*: 18.

14. Whitefield, *Account of God's Dealings*: 24.

15. Ibid.: 25.

16. George Whitefield, "The Pharisee and Publican," in Smith, ed., *Fifteen Sermons*: 152–160.

17. Whitefield, *Account of God's Dealings*: 25.

18. Ibid.: 26.

19. Ibid.

20. London Metropolitan Archives, P154/11 SP 2/9.

21. Ibid.

22. John Wesley, *A Sermon on the Death of the Rev. Mr. George Whitefield. Preached at the Chapel in Tottenham-Court-Road and at the Tabernacle near Moorfields, on Sunday, November 18, 1770* (London: Holt, 1770): 27.

23. Lambert, *"Pedlar in Divinity"*: 11.

24. Wesley, *A Sermon*: 28.

25. Ibid.: 28–30; Nancy Ruttenburg, "George Whitefield: Spectacular Conversion, and the Rise of Democratic Personality." Eighteenth-Century Cultural Studies series, *American Literary History* 5, no. 3 (Autumn 1993): 433.

26. 2 Samuel 16:13, in *The Good News Bible*, 2nd ed. (New York: American Bible Society, 1992): 377.

27. George Whitefield, *A Short Account of God's Dealings with the Reverend George Whitefield, A.B., Late of Pembroke-College Oxford from His Infancy to His Entering into the Holy Orders* (London, 1740): 35.

28. Ibid.: 35, 51.

29. Ibid.: 54–55.

30. Ibid.: 56.

31. Ibid.: 62.

32. Abel Stevens, *The Women of Methodism: Its Three Foundresses, Susanna Wesley, the Countess of Huntingdon, and Barbara Heck: With Sketches of their Female Associates and Successors in the Early History of the Denomination* (New York: Carlton and Porter, 1866): 147

33. Whitefield, *Short Account of God's Dealings*: 62.

34. Ibid.: 63.

35. Ibid.

36. Ibid.

37. Ibid.: 64.

Notes

38. Ibid.: 66.

39. Ibid.: 71.

40. Kathy W. Ross and Rosemary Stacy, "John Wesley and Savannah," at http://www.sip.armstrong.edu/Methodism/wesley.html (accessed March 29, 2011). On the allegations surrounding Charles Wesley, see Alex Hudson, "The Secret Code of Diaries," *BBC Today*, August 29, 2008, at http://news.bbc.co.uk/today/hi/today/newsid_7586000/7586683.stm (accessed March 29, 2011). Charles Wesley also had a falling out with Oglethorpe. See entries starting Thursday, March 25, 1736, in *The Diary of Charles Wesley*, Wesley Center Online, at http://wesley.nnu.edu/charles-wesley/the-journal-of-charles-wesley-1707-1788/the-journal-of-charles-wesley-march-9-august-30-1736/ (accessed March 31, 2011).

41. Whitefield, *Account of God's Dealings*: 32.

42. Ibid.: 6, 7. Note it is clear that although Whitefield did not self-identify as an evangelical, he nonetheless admired them—the autobiography particularly notes their lack of "false piety" and willingness to recognize "the dark side of human character" vis-à-vis an example of "evangelicals not hesitating to mention of Jesus casting "sin out of Mary Magdalene seven times."

43. "George Whitefield, 1714–1770," in *Historical Portraits . . . 1700–1800*, ed. Emery Walker, Charles Robert Leslie Fletcher, and Harold Beresford Butler (London: Clarendon Press, 1919): 27.

44. As opposed to an established, or national church.

45. Christopher Hill, *Puritanism and Revolution: The English Revolution of the 17th Century* (New York: Schocken Books, 1964): 5

46. John Locke, *A Letter Concerning Toleration*, 3rd ed. (1689; Boston, 1943): A3.

47. Ibid.

48. *The Fundamental Constitutions of Carolina*, March 1, 1663. See Articles 97, 100–103, Yale Law School, The Avalon Project: Documents in Law, History and Diplomacy, at http://avalon.law.yale.edu/17th_century/nc05.asp (accessed January 4, 2012).

49. Ibid.: 3.

50. Ibid.: 10–11.

51. Ibid.

52. 1 Peter 1:3 and John 3:7, in *Good News Bible*: 1472, 1483.

53. John Wesley, "Sermon 45: The New Birth (c. 1743)," quoted in the 1876 edition, edited by Thomas Jackson, The United Methodist Global Ministries website, at http://new.gbgm-umc.org/umhistory/wesley/sermons/45/ (accessed February 7, 2012).

54. Ava Chamberlain, "Self-Deception as a Theological Problem in Jonathan Edwards's 'Treatise Concerning Religious Affections,'" *Catholic History* 63, no. 4 (December 1994): 541–556; Bonomi, *Under the Cope of Heaven*, 139–152.

Notes

55. Richard L. Bushman, *From Puritan to Yankee: Character and the Social Order in Connecticut, 1690–1765* (Cambridge, MA: Harvard University Press, 1967): 182–195, 235–266.

56. George Whitefield, *A Further Account of God's Dealings with the Rev. Mr. George Whitefield . . . from his Ordination to his Embarkment to Georgia. . . .* (London, 1747): 14.

57. Ibid.: 23–24.

58. Ibid.: 24.

59. Ibid.

60. Ibid.

61. Christopher Beneke, *Beyond Toleration: The Religious Origins of American Pluralism* (New York: Oxford University Press, 2008): 139.

62. Ibid.: 17.

63. Locke, *A Letter Concerning Toleration*: 12.

64. Ibid.: 25.

65. As St. John of Damascus argued, "one who honors the martyr, honors God." Saint John of Damascus, *Three Treatises on the Divine Images, Treatise I* (New York: St. Vladimir's Seminary Press, 2003): 52. In defending Whitefield and his motives as pure, his followers honored Whitefield as a disseminator of God's message.

66. Whitefield, *A Further Account*: 25.

67. Lambert, *"Pedlar in Divinity"*: 5. In the context of Christian iconography, there are also archetypes, or paradigms, of what God is going to bring about (Saint John of Damascus, *Three Treatises on the Divine Images, Treatise I*: 25). The reproduction and distribution of Whitefield's likeness as a symbol of profound change in eighteenth-century religious culture can therefore be understood as an aspect of his development as an icon.

68. Whitefield, *A Further Account*: 26.

69. Stout, *Divine Dramatist*: xiv.

70. Journal Entries, January 9, 1738, January 18, 1738, in *George Whitefield's Journals* (hereafter *GWJ*) *(1738–1741)*, ed. William V. Davis (Gainesville, FL: Scholars' Facsimiles & Reprints, 1969): 95, 102.

71. Journal Entry, February 8, 1738, in ibid.: 115.

72. *A Brief and Impartial Account of the Character and Doctrines of Mr. Whitefield and Mr. Wesley: In a Letter from London, September 1743* (Edinburgh, 1743): 10.

73. Timothy H. Breen, "An Empire of Goods: The Anglicization of Colonial America, 1680–1776," *Journal of British Studies* 25 (1986): 473; Susan O'Brien, "Eighteenth-Century Publishing Networks in the First Years of Transatlantic Evangelicalism," in *Evangelicalism: Comparative Studies of Popular Protestantism in North America, the British Isles, and Beyond*, ed. Mark A. Noll, David W.

Notes

Bebbington, and George A. Rawlyk (New York: Oxford University Press, 1994): 39.

74. Mills Lane, ed., *General Oglethorpe's Georgia: Colonial Letters, 1733-1743*, vol. 1: xvi.

75. Betty Wood, *Slavery in Colonial Georgia: 1730-1775* (Athens: University of Georgia Press, 2007): 2; Kenneth Coleman, *Colonial Georgia: A History* (New York: Charles Scribner's Sons, 1976): 17-20.

76. Frances Harold, "Colonial Siblings: Georgia's Relationship with South Carolina during the Pre-Revolutionary Period," *Georgia Historical Quarterly* 73, no. 4 (Winter 1989): 707-708; Alan Gallay, *The Formation of a Planter Elite: Jonathan Bryan and the Southern Colonial Frontier* (Athens, GA: University of Georgia Press, 1989): 18-23.

77. Lane, ed., *General Oglethorpe's Georgia*, vol. 1: xv; Coleman, *Colonial Georgia*: xxvii.

78. Lane, ed., *General Oglethorpe's Georgia*, vol. 1: xxvii.

79. Gallay, *Formation of a Planter Elite*: 23-29.

80. Thomas Gapen to the Trustees, June 13, 1735, James Oglethorpe to the Trustees, June 1736, and Thomas Causton to the Trustees, February 24, 1737, in Lane, ed., *General Oglethorpe's Georgia*, vol. 1: xv; Coleman, *Colonial Georgia*: 268-276. For a more in-depth analysis of the Spanish-Yamasee alliance, see Steven J. Oatis, *A Colonial Complex: South Carolina's Frontier in the Era of the Yamasee War, 1680-1730* (Lincoln: University of Nebraska Press, 2004). For a description of British-Indian relations in South Carolina during this period, see David M. Ramsay, *History of South Carolina from its First Settlement in 1670 to the Year 1808*, vol. 1 (Philadelphia: W.J. Duffie, 1858): 31-53, 84-124.

81. Lane, ed., *General Oglethorpe's Georgia*, vol. 1: xxxii-xxxiii.

82. Ibid.

83. Gallay, *Formation of a Planter Elite*: 23.

84. Journal Entry, June 2, 1738, in W. V. Davis, ed., *GWJ*: 151.

85. Journal Entry, May 19, 1738, in ibid.: 150.

86. "Mr. Franklin; A Minister's Duty to Men...," *Pennsylvania Gazette*, no. 910 (May 22, 1746): 1; "Advertisement," *Georgia Gazette*, no. 99 (February 21, 1765): 3; "Advertisement," *Boston Evening Post*, no. 1545 (April 15, 1765): 1.

87. Journal Entry, June 2, 1738, in W. V. Davis, ed., *GWJ*: 151-152.

88. Sally Schwartz, *"A Mixed Multitude": The Struggle for Toleration in Colonial Pennsylvania* (New York: New York University Press, 1987). While limited in scope to Pennsylvania, this study is still useful for understanding the challenges that pluralism created among early settlers.

89. Journal Entry, June 5, 1738, in W. V. Davis, ed., *GWJ*: 152.

90. Journal Entry, June 24, 1738, in ibid: 153.

Notes

91. Ibid.

92. Along the lines of what Beneke and Remer discuss, though it is important that, like many eighteenth-century religious commentators, Whitefield's acceptance was more forthcoming when the other religious society was either complementary to his beliefs or when he did not believe it to be large or visible enough to undermine him. Beneke, *Beyond Toleration*: 17; Remer, *Humanism*: 6.

93. Journal Entry, June 24, 1738, in W. V. Davis, ed., *GWJ*: 153.

94. Benjamin Ingham to Sir John Phillips, September 15, 1736 in Lane, Ibid: 279. Note: Sir John Phillips was Whitefield's sponsor for his missionary work in Oxford before Whitefield undertook his first voyage to Georgia.

95. Ramsay, *History of South Carolina*, vol.1: 15.

96. Ibid.

97. Remer, *Humanism*: 6.

98. "Huguenot Quarrel (1726)," in *A Documentary History of Religion in America*, ed. Edwin S. Gaustad and Mark A. Noll: 118–120.

99. Anonymous Fragment Objecting to the Appointment of Colonel N, FP, vol. 10: General Correspondence, 1735–?: South Carolina, f. 243, LPL. Note: The fragment is undated, but LPL staff dates it as belonging to the proprietary period.

100. Ramsay, *History of South Carolina*, vol. 1: 19–20.

101. Ibid., vol. 2: 3.

102. East Apthrop, "Considerations on the Institution and Conduct of the Society for the Propagation of the Gospel in Foreign Parts" (Boston: Green and Russell, 1818): 9, 13, 21 and Jonathan Mayhew, "Observations on the Charter and Conduct of the Society for the Propagation of the Gospel" (Boston: Richard and Draper, 1804): 35

103. Ramsay, *History of South Carolina*, vol. 1: 3.

104. Ibid.

105. Thomas Morrit to Bishop Gibson, Feb. 3, 1734/5, FP, vol. 10: General Correspondence, 1735–?: South Carolina, ff. 3–4, LPL.

106. Correspondence: Wardens and Vestry of St. James' Parish, Santee to Bishop Gibson, Apr. 17, 1735; Alexander Garden to Bishop Gibson, May 15, 1735; Wardens and Vestry of Prince Frederick's Parish to Bishop Gibson, May 25, 1735; Thomas Morrit to Bishop Gibson, Sept. 18, 1735 and Alexander Garden to Bishop Gibson, May 4, 1739, ibid.: ff. 5–6, 7–10, 11–12, 15–16 and 54–55, LPL.

107. Journal Entry, August 28, 1738, in W. V. Davis, ed., *GWJ*: 159.

108. Ibid.

109. Journal Entry, Dec. 9, 1738, in ibid.

110. Stout, *Divine Dramatist*: 64.

111. Saint John of Damascus, *Three Treatises on the Divine Images*, Treatise I, 29.

112. Journal Entry, January 25, 1739, in W. V. Davis, ed., *GWJ*: 195.

Notes

113. Journal Entry, December 10, 1738, in ibid.

114. David S. Lovejoy, *Religious Enthusiam in the New World: Heresy to Revolution* (Cambridge, MA: Harvard University Press, 1985).

115. *A Letter from the Reverend George Whitefield to the Religious Societies, Lately Formed in England and Wales* (Philadelphia, 1739): 5–6.

116. William Penn, *Primitive Christianity Revived in the Faith and Practice of the People Called Quakers* (Salem, MA: George F. Read, 1844). In invoking early Christians who met at considerable risk to themselves, Whitefield also implied a potential martyrdom. Saint John of Damascus, *Three Treatises on the Divine Images, Treatise III*: 52.

117. *A Letter from the Reverend George Whitefield*: 6.

118. Journal Entries, January 5 and 22, 1739, in W. V. Davis, ed., *GWJ*: 189, 194.

119. Lovejoy, *Religious Enthusiasm*: 186.

120. Ibid.: 149.

121. Quoted in Tyerman, *Life of the Rev. George Whitefield*, vol. 1: 152.

122. Ibid.

123. Ibid.

124. Journal Entry, January 14, 1739, in W. V. Davis, ed., *GWJ*: 192. Another example appears in his entry for January 21, 1739, in ibid.: 193.

125. Ibid.; Gal. 1:8, Saint John of Damascus, *Three Treatises on the Divine Images, Treatise II*, 57. For an explanation of the fourth type of icon, see Saint John of Damascus, *Three Treatises on the Divine Images, Treatise III*, 98.

126. Journal Entry, January 17, 1739, in W. V. Davis, ed., *GWJ*: 193.

127. William Wainwright, "Jonathan Edwards," *The Stanford Encyclopedia of Philosophy* (Fall 2009 edition), Edward N. Zalta, ed., at http://plato.stanford.edu/archives/fall2009/entries/edwards (accessed on February 7, 2012).

128. Tyerman, *Life of the Rev. George Whitefield*, vol. 1: 179, 186, and Andrew Delbanco, *The Death of Satan: How Americans Have Lost the Sense of Evil* (New York: Farrar, Straus and Giroux, 1996): 86–88.

129. Charles Wesley Lowry, Jr., "Spiritual Antecedents of Anglican Evangelicalism," in *Anglican Evangelicalism*, ed. Alexander C. Zabriske (Philadelphia: Church Historical Society, 1943): 40

130. Butler, *Awash in a Sea*: 178.

131. Ibid.: 179.

132. Journal Entry, January 26, 1739, in W. V. Davis, ed., *GWJ*: 195.

133. Ibid.: 196.

134. Journal Entry, March 6, 1739, in ibid.: 221.

135. Bonomi, *Under the Cope of Heaven*, 162; Pestana, *Protestant Empire*: 220; Butler, *Awash in a Sea*: 170–172.

136. Stout, *Divine Dramatist*: 1–15.

Notes

137. Journal Entry, February 6, 1739, in W. V. Davis, ed., *GWJ*: 200. Whitefield also reported being well received by the bishop of Bristol on May 30, 1739, and receiving his benediction for Georgia. Journal Entry, May 30, 1739, in ibid.: 271.

138. Ibid.

139. "From George Whitefield's Journal," Monday, November 19, 1739, *Boston Evening Post*, no. 224: 1.

140. Ibid.

141. Ibid.

142. Whitefield to the Archbishop, Tottenham Court, Feb. 12 1768, *SPG*, vol. XI: *Correspondence: American Colonies, 1703–1803*, ff. 262–263, LPL.

143. "From George Whitefield's Journal," Monday, November 19, 1739, *Boston Evening Post*, no. 224: 1.

144. Journal Entry, February 23, 1739, in W. V. Davis, ed., *GWJ*: 215–216.

145. Journal Entries, February 25–28, 1739, in ibid.: 216–218.

146. Journal Entry, May 12, 1739, in ibid.: 259.

147. Journal Entries, May 9 and 19, 1739, in ibid.: 261–262, 265–266.

148. Ibid.

149. Journal Entries, May 18 and 21, 1739, in ibid.: 261, 267.

150. Ibid.: 281.

151. Linda Colley, *Britons: Forging the Nations, 1707–1837* (New York: Yale University Press, 1992): 71.

152. Journal Entry, June 7, 1739, in W. V. Davis, ed., *GWJ*: 281.

153. Journal Entry, June 21, 1739, in ibid.: 287; Ruttenburg, "George Whitefield": 436.

154. Journal Entry, July 6, 1739, in W. V. Davis, ed., *GWJ*: 294.

155. Journal Entry, July 3, 1739, in ibid.: 292.

156. Ibid.

157. Journal Entries, July 19, 20, and 23, 1739, in ibid.: 303–307.

158. Journal Entry, August 14, 1739, in ibid.: 321.

159. Ola Elizabeth Winslow, *Jonathan Edwards, 1703–1758: A Biography* (New York: Macmillan Company, 1940): 176–178.

160. Ibid.: 179.

161. Advertisements, *American Mercury Weekly* (Philadelphia), no. 1039 (November 22–29, 1739): 3; *Boston Evening Post*, no. 228 (December 17, 1739): 2.

162. Winslow, *Jonathan Edwards*: 178.

163. Beneke, *Beyond Toleration*: 55–56; *Mr. Whi__d's Soliloquy, or a Serious Debate with Himself what Course He Shall Take* (Boston, 1745), lines 69–77; Benjamin Prescott, *A Letter to the Reverend Mr. Whitefield, An Itinerant Preacher* (Boston, 1745), 3; George Gillespie, *Remarks upon Mr. Whitefield, Proving Him a Man under Delusion* (Philadelphia, 1744), front matter.

Notes

164. Butler, *Awash in a Sea*: 187.
165. Beneke, *Beyond Tolerance*: 81–82.
166. Ibid.: 63.

Chapter Two

1. Lambert, "*Pedlar in Divinity*": 11.
2. William Penn, "The Great Case of Liberty of Conscience (1670)," in ibid.: 130–131.
3. Ibid.: 135.
4. Bonomi, *Under the Cope of Heaven*: 169.
5. William Penn to James Logan, February 20, 1705, in *Correspondence between William Penn and James Logan*, ed. Edward Armstrong, vol. 2 (New York: AMS Press, 1872): 14. There was also a concern that the growing wealth in the colonies was corrupting Quaker morals. See Isaac Norris to Jonathan Dickenson, August 31, 1705, in ibid.: 81.
6. Penn, "A Seasonable Caveat against Popery (1670)," in ibid.: 165.
7. Ibid.: 167.
8. Ibid.: 179.
9. Bonomi, *Under the Cope of Heaven*, 90.
10. Ibid.: 90, 168.
11. Ibid.
12. Charles Gookin, Address to the Pennsylvania Assembly, July, 29, 1709, in *Pennsylvania Archives*, eighth series: *Votes and Proceedings of the House of Representatives of the Province of Pennsylvania, Oct. 14, 1707–Aug. 6, 1726*, ed. Gertrude MacKinney, vol. 2 (Philadelphia: S.I., s.n., 1931): 869.
13. Votes of the Assembly, April 13, 1709, in ibid.: 845.
14. Journal Entry, November 3, 1739, in W. V. Davis, ed., *GWJ*: 337.
15. This refers back to the historiography of the development of the ideology of religious toleration. See especially Beneke, *Beyond Tolerance*; Remer, *Humanism*; and Schwartz, "*A Mixed Multitude*."
16. Bonomi, *Under the Cope of Heaven*, 146–147.
17. Hoffer, *When Benjamin Franklin . . .* : 9–22.
18. Lois W. Banner, "Religious Benevolence as Social Control: A Critique of an Interpretation," *Journal of American History* 60, no. 1 (June 1973): 27.
19. Ibid.; Journal Entry, September 19, 1740, in W. V. Davis, ed., *GWJ*: 458.
20. Ibid.: 342.
21. "Philadelphia, Nov. 8," *New-England Weekly Journal*, no. 657 (November 20, 1739): 2. In particular, this is a form of veneration as described in Saint John of Damascus, *Three Treatises on the Divine Images*, Treatise I: 27.

Notes

22. "From the *Pennsylvania Gazette*, On Hearing George Whitefield at the New Building in Philadelphia," *Gentleman's Magazine* (January 1, 1741): 70.

23. Ibid.

24. "A Letter from Rev. Mr. Whitefield, to Some Church-Members of the Presbyterian Perswasion, New York, Nov. 1, 1740," *Gentleman's Magazine* (January 1, 1741): 53.

25. Ibid.

26. Ibid.

27. Ibid.

28. "Advertisement: Just Published," *Pennsylvania Gazette* (November 13, 1740): 2.

29. Ibid.

30. Matthew Tindall, *The Rights of the Christian Church Asserted* . . . (1709).

31. Isaac Norris to Joseph Pike, February 24, 1707, in *Correspondence between William Penn and James Logan*, vol. 2 (New York: AMS Press, 1872): 210–211.

32. Ibid.: 67.

33. Ibid.: 69.

34. Journal Entry, November 13, 1739, in W. V. Davis, ed., *GWJ*: 343.

35. Ibid.

36. Journal Entry, November 14, 1739, in ibid.: 344.

37. Francis Bazley Lee, *New Jersey as a Colony and as a State: One of the Original Thirteen*, vol. 1 (New York: Publishing Society of New Jersey, 1902): 332–333.

38. "Mr. Arnold's Letter against the Reverend Mr. George Whitefield, Answer'd, by Magnus Falconar, Marriner. To the Inhabitants of New-York," *American Weekly Mercury*, no. 1039 (November 22–29, 1739): 1.

39. Ibid.

40. Ibid.

41. Ibid.

42. One of the criticisms against divine images involved the preservation of traditions as well as "suspicion" of the "decline in the smallest degree of perfection" of those traditions. This is one of many such examples in the reaction against Whitefield as an icon of revivalism. Saint John of Damascus, *Three Treatises on the Divine Images, Treatise I*: 20.

43. Archibald Cummings to Bishop Gibson, Philadelphia, November 17, 1739, FP, vol. 7: General Correspondence, Pennsylvania, 1680–1762: ff. 246–247, LPL.

44. Archibald Cummings, *The Danger of Breaking Christian Unity, in Two Sermons, Preached June 12, 1737* (Philadelphia: Printed and Sold by Andrew Bradford, 1737): 15.

45. Postscript: Archibald Cummings to Bishop Gibson, July 18, 1737, in ibid.: A3.

Notes

46. Ibid.

47. Alexander Malcolm to Bishop Gibson, Marblehead, July 6, 1747, FP, vol. 5: General Correspondence, Massachusetts, 1730–1750: ff. 305–306, LPL.

48. Francis Makemie, Sermon, March 2, 1706, in ibid.: f. 413.

49. See, e.g., Advertisements: *New-York Journal*, January 14, 1733; *New-York Gazette*, December 6, 1747. See also November 2, 1747, and November 6, 1749.

50. Clark, *Public Prints*: 170.

51. "New York, Nov. 18," *Boston Gazette*, no. 1036 (November 29–December 3, 1739): 3.

52. "Old New York and Trinity Church, Minutes of the Council," in *Collections of the New-York Historical Society for the Year 1870*, vol. 3 (New York: Printed for the Society, 1871): 283–284.

53. Ibid.; Advertisement, *Boston News-Letter*, no. 1919 (December 25, 1740–January 1, 1741): 2.

54. Journal Entry, November 15, 1739, in W. V. Davis, ed., *GWJ*: 344.

55. Ibid.: 345.

56. Ibid.

57. Ibid.

58. Beneke, *Beyond Tolerance*: 17. This also ties into the tensions between icon and orthodoxy, but this time with Whitefield asserting himself as the "pure" image. Saint John of Damascus, *Three Treatises on the Divine Images, Treatise I*: 19–20.

59. Journal Entry, November 18, 1739, in W. V. Davis, ed., *GWJ*: 347.

60. "From the Gentleman's Magazine for May, 1739," *Boston Evening Post*, no. 214 (September 17, 1739): 1

61. Ibid.

62. Delbanco, *Death of Satan*.

63. Journal Entry, November 23, 1739, in W. V. Davis, ed., *GWJ*: 351.

64. Butler, *Awash in a Sea*: 143.

65. Journal Entry, November 25, 1739, in W. V. Davis, ed., *GWJ*: 352–353.

66. Journal Entry, November 27, 1739, in ibid.: 354–355.

67. Journal Entry, November 28, 1739, in ibid.: 357.

68. Journal Entries, November 29–December 6, 1739, in ibid.: 358–363.

69. Journal Entry, December 8, 1739, in ibid.: 366.

70. A. Owen Aldridge, "Natural Religion and Deism in America before Ethan Allen and Thomas Paine," *William and Mary Quarterly*, third series, 54, no. 4 (October 1997): 836.

71. I. Woodbridge Riley, "The Rise of Deism in Yale College," *American Journal of Theology* 9, no. 3 (July 1905): 474.

72. Bonomi, *Under the Cope of Heaven*: 179, 186; Delbanco, *Death of Satan*: 86–88.

Notes

73. Aldridge, "Natural Religion and Deism": 837.
74. Ibid.: 839.
75. Hoffer, *When Benjamin Franklin* . . . .
76. Ibid.
77. Aldridge, "Natural Religion and Deism": 16.
78. *Oath of Obedience*, 3 James I, chap. 4. See also Arthur P. Scott, *Criminal Law in Colonial Virginia* (Chicago: University of Chicago Press, 1930): 243–244.
79. "Act III: Against Persons that Refuse to have their Children Baptised," in *The Statutes at Large; Being a Collection of all the Laws of Virginia, from the First Session of the First Legislature, in the Year 1619*, ed. William Waller Hening, vol. 2 (New York: R & W & G Bartow, 1823): 165–166.
80. Bonomi, *Under the Cope of Heaven*: 17, 42, 46.
81. Ibid.: 42–43, 46, 50. As Bonomi notes, the SPG's lack of support can be attributed to the fact that in Virginia there was an established church (unlike Pennsylvania, Delaware, New Jersey, Rhode Island, and much of New York) and dissenters were not a significant threat, as they were in more religiously pluralist colonies like North and South Carolina.
82. Mr. Blair to the bishop of London, Williamsburgh in Virginia, November 18, 1714, in *Historical Documents Relating to the American Colonial Church*, vol. 1: *Virginia*, ed. William Stevens Perry (New York: AMS Press, 1969): 130.
83. Wednesday, January 9, 1741, in *Journal of a Voyage from London to Savannah in Georgia in Three Parts*, by George Whitefield (London: W. Strahan, 1741): 85.
84. Arthur P. Scott, *Criminal Law in Colonial Virginia* (Chicago: University of Chicago Press, 1930): 245–246.
85. Ibid.: 246.
86. Journal Entry, December 11, 1739, in W. V. Davis, ed., *GWJ*: 367.
87. Journal Entries, December 14, 16, 1739, in ibid.: 368–369.
88. Journal Entry, January 5, 1740, in ibid.: 382.
89. Journal Entry, January 6, 1740, in ibid.
90. Ibid.
91. For discussions of British high culture, see especially John Brewer, *The Pleasures of the Imagination: English Culture in the Eighteenth Century* (New York: Routledge, 2013); David Hancock, *Citizens of the World: London Merchants and the Integration of the British Atlantic Community, 1735–1785* (New York: Cambridge University Press, 1997); and Paul Langford, *A Polite and Commercial People: England 1727–1783* (New York: Oxford University Press, 1994).
92. Alexander Garden to Bishop Gibson, June 12, 1739, FP, vol. 10: General Correspondence: South Carolina, 1735–?, ff. 56–57, LPL.
93. Bonomi, *Under the Cope of Heaven*: 143.

Notes

94. George Whitefield, *Letter to the Inhabitants of Maryland, Virginia, North and South Carolina, Concerning Their Negroes* (Philadelphia, 1740).

95. Ibid.

96. Alexander Garden, *Mr. Commissary Garden's Six Letters to the Rev. Mr. George Whitefield* (Charles Town, SC: Peter Timothy, 1740; repr. Boston: T. Fleet, 1740), text-fiche, 52. See also Fred Witzig, "'Coining Dupes and Catching Fools,' or 'A Little Heaven on Earth?': Philanthropy and Rhetoric in the Great Awakening" (paper presented at the Annual Meeting of the American Studies Association, Baltimore, MD, October 23, 2011): 3–4, 6.

97. Journal Entry, March 14, 1740, in W. V. Davis, ed., *GWJ*: 397.

98. Leigh Eric Schmidt, "'The Grand Prophet,' Hugh Bryan: Early Evangelicalism's Challenge to the Establishment and Slavery in the Colonial South." *South Carolina Historical Magazine* 87, no. 4 (October 1986): 240

99. Harvey H. Jackson, "Hugh Bryan and the Evangelical Movement in Colonial South Carolina," *William and Mary Quarterly*, third series, 43, no. 4 (October 1986): 596.

100. Schmidt, "Grand Prophet": 240.

101. "Charles-Town," January 15, 1740, *New-York Weekly Journal*, no. 378 (March 2, 1740): 4. Curiously, this incident does not appear in Whitefield's journal.

102. Schmidt, "Grand Prophet": 240.

103. Journal Entry, March 14, 1740, in W. V. Davis, ed., *GWJ*: 398.

104. Ibid.

105. "Advertisement: Six Letters to the Rev. Mr. George Whitefield," *Boston Evening Post*, no. 273 (October 27, 1740): 4.

106. Alexander Garden, Letter One to the Reverend Mr. Whitefield, July 30, 1740, in *Mr. Commissary Garden's Six Letters*: 5.

107. Romans 1:17, in *Good News Bible*: 1349.

108. Letter One to the Reverend Mr. Whitefield, March 17, 1739, in *Mr. Commissary Garden's Six Letters*: 5.

109. Letter Three to the Reverend Mr. Whitefield, April 8, 1740, in ibid.: 8. Also pertinent to debates over an icon's perfection or purity is Saint John of Damascus, *Three Treatises on the Divine Images, Treatise I*: 19–20.

110. Mr. Whitefield's Answer to the Reverend Mr. Garden, March 18, 1739, in *Mr. Commissary Garden's Six Letters*: 6. Note: This only responds to Garden's first letter.

111. Journal Entry, March 14, 1740, in W. V. Davis, ed., *GWJ*: 398.

112. Ibid.

Notes

113. Alexander Garden to Bishop Gibson, January 28, 1740, FP 10, General Correspondence: South Carolina, 1735–?, ff.: 67–68, LPL.

114. Journal Entry, March 16, 1740, in W. V. Davis, ed., *GWJ*: 399. See "imagery" as described in Saint John Damascus, *Three Treatises on the Divine Images, Treatise II*: 61.

115. Letter Six to the Reverend Mr. Whitefield, in *Mr. Commissary Garden's Six Letters*: 53.

116. Alexander Garden to the Bishop of London, July 30, 1741, FP, vol. 10, ff. 86–87, LPL.

117. Ibid.

118. For analysis of the criticisms of the Bethesda Orphan House by Garden and his allies, see Witzig, "'Coining Dupes'": 6–7.

119. Alexander Garden to Bishop Gibson, Charles Town, July 30, 1741, FP, vol. 10: General Correspondence: 1735–?, South Carolina: ff. 86–87, LPL.

120. Ibid.

121. Ibid.

122. Alexander Garden to Bishop Gibson, Charles Town, August 1740, and Garden to Bishop Gibson, Charles Town, January 7, 1743 [extract], FP, vol. 10: General Correspondence: 1735–?, South Carolina: ff. 106–107, LPL.

123. Alexander Garden, *Take Heed of How Ye Year: A Sermon Preached in the Parish Church of St. Philip Charles-Town, in South Carolina on Sunday the 13th of July, 1740: A Preface, Containing Some Remarks on Mr. Whitefield's Journals* (Charles Town: Peter Timothy, 1740): 5.

124. Ibid.

125. Ibid.

126. Ibid.: 4.

127. Ibid.

128. Advertisement, *Boston Evening Post*, no. 359 (June 21, 1742): 2

129. Alexander Garden to Bishop Gibson, Charleston, July 12, 1750, FP, vol. 40: General Correspondence: South Carolina, 1735–?: ff. 134–135, LPL.

130. Whitefield to Bishop Gibson, On Board the Savannah Bound from Charlestown to Boston, September 8, 1740, FP, vol. 10: General Correspondence: 1735–?, South Carolina: ff. 63–64, LPL.

131. Whitefield to Bishop Gibson, June 9, 1741, MS Film 773, MS 1123/Item 26, LPL.

132. Ibid.

133. Ibid.

134. Ibid.

135. W. Sharpe to the Bishop of London, Council Office, May 15, 1742, FP, vol. 10: General Correspondence: 1735–?, South Carolina: ff. 104–105, LPL.

136. T. S. Kidd, *Great Awakening*: 72.

Notes

137. Ibid.
138. Saint John of Damascus, *Three Treatises on the Divine Images*, Treatises I and III: 19–20, 98.
139. Ibid.
140. Journal Entry, April 15, 1740, in W. V. Davis, ed., *GWJ*: 404.
141. "A Second Letter from the Rev. Mr. Whitefield to a Friend in London," *Pennsylvania Gazette*, no. 593 (April 24, 1740): 1.
142. Journal Entry, April 15, 1740, in W. V. Davis, ed., *GWJ*: 404.
143. Gilbert Tennent, *The Examiner, Examined*. . . . (Philadelphia, 1743): 42.
144. Ibid.: 5.
145. Ibid.: 9–10.

Chapter Three

1. This can be connected to St. John of Damascus's discussion about the "purity" of an icon. Gal. 1:8; Saint John of Damascus, *Three Treatises on the Divine Images*, Treatise II: 57. For a discussion of the broader clashes between popular Protestantism and Anglicanism, see especially Pestana, *Protestant Empire*.
2. Colin Kidd, *Forging of Races*: 54–78; Brown and Webb, *Race in the American South*: 119.
3. Nicholas M. Beasley, *Christian Ritual and the Creation of British Slave Societies, 1650–1900* (Athens: University of Georgia Press, 2010): 1–20, 54–84.
4. Wheeler, *Complexion of Race*: 54.
5. Christopher Leslie Brown, *Moral Capital: Foundations of British Abolitionism* (Chapel Hill: University of North Carolina Press, 2005): 67.
6. Ibid.: 68.
7. By virtue of his inexorable campaign against Whitefield, Garden in many ways became the iconoclast to Whitefield's icon. In trying to undermine Whitefield's image, Garden, by extent, sought to undermine revivalism and reassert the orthodoxy of the Anglican Church.
8. Glasson, *Mastering Christianity*: 47–55.
9. Charles F. Irons, *The Origins of Proslavery Christianity: White and Black Evangelicals in Colonial and Antebellum Virginia* (Chapel Hill: University of North Carolina Press, 2008): 29.
10. "Godwyn, Morgan (*bap.* 1640, *d.* 1685x1709)," by Betty Wood, in *Oxford Dictionary of National Biography*, ed. Lawrence Goldman, Oxford: Oxford University Press, online ed., at http://www.oxforddnb.com/view/article/10894 (accessed February 18, 2012).
11. Irons, *Origins of Proslavery Christianity*: 29.
12. Quoted in ibid.: 29.

13. Brown, *Moral Capital*: 69–71.
14. Ibid.
15. Ibid.: 33–101.
16. C. Kidd, *Forging of Races*, 19–120.
17. Alexander Hewatt, *An Historical Account of the Rise and Progress of the Colonies of South Carolina and Georgia*, vol. 1 (London, 1779): 21.
18. Booker T. Washington and W. E. Burghardt Du Bois, *The Negro in the South: His Economic Progress in Relation to His Moral and Religious Development* (Philadelphia: George W. Jacobs, 1907): 58.
19. Alan Gallay, "The Origins of Slaveholders' Paternalism: George Whitefield, the Bryan Family, and the Great Awakening in the South," *Journal of Southern History* 53, no. 3 (August 1987): 369–370.
20. Leland J. Bellot, "Evangelicals and the Defense of Slavery in Britain's Old Colonial Empire," *Journal of Southern History* 37, no. 1 (February 1971): 20.
21. Gallay, "Origins of Slaveholders' Paternalism": 370.
22. Gregory D. Massey, "Limits of Antislavery Thought in the Revolutionary Lower South: John Laurens and Henry Laurens," *Journal of Southern History*, 63, no. 3 (August 1997): 499. Essentially, Whitefield assigned slaves a qualified humanity, which undermined the process of race-making in the early eighteenth-century. Brown and Webb, *Race in the American South*: 119.
23. David Brion Davis, *The Problem of Slavery in the Age of Revolution, 1770–1823* (Ithaca, NY: Cornell University Press, 1975): 41.
24. Massey, "Limits of Antislavery Thought": 498–500.
25. Ibid.: 501.
26. David Brion Davis, *Problem of Slavery*: 39; Brown and Webb, *Race in the American South*: 119.
27. Journal Entry, June 21, 1739, in W. V. Davis, ed., *GWJ*: 287; Ruttenburg, "George Whitefield": 436.
28. Mark 6:34, in *The Holy Bible: King James Version* (New York: American Bible Society, 1980): 42.
29. Hebrews 13:20, in ibid.: 230.
30. Genesis 4:2, in ibid.: 2.
31. Genesis 4:2, 12:16, 29:9, in ibid.: 2, 11, 28. All of this invocation of scriptural imagery can be connected to Whitefield positing himself as an example of "good things to come" as well as conveying a "faint image of God." Saint John of Damascus, *Three Treatises on the Divine Images, Treatises I and II*: 29, 57.
32. Journal Entries for May 9 and 19, 1739, in W. V. Davis, ed., *GWJ*: 261–262, 265–266.
33. Bellot, "Evangelicals and the Defense of Slavery": 15.
34. Ibid.: 16–17

Notes

35. Salley, *Narratives*, p. 67, and Craven, *Southern Colonies*, p. 330, quoted in B. Wood, *Slavery in Colonial Georgia*: 17.

36. *Fundamental Constitutions of Carolina*, March 1, 1669, at http://avalon.law.yale.edu/17th_century/nc05.asp (accessed August 29, 2011).

37. John B. Boles, *Black Southerners, 1619-1869* (Lexington: University Press of Kentucky, 1983): 32.

38. Philip D. Morgan, "Black Life in Eighteenth-Century Charleston," in *Perspectives in American History, New Series*, vol. 1, ed. Bernard Bailyn, Donald Fleming, and Stephan Thernstrom (New York: Cambridge University Press for the Charles Warren Center for Studies in American History, 1984): 188.

39. Philip M. Hammer, ed. *Papers of Henry Laurens*, vol. 9: *Apr. 19, 1773-Dec. 12, 1774* (Columbia: University of South Carolina Press, 1981): 578n.

40. R. C. Nash, "South Carolina and the Atlantic Economy in the Late Seventeenth and Eighteenth Centuries," *Economic History Review*, new series, 45, no. 1 (January 1995): 15.

41. Ibid.: 16-23.

42. R. C. Nash, "Trade and Business in Eighteenth-Century South Carolina: The Career of John Guerard," *South Carolina Historical Magazine* 96, no. 1 (January 1995): 6.

43. Ibid.: 9-12.

44. "A Letter from the Rev. Mr. George Whitefield, to the Inhabitants of Maryland, Virginia, North and South Carolina," *Pennsylvania Gazette*, no. 592 (April 17, 1940): 1. Note that his letter was originally written on January 23, 1739. It is not insignificant that it was reproduced in several colonial papers in the spring of 1740.

45. Ibid.

46. Stein, "George Whitefield on Slavery": 244.

47. David H. Corkran, *The Creek Frontier, 1540-1783* (Norman: University of Oklahoma Press, 1967): 52-53.

48. Julie Anne Sweet, *Negotiating for Georgia: British-Creek Relations in the Trustee Era, 1733-1752* (Athens: University of Georgia Press, 2005): 99.

49. Ibid.: 246-247.

50. Hewatt, *Historical Account*, vol. 2: 23.

51. Benjamin Martyn to Governor Robert Johnson of South Carolina, October 18, 1732, Trustees Office, Palace Court, Westminster, C.O. 5/666, in *Colonial Records of the State of Georgia: Trustees' Letter Book, 1732-1738*, ed. Kenneth Coleman and Milton Ready, vol. 29 (Athens: University of Georgia Press, 1985): 1.

52. Stein, "George Whitefield on Slavery": 246-247.

53. Hewatt, *Historical Account*: 150-151.

Notes

54. Benjamin Martyn to Samuel Eveleigh at Charles Town, May 1, 1735, Westminster, C.O. 5/666, in Coleman and Ready, eds., *Colonial Records of the State of Georgia*: 66

55. Ibid.

56. Ibid.

57. Ibid.

58. Sarah B. Gober Temple and Kenneth Coleman, *Georgia Journeys* (Athens: University of Georgia Press, 1961): 14.

59. Ralph Betts Flanders, *Plantation Slavery in Georgia* (Cos Cob, CT: John E. Edwards, 1967): 10–11.

60. Ibid.: 24.

61. Common Council Authorization to Constables of Savannah to Seize Any Blacks or Negroes Found in Georgia. Sept. 24, 1735, C.O. 5/670 in *Colonial Records of the State of Georgia: Entry Books of Commissions, Powers, Instructions, Leases, Grants of Land, Etc, by the Trustees, 1732–1738*, ed. Kenneth Coleman, vol. 32 (Athens: University of Georgia Press, 1989): 177–178.

62. Flanders, *Plantation Slavery*: 16.

63. See especially Goetz, *Baptism of Early Virginia*: 86–137, and C. Kidd, *Forging of Races*: 19–78.

64. Stein, "George Whitefield on Slavery": 243, 248–356.

65. *A Letter to the Negroes Lately Converted to Christ in America* . . . (London: J. Hart, 1740): 2.

66. Ibid.: 17.

67. Ibid.

68. Ibid.: 19.

69. Ibid.: 21.

70. Commissaries were special appointees by the bishop of London who oversaw Anglican affairs in rural parts of England and, starting in 1689, the British colonies in the Americas.

71. "A Letter from the Reverend Mr. George Whitefield, to the Inhabitants of Maryland, Virginia, North and South Carolina," *Pennsylvania Gazette*, no. 592 (April 17, 1740): 1; *New-England Weekly Journal*, no. 680 (April 29, 1740): 1.

72. Ibid.

73. Ibid. This is germane to Colin Kidd's description of "race as a scriptural problem." C. Kidd, *Forging of Races*: 19–53.

74. Valeri, *Heavenly Merchandize*: 12; George Whitefield, "The Pharisee and Publican," in Smith, ed., *Fifteen Sermons*: 152–160; Breen, "An Empire of Goods": 473; Lambert, *"Pedlar in Divinity"*: 13; Hoffer, *When Benjamin Franklin* . . . : 37.

75. T. S. Kidd, *Great Awakening*, 91; W. V. Davis, ed., *GWJ*: 486–488.

76. Vincent Carretta, *Phillis Wheatley: Biography of a Genius in Bondage* (Athens: University of Georgia Press, 2011): 29.

Notes

77. Ibid.
78. As noted by Wheeler in her discussion of categories of difference in the British Atlantic. Wheeler, *Complexion of Race*: 1–89.
79. Journal Entry, Wednesday, January 2, 1740, in George Whitefield, *A Continuation of Mr. Whitefield's Journal, from his Embarking after the Embargo* (London, 1740): 78.
80. Ibid.: 78.
81. Ibid.: 79.
82. Ibid.
83. Ibid.
84. Philip D. Morgan, *Slave Counterpoint: Black Culture in the Eighteenth-Century Chesapeake and Lowcountry* (Chapel Hill: University of North Carolina Press, 1998): 408, 418.
85. His views were driven by the complexities of how "race" was understood in the eighteenth century. See especially Goetz, *Baptism of Early Virginia*; Wheeler, *Complexion of Race*: 1–89; and C. Kidd, *Forging of Races*, 1–120.
86. Stein, "George Whitefield on Slavery": 246.
87. Ibid.: 246–247.
88. Robert Pringle, Charles Town, to John Richards, London, September 26, 1739, quoted in Mark M. Smith, ed., *Stono: Documenting and Interpreting a Southern Slave Revolt* (Columbia: University of South Carolina Press, 2005): 9.
89. Detailed Reports on the Salzburger Emigrants Who Settled in America ..., quoted in ibid.: 10.
90. South Carolina Slave Code of 1740, Acts of the South Carolina General Assembly, 1740, #670, South Carolina Department of Archives and History, Columbia, South Carolina.
91. For further analysis of some African American dance rituals with links to conjure, see Jeffrey E. Anderson, *Conjure in African American Society* (Baton Rouge: Louisiana State University Press, 2007): 45–49, 57, 66–67, 91–92, 100, 114, 136.
92. Banner, "Religious Benevolence": 25.
93. A Letter to Mr. B., South Carolina, October 25, 1747, Whitefield, *Works*, vol. 2: 141.
94. See National Archives, United Kingdom (formerly the Public Record Office), at http://www.nationalarchives.gov.uk/pathways/blackhistory/rights/slave_free.htm (accessed 17 February 17, 2012).
95. Whitefield, *Works*, vol. 2: 90.
96. To the Honourable Trustees in Georgia, Gloucester, December 6, 1748, in ibid.: 208.
97. Ibid.
98. Ibid.

99. Ibid.: 209.

100. Ibid.

101. To the Countess of H, London, November 14, 1748, in ibid.: 201.

102. This is also consistent with Whitefield's efforts to paint himself as a symbol, or at least a forbearer, of "good things to come;" in this case, economic prosperity. Saint John of Damascus, *Three Treatises on the Divine Images*, Treatise I: 29.

103. Quoted in B. Wood, *Slavery in Colonial Georgia*: 83.

104. Ibid.

105. Quoted in ibid.

106. Ibid.

107. Ibid.: 85.

108. Letter to Mr. B., Bristol, March 22, 1751, in *The Works of the Reverend George Whitefield*, by George Whitefield, vol. 2: 404–405.

109. "A Letter from the Rev. Mr. George Whitefield, to the Inhabitants of Maryland, Virginia, North and South Carolina," April 17, 1740, *Pennsylvania Gazette*, January 23, 1740, in Whitefield, *Works*, vol. 4; Whitefield to Mr. B., Bristol, March 22, 1751, in ibid., vol. 2: 404–405.

110. Whitefield to Mr. B., Bristol, March 22, 1751, in ibid., vol. 2: 404-405. It is also possible to make a connection between Whitefield serving as an icon of "good things to come," as a divine figure to oversee the spiritual well-being of slaves. Saint John of Damascus, *Three Treatises on the Divine Images*, Treatise I: 29.

111. Jackson, "Hugh Bryan and the Evangelical Movement": 600.

112. Gallay, *Formation of a Planter Elite*: 37.

113. Quoted in ibid.: 37–38.

114. This was a calculated attempt to undermine Whitefield's credibility as an icon of revivalism as well as the religious truth of revivalism itself.

115. *South Carolina Gazette*, October 3, 1741; Witzig, "'Coining Dupes'": 7.

116. In essence, this campaign was responding to iconoclastic efforts to undermine him as a visible symbol of revivalism.

117. "Mr. Franklin; A Minister's Duty to Men . . . ," *Pennsylvania Gazette*, no. 910 (May 22, 1746): 1; Advertisement, *Georgia Gazette*, no. 99 (February 21, 1765): 3; Advertisement, *Boston Evening Post*, no. 1545 (April 15, 1765): 1

118. Saint John of Damascus, *Three Treatises on the Divine Images*, Treatise III: 98.

119. This is another example of Whitefield as icon of "good things to come." Ibid.: 29.

120. It is worth noting the similarities between *polite* and the Greek word *politēs*, which is a derivative of *polis*, or city-state. It indicates a political

shrewdness that Whitefield lacked and that helped his opponents paint him as outside of the *polis*.

121. Glasson, *Mastering Christianity*: 113.

122. The school failed, and the slaves were sold.

123. Albert J. Raboteau, *Canaan Land: A Religious History of African Americans* (New York: Oxford University Press, 2001): 3–39.

124. Martha Simmons and Frank A. Thomas, eds., *Preaching with Sacred Fire: An Anthology of African American Sermons, 1750 to the Present* (New York: W.W. Norton, 2010): 21

125. Ibid.

126. Jackson, "Hugh Bryan and the Evangelical Movement": 594.

127. Sylvia Frey and Betty Wood, *Come Shouting to Zion: African American Protestantism in the American South and British Caribbean to 1830* (Chapel Hill: University of North Carolina Press, 1998): 82, 84.

128. Ibid.

129. Ibid.: 84.

130. Glasson, *Mastering Christianity*: 111–138.

131. Vincent Carretta, ed., *Olaudah Equiano, The Interesting Narrative and Other Writings* (New York: Penguin Books, 2003): ix—xxx, 131—146; Carretta, *Phillis Wheatley*: 73; John Marrant, *A Narrative of the Lord's Wonderful Dealings with John Marrant, a Black* (London, 1788): 8.

132. See David Hume, *Of National Characters* (1742); Immanuel Kant, *The Difference Between the Races of Man* (1775); and Edward Long, *The History of Jamaica* (1774). The relevant passages of text can be found in Isaac Kramnick, ed., *The Portable Enlightenment Reader* (New York: Viking, 1995): 629, 638, 644. See also Franklin W. Knight, "Race and Identity in the New World," in *Assumed Identities: The Meanings of Race in the Atlantic World*, ed. John D. Garrigus and Christopher Morris (College Station: Texas A&M Press, 2010): 4–5.

Chapter Four

1. J. M. Bumsted, "Revivalism and Separatism in New England: The First Society of Norwich, Connecticut as a Case Study." *William and Mary Quarterly*, third series, 24, no. 4 (October 1967): 588.

2. Ibid. On perceptions of revivalism in New England during the (First) Great Awakening, see especially Lambert, *Inventing the "Great Awakening"*: 21–53, 62–82.

3. Pestana, *Protestant Empire*: 73.

4. Ibid.: 122.

Notes

5. Ibid.: 210.
6. Ibid.
7. Ibid.
8. Cotton Mather and Zebidiah Boylston, *Some Account of What is Said of Inoculating or Transplanting the Small Pox. By the Learned Dr. Emanuel Timonius, and Jacobus Pylarinus* (Boston, 1721).
9. Valeri, *Heavenly Merchandize*: 211.
10. Ibid.: 210, 234; Delbanco, *Death of Satan* (1995).
11. Harry S. Stout, *The New England Soul: Preaching and Religious Culture in Colonial New England* (New York: Oxford University Press, 2011): 127.
12. George Marsden, *Jonathan Edwards: A Life* (New Haven, CT: Yale University Press, 2008): 3.
13. *A Letter of Mr. John Cottons, Teacher of the Church in Boston, in New-England, to Mr. Williams, a Preacher There* (London: Benjamin Allen, 1643), also in John Cotton, *The New England Way* (New York: AMS Press, 1983): 15.
14. Stout, *New England Soul*, 185.
15. Joseph Belcher, *George Whitefield: A Biography, with Special References to his Labors in America* (New York: American Tract Society, 1857): 149.
16. Ibid.
17. Bushman, *From Puritan to Yankee*: 107–121.
18. Ibid.
19. Ibid.
20. Michael Crawford, "Origins of the Eighteenth-Century Evangelical Revival: England and New England Compared," *Journal of British Studies* 26, no. 4 (October 1987): 369. Bushman, *From Puritan to Yankee*: 183–195; James A. Henretta, *The Evolution of American Society, 1700–1815: An Interdisciplinary Analysis* (New York: DC Heath, 1973): 134–138.
21. Crawford, "Origins of the Eighteenth-Century Evangelical Revival": 369
22. Ibid.
23. Timothy Cutler to Bishop Gibson, Boston, February 4, 1730, FP, vol. 5: General Correspondence, 1730–1750, ff. 1–2, LPL.
24. Noll, *America's God*: 44.
25. Perry Miller, *The New England Mind: The Seventeenth Century* (New York: Macmillan, 1939): 3–37.
26. Valeri, *Heavenly Merchandize*: 210–211.
27. Miller, *New England Mind*: 46–47.
28. Ibid.: 47.
29. Ibid.
30. James F. Cooper, *Tenacious of Their Liberties: The Congregationalists in Colonial Massachusetts* (New York: Oxford University Press, 1999): 197

Notes

31. Ibid.: 200.

32. Marsden, *Jonathan Edwards*: 201–213

33. Saint John of Damascus, *Three Treatises on the Divine Images*, Treatise I: 29. For more on the impact of Whitefield's visit to Northampton on his image, and on revivalism as a whole, see Lambert, *Inventing the "Great Awakening"*: 69–82.

34. Delbanco, *Death of Satan*: 86–88.

35. Saint John of Damascus, *Three Treatises on the Divine Images*, Treatise I: 29.

36. Biographical Sketch, *Guide to the Benjamin Colman Papers*, Massachusetts Historical Society, Boston, MA (hereafter MHS).

37. Jonathan Edwards to Benjamin Colman, March 9, 1740, Papers of Benjamin Colman, MHS.

38. Benjamin Colman's Preface to Josiah Smith, *The Character, Preaching, &c of George Whitefield* (Boston: Rogers for Edwards and Foster, 1740): iii. See also Saint John of Damascus, *Three Treatises on the Divine Images*, Treatise II: 61.

39. Benjamin Colman's Preface to Smith, *Character, Preaching, &c*: vi; Saint John of Damascus, *Three Treatises on the Divine Images*, Treatise II, 61.

40. Damascus, *Three Treatises on the Divine Images*, Treatise II: 61.

41. Belcher, *George Whitefield*: 266.

42. Crawford, "Origins of the Eighteenth-Century Evangelical Revival": 377; Cooper, *Tenacious of Their Liberties*: 198–199.

43. Cooper, *Tenacious of Their Liberties*: 198-199.

44. Ibid.

45. Ibid.: 378.

46. Cotton, *New England Way*: 5.

47. J. M. Bumsted, "Orthodoxy in Massachusetts: The Ecclesiastical History of Freetown, 1683–1776," *New England Quarterly* (hereafter *NEQ*), 43, no. 2 (June 1970): 274.

48. Norman Pettit, "Prelude to Mission: Brainerd's Expulsion from Yale," *NEQ* 59, no. 1 (March 1986): 46.

49. Ibid. 29.

50. Ibid.: 47.

51. Eleazar Wheelock, *A Continuation of the Narrative of the Indian Charity-School, Begun in Lebanon, in Connecticut; Now Incorporated with Dartmouth-College, in Hanover, in the Province of New-Hampshire* (Hartford, CT: Ebenezer Watson, 1773).

52. For more detailed treatments of revivalism among Native Americans, see especially Linford D. Fisher, *The Indian Great Awakening: Revivalism and the Shaping of Native Cultures in Early America* (New York: Oxford University Press, 2012), and Edward E. Andrews, *Native Apostles: Black and Indian Missionaries in the British Atlantic World* (Cambridge, MA: Harvard University Press, 2013).

Notes

53. W. DeLoss Love, *Sansom Occom and the Christian Indians of New England* (Syracuse, NY: Syracuse University Press, 2000): 33.

54. The literature on New England slavery and antislavery is vast, but see especially the collection of essays in *Slavery/Antislavery in New England: The Dublin Seminar for New England Folklife, Annual Proceedings, June 20-22, 2003*; Catherine Adams and Elizabeth H. Pleck, *Love of Freedom: Black Women in Colonial and Revolutionary New England* (New York: Oxford University Press, 2010), and Vincent Carretta, *Phillis Wheatley: Biography of a Genius in Bondage* (Athens, GA: University of Georgia Press, 2011).

55. Carretta, *Phillis Wheatley*: 33.

56. The excitement his visits generated can be factored into the "invention" of the Great Awakening, as described by Frank Lambert in *Inventing the "Great Awakening."*

57. "From the Rev. Mr. Whitefield's Journal, Jul. 9," *Boston Evening Post*, no. 224 (November 19, 1739): 1.

58. Ibid.

59. The challenges to his orthodoxy were, of course, problematic in terms of his "divine image." Saint John of Damascus, *Three Treatises on the Divine Images, Treatise I*: 19-20.

60. *The Wonderful Narrative: or, A Faithful Account of the French Prophets, Their Agitations, Extasies and Inspirations* (Boston, 1742): 2, quoted in T. H. Breen and Timothy Hall, "Structuring Provincial Imagination: The Rhetoric and Experience of Social Change in Eighteenth-Century New England," *American Historical Review* 103, no. 5 (December 1998): 1411.

61. Ibid.

62. Ibid.: 1412.

63. Belcher, *George Whitefield*: 152.

64. Journal Entry, Sunday, September 14, 1740, in W. V. Davis, ed., *GWJ*: 452, and Belcher, *George Whitefield*: 153.

65. Ibid.

66. Belcher, *George Whitefield*: 154.

67. Journal Entry, September, 16, 1740, in W. V. Davis, ed., *GWJ*: 456.

68. Ibid.

69. Ibid.

70. Ibid.

71. September 18, 1740, in ibid.: 458.

72. Benjamin Colman to Unknown, October 7, 1740, *Papers of Benjamin Colman*, MHS. Note: The letter is sufficiently faded so that the intended recipient's name is no longer readable.

73. Ibid.

Notes

74. Ibid.

75. Foxcroft fell under criticism in 1745 for exposing his congregation to "Errors and mischief." See *A Letter to the Reverend Thomas Foxcroft* (Boston, 1745), MHS.

76. Belcher, *George Whitefield*: 157.

77. Winslow, *Jonathan Edwards*: 187.

78. Journal Entry, September 19, 1740, in W. V. Davis, ed., *GWJ*: 458.

79. Ibid.

80. Ibid.

81. Ibid.: 458–459.

82. Ibid.: 459–460.

83. "To the Rev. Mr. George Whitefield in Lynn, July 3, 1745," *Boston Evening Post*, no. 518 (July 15, 1745): 1.

84. Ibid.

85. Christopher Grasso, *Speaking Aristocracy* (Chapel Hill: University of North Carolina Press, 1999).

86. "To the Rev. Mr. George Whitefield in Lynn, July 3, 1745," *Boston Evening Post*, no. 518 (July 15, 1745): 1.

87. Ibid.

88. Journal Entry, September 29, 1740, in W. V. Davis, ed., *GWJ*: 466.

89. In the context of an "invented great awakening," Whitefield also had the problem of being seen as what Frank Lambert describes as "imported divinity" in a region where authority at the congregational level (as opposed to a church hierarchy) was highly prized. Lambert, *Inventing the "Great Awakening"*: 87–124.

90. Belcher, *George Whitefield*: 162.

91. Ibid.: 163.

92. William Buell Sprague, *Annals of the American Pulpit: Unitarian Congregational, 1865* (n.p.: Robert Carter and Brothers, 1865): 132.

93. *The England Historical and Genealogical Register 1863*, vol. 17 (Westminster, MD: Heritage Books, 1994): 234.

94. Richard Pateshall, *Pride Humbled, Mr. Hobby Chastised: Being some Remarks on Said Hobby's Piece, Entitled, a Defence of the Itinerancy and the Conduct of the Rev. Mr. Whitefield. In a Letter to the Reverend Mr. William Hobby, Pastor of the First Church in Reading* (Boston: Draper, 1745): 1.

95. Ibid.: 2.

96. "The Way of the Churches of Christ in New England" (1645), in Cotton, *New England Way*: 101–102.

97. Ibid.: 67–69.

98. Pateshall, *Pride Humbled*: 4.

99. Ibid.: 5.

Notes

100. Ibid.

101. "Thursday Next May Be Published," *Boston Evening Post*, no. 493 (January 21, 1745): 2.

102. Whitefield, *Works*, vol. 4: 88.

103. Marsden, *Jonathan Edwards*: 11.

104. Connecticut's first commissary was the Reverend Dr. Samuel Johnson, appointed in 1742.

105. Marsden, *Jonathan Edwards*: 60.

106. Ibid.: 63–64.

107. Ibid.: 59.

108. Ibid.: 202.

109. Ibid.: 178.

110. Ibid.: 180.

111. Belcher, *George Whitefield*: 181.

112. Ibid.

113. Ibid.: 183.

114. Journal Entry, October 21, 1740, in W. V. Davis, ed., *GWJ*: 480.

115. Ibid.

116. Ibid.

117. Ibid.

118. Belcher, *George Whitefield*: 256.

119. Ibid.: 258.

120. Ibid.

121. Ibid.: 259.

122. Ibid.

123. Ibid. This also fits with St. John of Damascus's fourth type of icon. Saint John of Damascus, *Three Treatises on the Divine Images*, Treatise II: 61.

124. Charles Chauncy, *The State of Religion, Since the Reverend Mr. George Whitefield's Arrival There* (Glasgow, 1742): 8, MHS.

125. Ibid.

126. Ibid.

127. Ibid. This is another example in which the religious orthodoxy or "truth" of Whitefield's message/reflection as an icon of revivalism was challenged. Saint John of Damascus, *Three Treatises on the Divine Images*, Treatise I: 19–20.

128. Ibid.

129. Charles Chauncy, *Seasonable Thoughts on the State of Religion in New England* (Boston: Rogers and Fowle, 1743: 1.

130. Ibid., 3.

131. Ibid.

132. Ibid.

Notes

133. Charles Chauncy, *A Letter to the Reverend Mr. Whitefield, Publically Calling Upon Him to Vindicate His Conduct, or Confess His Faults* (Boston, 1745): 1, MHS. Note: There is no evidence to indicate that Chauncy really ever supported Whitefield's invitation to Boston. His language in this letter was probably a function of etiquette rather than a sincere claim of past support.

134. Ibid.

135. Ibid.

136. Ibid.: 2.

137. Saint John of Damascus, *Three Treatises on the Divine Images, Treatise I*: 19–20.

138. Belcher, *George Whitefield*: 269.

139. Lambert, *Inventing the "Great Awakening"*: 82–124.

140. *A Letter from Two Neighbouring Associations of Ministers in the Country, to the Associated Ministers of Boston and Charlestown, Relating to the Admission of Mr. Whitefield into their Pulpits* (Boston, 1745): 2. A similar pamphlet, *The Sentiments and Resolutions of an Association of Ministers*, was published and sold early in 1745: "This Day Published," *Boston Evening Post*, no. 495 (February 4, 1745): 3.

141. *A Letter from Two Neighbouring Associations*: 7.

142. Ibid.: 2.

143. Ibid.: 3. The conflation of Whitefield with these "unschooled itinerants," in their view, tainted his status as an icon. Saint John of Damascus, *Three Treatises on the Divine Images, Treatise I*: 19–20.

144. "An Extract from a Letter of Doctor Benjamin Colman, Boston, May 15, 1742," in Chauncy, *State of Religion*: 42, MHS.

145. Ibid.

146. Belcher, *George Whitefield*: 263.

147. Ibid.

148. Ibid.: 266.

149. Ibid.

150. Crawford, "Origins of the Eighteenth-Century Evangelical Revival": 371.

151. *Letter to a Gentleman, Containing a Plea for the Rights of Conscience, in Things of a Religious Nature, by a Dissenting Protestant* (Boston: Kneeland, 1753): 2.

152. Ibid.

153. Ibid.

154. Belcher, *George Whitefield*: 270.

155. Ibid.

156. Ibid.: 356.

157. Ibid.: 412. His wife was Welsh widow Elizabeth James, whom he met through Welsh Methodist Howell Harris. By most accounts, the marriage was not a happy one.

Notes

158. Ibid.: 425.

159. Ibid.

160. "To the Printers of the Pennsylvania Gazette," *Pennsylvania Gazette*, no. 1812 (September 15, 1763): 2.

161. Quoted in John Piper, *Tested By Fire: The Fruit of Suffering in the Lives of John Bunyan, William Cowper, and David Brainerd* (Downers Grove, IL: InterVarsity Press, 2001): 127–128.

162. For further discussion of revivalism among Native Americans, see especially Fisher, *Indian Great Awakening*, and Andrews, *Native Apostles*.

163. Piper, *Tested By Fire*: 21.

164. Joanna Brooks, ed., *The Collected Writings of Sansom Occom, Mohegan: Leadership and Literature in Eighteenth-Century Native America* (New York: Oxford University Press, 2006): 162.

165. Ibid.: 163.

166. To Eleazar Wheelock, July 24, 1771, in ibid.: 99. Note: Occom's concerns were not without merit. Wheelock had complained in his "Continuation of the Narrative of the Indian Charity-School" (1771) about the "bad conduct" of the Native American alumni and said he believed that "white students were better candidates for the ministry." See Brooks, ed., *Collected Writings of Sansom Occom*: 98n68.

167. Ibid.: 99.

168. Journal Entry, Sunday, April 2, 1786, in ibid.: 334.

169. Ibid.

170. Marrant, *A Narrative*: 19–28.

171. "Prince Hall Masonry," in *Encyclopedia of African American History*, ed. Leslie M. Alexander and Walter C. Rucker, vol. 1 (New York: ABC-CLIO, 2010): 243.

172. John Marrant, *A Sermon Preached on the 24th Day of June 1789, Being the Festival of St. John the Baptist, at the Request of the Right Worshipful the Grand Master Prince Hall, and the Rest of the Brethren of the African Lodge of the Honorable Society of Free and Accepted Masons in Boston. By the Reverend Brother Marrant, Chaplain.* (Boston, 1789): 3.

173. Ibid.: 5.

174. "Prince Hall Masonry": 243.

175. Mark Noll has convincingly argued that Whitefield was not, in fact, the composer of his own funeral hymn. Mark Noll, "George Whitefield, Hymnody, and Evangelical Spirituality (keynote, Whitefield at 300: Tercentenary Conference, Pembroke College, Oxford, June 27, 2014).

176. Luke Tyerman, *The Life of the Rev. George Whitefield, BA., of Pembroke College, Oxford* (London: Hodor, ca. 1819): 316. Note: Whitefield's mentor, John Wesley, is the originator of "The World is Now My Congregation," but Whitefield echoed it frequently.

Notes

177. Geoffrey Cubitt, *History and Memory* (New York: Manchester University Press, 2007): 141.

178. Maurice Halbwachs, *On Collective Memory* (Chicago: University of Chicago Press, 1992): 88–119.

179. Ibid.: 88.

180. Cubitt, *History and Memory*: 141.

Chapter Five

1. Robert H. Abzug, *Cosmic Crumbling: American Reform and the Religious Imagination* (New York: Oxford University Press, 1994): 6.

2. Ibid.: 5.

3. Ibid.: 13.

4. Quoted in Hatch, *Democratization of American Christianity*: 18. One feature of the later part of the First Great Awakening and the Second Great Awakening was what Lambert calls a "warning against 'Spiritual Directors,'" which denoted essentially a resistance against (particularly) "Anglican clergymen who sought to extend their power and influence." Anticlerical sentiment existed in both the old world and the new. Lambert, *Founding Fathers*: 187–193.

5. It also served as an underpinning of the early black church. The literature is vast, but see especially Sylvia Frey and Betty Wood, *Come Shouting to Zion: African American Protestantism in the American South and British Caribbean to 1830* (Chapel Hill, NC: University of North Carolina Press, 1998); Richard S. Newman, *Freedom's Prophet: Bishop Richard Allen, the AME Church, and the Black Founding Fathers* (New York: New York University Press, 2009); C. Eric Lincoln and Lawrence H. Mamiya, *The Black Church in the African American Experience* (Durham, NC: Duke University Press, 1990); and Henry H. Mitchell, *Black Church Beginnings: The Long-Hidden Realities of the First Years* (Grand Rapids, MI: Wm. B. Eerdmans, 2004).

6. Religious pluralism pre-dated and survived the American Revolution, complicating the American religious landscape. Pestana, *Protestant Empire*: 100–179

7. Abzug, *Cosmic Crumbling*, 5. See also Lambert's "revolution of religion" in Lambert, *Founding Fathers*, 207–235.

8. Halbwachs, *On Collective Memory*: 88.

9. Quoted in Abzug, *Cosmic Crumbling*: 19.

10. Harry Levin, "Society as Its Own Historian," in *Contexts of Criticism*, by Harry Levin (Cambridge, MA: Harvard University Press, 1958): 171–189; Michael Kammen, *Mystic Chords of Memory: The Transformation of Tradition in American Culture* (New York: Vintage Books, 1991): 17.

Notes

11. Halbwachs, *On Collective Memory*: 52.
12. Quoted in Kammen, *Mystic Chords*: 40.
13. Ibid.
14. Ibid.
15. Ruttenburg, "George Whitefield": 436.
16. Hatch, *Democratization of American Christianity*: 11.
17. Kammen, *Mystic Chords*: 40.
18. As a counter to scripture used to justify slavery, Christianized blacks would have been aware of biblical images, such as Moses leading the Jews out of slavery in Egypt, and would undoubtedly have made the connections with transatlantic slavery. Exodus 13, 14, in *Good News Bible*: 81–85. J. William Harris, "Book Talk: The Hanging of Thomas Jeremiah: A Free Black Man's Encounter with Liberty," October 5, 2013, Massachusetts School of Law, Andover, MA.
19. This is also connected with the origins of the black church and resistance to slavery generally. See especially Sylvia Frey, *Water from the Rock: Black Resistance in a Revolutionary Age* (Princeton, NJ: Princeton University Press, 1992): 243–283. Resistance to the creation of black churches, including by Quakers (owing to the singing of psalms as part of worship), vexed black and white Christians alike. Abzug, *Cosmos Crumbling*: 26.
20. Abzug, *Cosmos Crumbling*: 9–76.
21. Ibid.: 16, 17. As Christopher Brown shows, antislavery sentiments driven by this blend of republicanism and religious ideology were not unique to the United States. Brown, *Moral Capital*.
22. Halbwachs, *On Collective Memory*: 141.
23. Hatch, *Democratization of American Christianity*: 13.
24. Halbwachs, *On Collective Memory*: 88–94.
25. Benedict Anderson, *Imagined Communities: Reflections on the Origins and Spread of Nationalism* (New York: Verso, 1983): 40.
26. Ibid.: 67–82.
27. Ibid.: 44.
28. Hatch, *Democratization of American Christianity*: 14.
29. "Art. 26, Remarks Upon the Life, Character, and Behavior of the Rev. George Whitefield." *Monthly Review*: 30 (January 1, 1764): 76, American Antiquarian Society Historical Periodical Collection (hereafter AASHPC), series 1, Worcester, MA.
30. Ibid.: 77.
31. Ibid.
32. "Article 27: A Letter to the Rev. Mr. George Whitefield," *Monthly Review* 40 (June 1769): 514, AASHPC, series 1. Note: In 1768 Whitefield wrote an angry letter to Durell, occasioned by the expulsion of six students from Oxford for "enthusiastic" tendencies. George Whitefield, "From a Letter to Dr. Durell, Vice Chancellor of

the University of Oxford; Occasioned by a Late Expulsion of Six Students," *Scots Magazine* 30 (May 1768): 232, AASHPC, series 1. This serves as an example of Frank Lambert's "warning against 'Spiritual Directors,'" a concern that, as Nathan Hatch shows, continued into the Second Great Awakening. See Lambert, *Founding Fathers*: 187–194, and Hatch, *Democratization of American Christianity*: 3–48.

33. "Article 27": 514. Note: In 1768, Whitefield wrote an angry letter to Durell, occasioned by the expulsion of six students from Oxford for "enthusiastic" tendencies. George Whitefield, "From a Letter to Dr. Durell, Vice Chancellor of the University of Oxford; Occasioned by a Late Expulsion of Six Students," *Scots Magazine* 30 (May 1768): 232, at AASHPC, series 1.

34. Whitefield, "From a Letter."

35. "Edinburgh, Sept. 15," *Pennsylvania Gazette*, no. 1044 (December 13, 1748): 2; "London, Oct. 26," *New-York Gazette*, no. 368 (February 5, 1750): 2; "New-York, July 29," *Boston Gazette*, no. 84 (August 6, 1754): 3; "Edinburgh, Sept. 14," *Boston Gazette*, no. 194 (December 18, 1758): 2; "New-York, Sept. 12," *Boston Post-Boy*, no. 318 (September 19, 1763): 3; "Boston, February 27, 1764," *Boston Evening Post*, no. 1486 (February 27, 1764): 3; "Providence, Feb. 18," *Pennsylvania Gazette* (March 1, 1764): 2; "Boston, June 7," *Boston News-Letter*, no. 3146 (June 7, 1764): 3; "Charles Town (South Carolina), November 30/December 7," *Pennsylvania Gazette* (January 3, 1765): 2; "Charles-Town, South-Carolina, January 26," *Boston Post-Boy*, no. 395 (March 11, 1765): 3; "Savannah, (in Georgia) February 21," *New-Hampshire Gazette* 9, no. 443 (April 4, 1765): 3.

36. "Charles-Town, South-Carolina, Jan. 26," *Boston Post-Boy*, no. 395 (March 11, 1765): 3. Whitefield's (unfulfilled) intentions concerning the Orphan House also appeared in the newspapers: "The Memorial of the Reverend George Whitefield, Clerk," *Georgia Gazette*, no. 94 (January 17, 1765): 2.

37. "James and Mary, Captain Sparks, is arrived in London from this Port," *Pennsylvania Gazette*, no. 1812 (September 15, 1763): 2.

38. "Edinburgh, Sept. 14," *Boston Gazette*, no. 194 (December 18, 1758): 2; "London, Oct. 17," *New-York Gazette*, no. 368 (February 5, 1750): 2.

39. "The Following is an Extract of a Letter from the Rev. Mr. George Whitefield to His Friend in This Town, May 11, 1763," *New-York Gazette*, no. 241 (July 25, 1763): 2.

40. "New-York, July 9," *New-York Gazette*, no. 292 (July 9, 1764): 3.

41. "Philadelphia," *Pennsylvania Gazette*, no. 1338 (August 15, 1754): 2.

42. "New-York, December 5," *Boston Gazette*, no. 454 (December 12, 1763): 3. Whitefield was known to have health concerns, including asthma and unidentified gastro-intestinal difficulties.

43. "New-York, July 23," *Boston Evening Post*, no. 1508 (July 30, 1764): 2.

44. "Fort Cumberland, September 3, 1764," *Newport Mercury*, no. 317 (October 1, 1764): 3.

Notes

45. John J. Currier, *History of Newburyport*, vol. 1: *1764–1905* (Newburyport, MA, 1906): 265, 270.

46. George Keith, *The Presbyterian and Independent Visible Churches in New England and Elsewhere* (Philadelphia, 1689). Not long after publishing this rejection of Presbyterianism, he also rejected Quakerism as having strayed too far from orthodox Christianity and became an Anglican minister in 1702, returning to the colonies as a missionary of the SGP. See "George Keith," *Oxford National Dictionary of Biography* (New York: Oxford University Press, 2004–2011). It is worth noting that these anti-Protestant screeds were contemporary with a series of witchcraft trials in New England, including that of Anne Good (1688); those during the Salem Hysteria (1692); and some in Connecticut, which included the trial of Elizabeth Clawson in Stamford (1692).

47. Ibid.

48. As was the practice in most dissenter denominations.

49. Currier, *History of Newburyport*, vol. 1: 265.

50. Call to Jonathan Parsons, *Old South Documents, Collection* 2, Box 4, Item 20, Archives of the Old South Presbyterian Church, Newburyport, MA (hereafter AOSPC).

51. Ibid.

52. Book of Records, Old South Presbyterian Church, ca. 1746–1868, AOSPC.

53. Belcher, *George Whitefield*: 438.

54. Ibid.: 439.

55. Robert V. Wells, "A Tale of Two Cities: Epidemics and the Rituals of Death in Eighteenth-Century Boston and Philadelphia," in *Mortal Remains: Death in Early America*, ed. Nancy Isenberg and Andrew Burstein (Philadelphia: University of Pennsylvania Press, 2003): 57. There also existed a tradition of Christian literature that contained instructions for the dying. The most well-known are "Tractus (and Speculum) Artis Bene Moriendi" (ca. 1415) and the tract that is often considered its literary bookend, Jeremy Taylor, *The Rules and Exercises of Holy Dying* (1651).

56. Journal Entry, August 16, 1769, in *The Literary Diary of Ezra Stiles*, ed. Franklin Bowditch Dexter, vol. 1: *January 1, 1769–March 13, 1776* (New York: Charles Scribner's Sons, 1901): 25

57. Belcher, *George Whitefield*: 440.

58. Ibid.: 438.

59. Ibid.: 441.

60. Wells, "Tale of Two Cities": 58.

61. Belcher, *George Whitefield*: 442.

62. This demonstrated a change in religious practice in the colonies. Richard L. Bushman's analysis of William Burgis's *A Southeast View of the Great Town of Boston in New England in America* (1722) revealed a conscious exaggeration of

Notes

steeples and bell towers that "rise to extravagant height above the low-lying city." Richard L. Bushman, *The Refinement of America: Persons, Houses, Cities* (New York: Knopf, 1992): 169.

63. Abzug, *Cosmos Crumbling*: 11.

64. Butler, *Awash in a Sea*: 110–112.

65. Bushman, *Refinement of America*: 169–180; Robert Whiting, *The Reformation of the English Parish Church* (New York: Cambridge University Press, 2010).

66. Butler, *Awash in a Sea*: 187.

67. Julia Stern, "The Politics of Tears: Death in the Early American Novel," in Isenberg and Burstein, eds., *Mortal Remains*: 119, and Nicole Eustace, *Passion Is the Gale: Emotion, Power, and the Coming of the American Revolution* (Chapel Hill: University of North Carolina Press, 2008).

68. Ibid.: 289.

69. David E. Stannard, *The Puritan Way of Death: A Study in Religion, Culture, and Social Change* (New York: Oxford University Press, 1977): 100.

70. Ibid.: 74.

71. Rev. George Whitefield to Thomas Deering, Esq, Boston, May 2, 1764, Sylvester Manor Archives, Box 142, Folder 32, Fales Library, New York University, New York, NY.

72. Stannard, *Puritan Way of Death*: 101.

73. Jack P. Greene, *The Intellectual Construction of America: Exceptionalism and Identity from 1492 to 1800* (Chapel Hill: University of North Carolina Press, 1992): 105.

74. The probate inventory of Whitefield's will reveals that at his death, his estate (less the lands) was worth £2,053 5s 1d. The 1,200 volumes in the Library of the Georgia Orphan House Bethesda Academy were valued at £265 10s 2d. Boyd Schlenther estimates that Whitefield's estate was valued at £150,000 in 2014 currency when he died, in Schlenther's, "'I Am Content to Wait Till the Day of Judgement for the Clearing Up of my Character': George Whitefield's Personal Life and Character" (keynote, Whitefield at 300, International Tercentenary Conference, Pembroke College, Oxford, June 27, 2014). Robert V. Williams, "George Whitefield's Bethesda: The Orphanage, the College, and the Library," *Library History Seminar*, no. 3, Proceedings (1968): 48. The debate over Whitefield's wealth is related to the question of whether revivalism could be construed as "polite." As Paul Langford notes, *politeness* and *politics* have the same roots and were used in a complimentary sense in the eighteenth century. Whitefield had the fiscal trappings of a "polite" eighteenth-century gentleman but lacked the political acumen—especially the respect for authority—to be accepted as a member of "polite" society. And while his writings were certainly commercial, it was a different sort of commercialism from that of merchants and planters. Langford, *A Polite and Commercial People*: 1–9, 59–122, 234–288.

Notes

75. Ibid.: 102.

76. Journal Entry, December 12, 1770, in Dexter, ed., *Literary Diary of Ezra Stiles*, vol. 1: 80. The funeral cost approximately £5,690, or $9,122 in 2011 money. See the value calculator at *Measuring Worth*, http://www.measuringworth.com (accessed November 13, 2013).

77. Stannard, *Puritan Way of Death*: 101.

78. Ibid.: 137.

79. Journal Entry, December 12, 1770, in Dexter, ed., *Literary Diary of Ezra Stiles*, vol. 1: 79.

80. Belcher, *George Whitefield*: 443.

81. Ibid.: 442. This scene, as reported, is suggestive of the version of the death of Jesus as reported in Mark 27:46, when Jesus cried out, "Eli, Eli, Lema Sabachthoni—My God, my God, why have you forsaken me?" While neither man was crucified, a similar hopelessness was conveyed.

82. Belcher, *George Whitefield*: 443.

83. When his fellow Anglican evangelical Josiah Smith died in 1781, he was similarly venerated. The Presbyterian Church of Philadelphia had him interred within the crypts of its Arch Street Church, between the tombs of Gilbert Tennent and Samuel Finley. See David Ramsay, *The History of the Independent or Congregational Church in Charleston, South Carolina from its Origin till the Year 1814* (Philadelphia: J. Maxwell, 1815): 16, tract A1, BA.

84. Belcher, *George Whitefield*: 436.

85. Tyerman, *Life of the Rev. George Whitefield*, vol. 2: 610.

86. Phillis Wheatley, *On the Death of that Celebrated Divine, and Eminent Servant of Jesus Christ, the Late Reverend, and Pious George Whitefield* (Boston, 1770): 1.

87. Ibid.: 5.

88. Wesley to Whitefield, London, August 9, 1740. From the copy reproduced at http://www.spurgeon.org/~phil/wesley.htm (accessed December 6, 2011).

89. Whitefield to Wesley, December 24, 1740, Bethesda, Georgia, at ibid.

90. Evidence of their reconciliation appears in a letter Whitefield wrote to Wesley, "Letter XXX. From the Rev. Mr. Whitefield, to the Rev. Mr. Wesley. Philadelphia, Sept. 25, 1764," *Methodist Magazine* 1 (August 1797): 380–381, AASHPC, series 1.

91. Tyerman, *Life of the Rev. George Whitefield*, vol. 2: 614.

92. Wesley, *A Sermon*: 19.

93. Ibid.: 20.

94. Ibid.: 25.

95. Tyerman, *Life of the Rev. George Whitefield*, vol. 2: 611.

96. Ibid.: 612.

97. Ibid.

Notes

98. Andrew Burstein, "Immortalizing the Founding Fathers: The Excesses of Public Eulogy," in Isenberg and Burstein, eds., *Mortal Remains*: 91.

99. Ibid.: 94.

100. Ibid.: 96.

101. Belcher, *George Whitefield*: 445.

102. Ibid.: 446.

103. Ibid.

104. Ibid.: 447. As Michael Kammen notes, the internments of high-profile figures became even more political in the nineteenth century. Kammen, *Digging Up the Dead*: 43–126.

105. Michael Meranze, "Major André's Exhumation," in Isenberg and Burstein, eds., *Mortal Remains*: 124.

106. Kammen, *Digging Up the Dead*, 169.

107. Ibid.

Chapter Six

1. "Description of New London . . . ," *Political Magazine & Parliamentary, Naval, Military & Literary Journal*, 2 (November 1781): 648, AASHPC, series 1.

2. Ibid.

3. Lambert, *Founding Fathers*: 138–139. Also note Erik Seeman argues that Protestants tended toward a "distaste for miracle stories," of which this is suggestive. Nonetheless, other examples of "miracles" attributed to divine figures followed. Most notable is the response people had to the storm that blocked the British troops' ability to march on Washington, D.C., during the War of 1812. See Erik R. Seeman, *Death in the New World: Cross-Cultural Encounters, 1492–1800* (Philadelphia: University of Pennsylvania Press, 2010): 141.

4. T. H. Breen, "'Baubles of Britain,': The American and Consumer Revolutions of the Eighteenth Century," *Past and Present*, no. 119 (May 1988): 77. See also Breen's longer analysis of the politicization of goods during the American Revolution: T. H. Breen, *The Marketplace of Revolution: How Consumer Goods Shaped American Independence* (New York: Oxford University Press, 2005).

5. Breen, "Baubles of Britain," 78.

6. Saint John of Damascus, *Three Treatises on the Divine Images*, Treatise I: 21. The literature on "nation" pre-dates modern ideas about nationalism. See, for example, Peter S. Onuf, *Jefferson's Empire: The Language of American Nationhood* (Charlottesville: University of Virginia Press, 2000). When St. John spoke of "nation," he was referring to all of Christendom, but it was a concept that could readily be imported into the politics of nationalism.

Notes

7. "Atteb y Parchedid Mr. Whitefield . . ." (Mr. Whitefield's Answer to the Bishop of London's Last Pastoral Letter) (n.p: Samuel and Felix Farley, 1740); "Llythyr Oddwrthy Parchedy" (Letters to Religious Societies)(n.p.: Argraph wyd yr Argraph—Wsg Newyyd, 1740); "Nadau'r Engedigaeth Newydd" (Marks of the New Birth) (n.p.: Felix Farley, 1739); and "Dischellian Satan" (Satan's Disciples) (n.p.: Lewis William, 1742). All at National Library of Wales, Aberystwyth.

8. George Whitefield, "Pregeth a Bregethwyd gan y Parchenchg, Tabernacle yn Lundain, Awst 30, 1769" (n.p.: Rhys Tomas, 1771); "Pregeth Ynghylch Rhods Gyda Duw" (Argraffwdyd, Wales: Ioan Ross, 1779), a translation of "Walking with God"; "Dwy Brugeth ar y Testynau Canlynd, sef . . ." (n.p.: Argraphwyd gan D. Jones, 1779), a translation of "Holy Spirit Convincing the World of Sin." All in National Library of Wales.

9. Memoirs of George Whitefield," *London Magazine* 39 (November 1770): 549, at AASHPC, series 1.

10. Ibid.: 552.

11. Ibid.

12. "Memoirs of George Whitefield," *Scots Magazine* 32 (November 1770): 591–593, at AASHPC, series 1.

13. "Memoires of the Life of the Rev. Mr. George Whitefield . . . ," *New-Jersey Magazine, or Weekly Advertiser* (December 1786): 44–49, at AASHPC, series 1.

14. Halbwach's chapter, "The Reconstruction of the Past," is especially pertinent here. Halbwachs, *On Collective Memory*: 46–51

15. "Advertisements—Eighteen Sermons Preached by the Late Rev. George Whitefield," *Scots Magazine* 34 (March 1772): 146–147, and *Monthly Review*, 46 (March 1772): 226–228, both at AASHPC, series 1.

16. "Art. 34: The Works of the Rev. George Whitefield," *Monthly Review* 47 (July 1772): 79–80, at AASHPC, series 1.

17. "Copy of the Transcript of the Rev. Mr. George Whitefield's Will . . ." *Scots Magazine* 33 (January 1771): 20–22, and *London Magazine* (February 1771): 65–67, both at AASHPC, series 1.

18. "Mr. George Whitefield's Will . . ." *New Jersey Magazine* (December 1786): 49–52.

19. "V. Memoirs of the Life of the Reverend George Whitefield, M.A. Late Chaplain to the Right Honourable the Countess of Huntingdon," *Critical Review by a Society of Gentlemen*, 34 (November 1772): 349–352, at AASHPC Collection, series 1. John Gillies was also a prolific author of writings central to the Great Awakening. Among other works, Gillies wrote *Historical Collections relating to the Success of the Gospel*, 2 vols. (Glasgow, 1754), and *Devotional Exercises on the New Testament*, 2 vols. (London, 1769). New editions of the Gillies memoir appeared after his death in 1796, some of which claimed new material. Jones, "'So Much Idolized by Some'": 17.

Notes

20. John Gillies, *Memoirs of Rev. George Whitefield* (London: Dilly, 1772): 221.
21. Ibid.: 223.
22. Cummings, *Danger of Breaking Christian Unity*: 15.
23. Ibid.: 3.
24. David Ceri Jones, Boyd Stanley Schlenther, and Eryn Mant White, *The Elect Methodists: Calvinistic Methodism in England and Wales, 1735–1811* (Cardiff, UK: University of Wales Press, 2012): 157–162.
25. Quoted in ibid.: 162. Mark Noll describes the Americanization of Calvinism (favored by the Countesses Connexion) as occurring in stages, beginning around 1793. Noll, *America's God*: 254–329.
26. Tyerman, *Life of the Rev. George Whitefield*, vol. 2: 613. Note: The memoir of Whitefield, which was critical, included additional sources missed by Gillies. Jones, "'So Much Idolized by Some'": 19.
27. Ibid.
28. Ibid.: 614.
29. Michael Walzer argued for a (Puritan) Calvinist saint who "ignored age-old customs and traditional loyalties to reconstruct the social order of seventeenth-century England." See Hatch, *Democratization of American Christianity*: 56, and Michael Walzer, *The Revolution of the Saints: A Study in the Origins of Radical Politics* (Cambridge, MA: Harvard University Press, 1965). For additional analysis of Whitefield eulogies, see Jones, "'So Much Idolized by Some'": 11–13.
30. Tyerman, *Life of the Reverend George Whitefield*, vol. 1: 269.
31. Butler, *Awash in a Sea*: 188.
32. Ibid.
33. Ibid.
34. Margaret Stratton, *The Living and the Dead: The Neapolitan Cult of the Skull* (Chicago: Columbia College Press, 2010): 5.
35. Ibid.: 6–7.
36. Elizabeth Reis, "Immortal Messengers: Angels, Gender, and Power in Early America," in Isenburg and Burstein, eds., *Mortal Remains*: 163.
37. Saint John of Damascus, *Three Treatises on the Divine Images, Treatise II*: 57.
38. Bonomi, *Under the Cope of Heaven*: 164.
39. Belcher, *George Whitefield*: 453.
40. Saint John of Damascus, *Three Treatises on the Divine Images, Treatise I*: 25.
41. Ibid.: 454.
42. Ibid.
43. Ibid.: 456.
44. Ibid.: 458.
45. The recurrent disturbance of Whitefield's remains for souvenirs and memorialization rituals had a precedent in Anglo-American history. After his

Notes

beheading, royalist supporters of King Charles I reportedly rushed the scaffold so that they could dip their handkerchiefs in their fallen king's blood. This collection of blood served as a symbol for a sort of "cult of the dead" for a king whom Philip Henry and other royalists saw as a martyr to their cause.

46. Wilfrid Bonser, "The Cult of Relics in the Middle Ages," *Folklore* 73 (Winter 1962): 234.

47. Ibid.: 235.

48. Ibid.

49. Butler, *Awash in a Sea*: 286.

50. Jon Butler, "Magic, Astrology and the Early American Religious Heritage, 1600–1760," *American Historical Review* 84, no. 2 (April 1979): 331–334, 342.

51. Clarence Edward Noble Macartney, *Six Kings of the American Pulpit* (New York: Ayer, 1971): 21.

52. Ibid.

53. "Letter XLIII," *Arminian Magazine* 1 (September 1778): 417–418.

54. Matthew Dennis, "Patriotic Remains: Bones of Contention in the Early Republic," in Isenburg and Burstein, eds., *Mortal Remains*: 137.

55. In the context of the American Revolution, religious iconography occasionally blended with the political.

56. Charles W. Akers, "Religion and the American Revolution: Samuel Cooper and the Brattle Street Church," *William and Mary Quarterly*, third series, 35, no. 3 (July 1978): 477.

57. Ibid.

58. "Patriotism! A Farce," *Newport Mercury*, no. 310 (August 13, 1764): 1.

59. The insertion of *Paradise Lost* is significant because it contained a number of the religious themes and politics of relevance to the English Revolution. See M. H. Abraham and Stephen Greenblatt, eds., *The Norton Anthology of English Literature*, vol. 1 (New York: W.W. Norton, 2000): 1785–1788. On John (Jack) Wilkes, see Peter D. G. Thomas, "Wilkes, John (1725–1797)," in *Oxford Dictionary of National Biography*, ed. H. C. G. Matthew and Brian Harrison (Oxford: Oxford University Press, 2004). See an online edition edited by Lawrence Goldman, May 2008, at http://www.oxforddnb.com/view/article/29410 (accessed April 6, 2012).

60. "Patriotism! A Farce": 1.

61. P. D. G. Thomas, "Wilkes, John (1725–1797)."

62. Ibid.

63. Ibid.

64. Ibid.

65. Ibid.

66. Noll, *America's God*: 76.

67. Kammen, *Mystic Chords*: 40.

Notes

68. "London, Oct. 14, To the Citizen," *Boston Post-Boy*, no. 23 (January 23, 1758): 1. Note: The writer suggests that "the Rev. Mr. Whitefield, and his Flock" are the only members of the "Divine" who have "thrown even a hint into his sermon, or in the list of his addresses of troubles and adversities." Whitefield may have mentioned the War in a sermon, but given that this appeared before the end of the Seven Years War and that no details are noted as to the nature of his sermon, it is, at best, weak evidence that Whitefield *might* have occasionally mentioned current events in his preaching. Since the tone of the notice is derisive toward Whitefield, it is likely that any political speech would have been reported as such.

69. Lambert, *Founding Fathers*: 209.

70. Ibid.

71. Ibid.: 135.

72. Noll, *America's God*: 47.

73. Ibid.: 77.

74. Ibid.: 79.

75. George Whitefield, *Represented in a Sermon: Preach'd at Philadelphia, on Sunday August 24, 1746. And Occasioned by the Suppression of the Late Unnatural Rebellion* (Philadelphia and London, 1746): 3.

76. Ibid.: 2.

77. Ibid.: 4.

78. Ibid.

79. Ibid.

80. Ibid.

81. Ibid.: 5.

82. Ibid.

83. Ibid.

84. George Whitefield, *Mr. Whitefield's Sermon on the Benefits of an Early Piety* (London, 1737): 4.

85. Ibid.: 7. See also George Whitefield, "Hymn XXXVI: The Divine Sovereignty," in *A Collection of Hymns for Social Worship*, 7th ed. (London, 1753): 142–143.

86. Mahaffrey, *Preaching Politics*; Stephen Mansfield, *Forgotten Founding Father: The Heroic Legacy of George Whitefield* (New York: Cumberland Press, 2001).

87. Saint John of Damascus, *Three Treatises on the Divine Images*, Treatise I: 25.

88. George Whitefield, "Ser. XI: The Burning Bush," in *Eighteen Sermons Preached by the Late George Whitefield*, ed. Andrew Gifford (London, 1771): 260.

89. George Whitefield, *The Almost Christian* (Boston, 1739): 5.

90. Ibid.: 6.

91. Remer, *Humanism*: 6; Beneke, *Beyond Tolerance*: 17.

Notes

92. Patricia Bonomi, "'Hippocrates Twins': Religion and Politics in the American Revolution," *The History Teacher* 29, no. 2 (February 1996): 141–142.
93. Ibid.
94. Noll, *America's God*: 76.
95. Ibid.
96. Quoted in ibid.
97. Lambert, *Founding Fathers*: 207–209.
98. Ibid: 180.
99. Ibid.
100. Ibid.: 181.
101. Hatch, *Democratization of American Christianity*: 17–46.
102. Ibid.: 11.
103. Lambert, *Founding Fathers and the Place of Religion in America*: 7.
104. Ibid.
105. Hatch, *Democratization of American Christianity*: 34.
106. Ibid.: 207.
107. Ibid.
108. Stout, *Divine Dramatist*: xiv.
109. Note: This is not the same as claiming him as an American.
110. Wheatley, "On the Death of the Rev. Mr. George Whitefield": 5–6.
111. Ibid.: 6.
112. "To the King's Most Excellent Majesty, 1768," in Phillis Wheatley, *Poems on Various Subjects, Religious and Moral* (London, 1773): 17. Note: This poem was published in 1773.
113. Wheatley, "On the Death of the Rev. Mr. George Whitefield," 6.
114. Noll, *America's God*: 77.
115. Ibid.
116. Ibid.
117. Bernard Bailyn, "The Origins of American Politics," in *Perspectives in American History, New Series*, vol. 1: *1967*, ed. Bernard Bailyn and Donald Fleming (Cambridge, MA: Charles Warren Center for Studies in American History at Harvard University, 1967): 9.
118. Ibid.
119. Eustace, *Passion Is the Gale*: 287.
120. Bellot, "Evangelicals and the Defense of Slavery": 20.
121. On English abolitionists' use of writs of habeas corpus to challenge slavery in England, see Peter D. Halliday, *Habeas Corpus: From England to Empire* (Cambridge, MA: Belknap Press, 2010).
122. For further analysis of the Somerset Case and its significance, see George Van Cleve, "Somerset's Case and Its Antecedents in Imperial Perspective," *Law

Notes

and History Review (Fall 2006), at http://www.historycooperative.org/journals/lhr/24.3/cleve.html (accessed February 17, 2012).

123. No. 294: From Anthony Benezet (May 20, 1774), in *In the Midst of Early Methodism: Lady Huntingdon and Her Correspondence*, ed. John R. Tyson and Boyd S. Schlenther (Lanham, MD: Scarecrow Press, 2006): 227.

124. Ibid.: 228.

125. Editorial Note in ibid.: 229.

126. No. 278: George Whitefield's Will (March 22, 1770), in ibid.: 214.

127. Editorial Note in ibid.: 229.

128. Carretta, *Phillis Wheatley*: 29.

129. Carretta, ed., *Olaudah Equiano*: 178-193.

130. Whitefield was in England at the time Equiano recalled seeing him in Philadelphia. Vincent Carretta believes that Equiano in fact saw Whitefield preach in Georgia in 1765. See Carretta, ed., *Olaudah Equiano*: 277n363.

131. Ibid: 132.

132. Ibid.

133. Ibid.

134. Ibid.

135. Carretta, *Phillis Wheatley*: 73.

136. Henry Louis Gates Jr., *The Trials of Phillis Wheatley: America's First Black Poet and Her Encounters with the Founding Fathers* (New York: Basic Books, 2003): 23.

137. Ibid.: 22.

138. Ibid.: 75.

139. See the Introduction in Phillis Wheatley, *Poems on Various Subjects, Religious and Moral* (London, 1773).

140. Wheatley, "On Being Brought from Africa to America," in ibid.: 18.

141. Stephanie E. Smallwood, *Saltwater Slavery: A Middle Passage from Africa to American Diaspora* (Cambridge, MA: Harvard University Press, 2008).

142. Carretta, ed., *Olaudah Equiano*: 52.

143. "To the Right Honourable William, Earl of Dartmouth," in Carretta, *Phillis Wheatley*: 73.

144. Ibid.: 74.

145. Ibid.

146. John Marrant, *A Narrative*: 8.

147. Ibid.: 9.

148. Ibid.

149. Ibid.: 10-11.

150. Ibid.: 19-28.

151. Ibid.: 12.

Notes

152. Ibid.: 39.

153. "Narrative of the Enslavement of Ottobah Cugoano, a Native of Africa; Published by Himself in the Year 1787," in *The Negro's Memorial; or, Abolitionist's Catechism; by an Abolitionist, 1781?-1836*, by Thomas Fischer (London: Printed for the Author and Sold by Hatchard and Co., 1825): 125.

154. Ibid.: 125–126.

155. Vincent Carretta, ed., *Quobna Ottobah Cugoano: Thoughts and Sentiments on the Evil of Slavery, and Other Writings* (New York: Penguin Books, 1999): 22.

156. Ibid.: 24.

157. Ibid.

158. Genesis: 9:20–27, in *Holy Bible: King James Version*: 8.

159. Carretta, ed., *Quobna Ottobah Cugoano*: xxiii: 33–34.

160. Simmons and Thomas, eds., *Preaching with Sacred Fire*: 56–57.

161. He found that a number of antislavery Congregationalists embraced him because of his accomplishments. See Ruth Bogin, "Notes and Documents: 'Liberty Further Extended': A 1776 Antislavery Manuscript by Lemuel Haynes," *William and Mary Quarterly*, third series, 40, no. 1 (January 1983): 86–87, 88.

162. Lemuel Haynes, "The Nature and Importance of True Republicanism . . . ," quoted in ibid.: 88.

163. See Simmons and Thomas, eds., *Preaching with Sacred Fire*: 60–61.

164. Ibid.: 61.

165. Ibid.: 61–62.

166. T. S. Kidd, *Great Awakening*: 214, 219.

167. Frey and Wood, *Come Shouting to Zion*: 82.

168. Ibid.: 84.

169. John Wood Sweet, *Bodies Politic: Negotiating Race in the American North, 1730–1830* (Baltimore, MD: Johns Hopkins University Press, 2003): 104.

170. Ibid.

171. See especially Joanna Brooks and John Salliant, eds., *"Face Zion Forward:" First Writers of the Black Atlantic* (Boston: Northeastern University Press, 2002).

172. J. W. Sweet, *Bodies Politic*: 105.

173. Hatch, *Democratization of American Christianity*: 3–48. On the early years of the black church, see also Mitchell, *Black Church Beginnings*: 70.

Epilogue

1. See Kammen, *Mystic Chords*: 62, and more generally on tradition, see Anderson, *Imagined Communities*: 1–48, 69–84, and Eric Hobsbawm and Terence Ranger, *The Invention of Tradition* (New York: Canto, 1992).

Notes

2. Kammen, *Digging Up the Dead*: 45. Also supported by Eliga Gould's analysis of American legal, political, intellectual, and diplomatic culture from the American Revolution on. See Eliga Gould, *Among the Powers of the Earth* (Cambridge, MA: Harvard University Press, 2012).

3. Halbwachs, *On Collective Memory*: 102, 103.

4. Kammen, *Digging Up the Dead*: 170–171.

5. Jones, "'So Much Idolized by Some'": 5.

6. Rev. William Larkin, *George Whitefield, Hero of Faith* (excerpts), First Presbyterian Church—ARP, Columbia, SC, November 3, 2004: 1, at http://www.ciu.edu/sites/default/files/academics/Lessons-from-a-preacher-George-Whitefield.pdf (accessed March 28, 2014).

7. Ibid.: 4.

8. Ibid.

BIBLIOGRAPHY

Primary Sources: Archival

Council of Gloucestershire Archives

Report: Suggested Removal from America to Westminster Abbey of Remains of George Whitefield. GBR/L/6/23/B856 (1930–1931)

Lambeth Palace Library

Fulham Papers
Miscellaneous Manuscripts
Records of the Society for the Propagation of the Gospel in Foreign Parts, American Colonies

London Metropolitan Archives

State Papers

New York University, Fales Library

Sylvester Manor Archives

Massachusetts Historical Society

Benjamin Colman Papers
Letters to Benjamin Colman, 1693–1747

National Archives (UK)

Colonial Office Records

Old South Presbyterian Church

Book of Records, Old South Presbyterian Church, ca. 1746–1868

Bibliography

Primary Sources: Historical Newspapers and Magazines

Alleghany Magazine, or Repository of Useful Knowledge
American Weekly Mercury
Arminian Magazine
Boston Evening Post
Boston Gazette
Boston News-Letter
Boston Post-Boy
Critical Review of a Society of Gentlemen
Evangelical Intelligencer
General Magazine
Gentlemen's Magazine
Georgia Gazette
London Magazine
Methodist Magazine
Monthly Journal
New-England Weekly Journal
New-Hampshire Gazette
New-Jersey Magazine, or Weekly Advertiser
New-York Gazette
Newport Mercury
New-York Journal
New-York Mercury
New-York Weekly Journal
Pennsylvania Gazette
Political Magazine & Parliamentary, Naval, Military & Literary Journal
Religious Remembrancer
Scots Magazine
South Carolina Gazette

Primary Sources

Alleine, Joseph. *An Alarm to Unconverted Sinners*. London, 1641.
Apthrop, East. *Considerations on the Institution and Conduct of the Society for the Propagation of the Gospel in Foreign Parts*. Boston: Green and Russell, 1818.
Benezet, Anthony. *A Caution and Warning to Great Britain and Her Colonies, in a Short Representation of the Calamitous State of the Enslaved Negroes in the British Dominions*. Philadelphia, PA: 1776.

Bibliography

A Brief and Impartial Account of the Character and Doctrines of Mr. Whitefield and Mr. Wesley: In a Letter from London, September 1743. Edinburgh, 1743.

Chauncy, Charles. *A Letter to the Reverend Mr. Whitefield, Publically Calling Upon Him to Vindicate His Conduct, or Confess His Faults.* Boston, 1745.

———. *Seasonable Thoughts on the State of Religion in New England.* Boston: Rogers and Fowle, 1743.

———. *The State of Religion, Since the Reverend Mr. George Whitefield's Arrival There.* Glasgow, 1742.

Clarkson, Thomas. *The History of the Rise, Progress and Accomplishment of the Abolition of the African Slave-Trade by the British Parliament.* Vol. 1. London: R. Taylor and Co., 1808.

Clement of Alexandria, Exhortation to the Heathen. 190 C.E.

In *Collections of the New-York Historical Society for the Year 1870.* 2 vols. New York: Printed for the Society, 1871.

Colman, Benjamin. *A Sermon Preach'd to a Very Crowded Audience, at the Opening of an Evening-Lecture, in Brattle-Street, Boston, Tuesday, October 21, 1740.* Boston, 1740.

Cummings, Archibald. *The Danger of Breaking Christian Unity, in Two Sermons, Preached June 12, 1737.* Philadelphia, PA: Printed and Sold by Andrew Bradford, 1737.

Davies, Samuels. *The Duty of Christians to Propagate their Religion Among Heathens, Earnestly recommended to the Masters of Negroe Slaves in Virginia . . .* London: J. Oliver, 1757.

Dexter, Franklin Boditch, ed. *The Literary Diary of Ezra Stiles.* Vol. 1: *January 1, 1769-March 13, 1776.* New York: Charles Scribner's Sons, 1901.

Fischer, Thomas. *The Negro's Memorial; or, Abolitionist's Catechism; by an Abolitionist, 1781?-1836.* London: Printed for the Author and Sold by Hatchard and Co., 1825.

Foxcroft, Thomas. *An Apology in Behalf of the Revd. Mr. Whitefield . . . Second Edition.* Boston, Rogers and Fowle, 1745.

Garden, Alexander. *Mr. Commissary Garden's Six Letters to the Rev. Mr. George Whitefield.* Boston, 1740.

———. *Take Heed of How Ye Hear: A Sermon Preached in the Parish Church of St. Philip Charles-Town, in South Carolina on Sunday the 13th of July, 1740: A Preface, Containing Some Remarks on Mr. Whitefield's Journals.* Charles Town: Peter Timothy, 1740.

Gillies, John. *Memoirs of the Life of the Reverend George Whitefield.* London: Dilly, 1772.

Gillespie, George. *Remarks upon Mr. Whitefield, Proving Him a Man under Delusion.* Philadelphia, 1744.

Hewatt, Alexander. *An Historical Account of the Rise and Progress of the Colonies of South Carolina and Georgia.* 2 vols. London, 1779.

Bibliography

Keith, George. *The Presbyterian and Independent Visible Churches in New England and Elsewhere*. Philadelphia, 1689.

Law, William. *The Absolute Unlawfulness of the Stage-Entertainment. Fully Demonstrated*. London, 1759.

Letter to a Gentleman, Containing a Plea for the Rights of Conscience, in Things of a Religious Nature, by a Dissenting Protestant. Boston: Kneeland, 1753.

A Letter of Mr. John Cotton, Teacher of the Church in Boston, in New-England, to Mr. Williams, a Preacher There. London: Benjamin Allen, 1643.

A Letter to the Negroes Lately Converted to Christ in America. London: J. Hart, 1740.

A Letter from the Reverend George Whitefield to the Religious Societies, Lately Formed in England and Wales. Philadelphia, 1739.

A Letter to the Reverend Thomas Foxcroft. Boston, 1745.

A Letter from Two Neighbouring Associations of Ministers in the Country, to the Associated Ministers of Boston and Charlestown, Relating to the Admission of Mr. Whitefield into their Pulpits. Boston, 1745.

Letters of the Late Reverend George Whitefield . . . Chaplain to the Rt. Hon. Countess of Huntingdon . . . in 3 volumes. London, 1772.

Liberty of Consciousness Asserted. Or, Persecution for Religion Condemned, by the Lawes of God, Nature, Reason. London, 1649.

Locke, John. *A Letter Concerning Toleration*. 3rd ed. Boston, 1943.

Marrant, John. *A Narrative of the Lord's Wonderful Dealings with John Marrant, a Black*. London, 1788.

———. *A Sermon Preached on the 24th Day of June 1789, Being the Festival of St. John the Baptist, at the Request of the Right Worshipful the Grand Master Prince Hall, and the Rest of the Brethren of the African Lodge of the Honorable Society of Free and Accepted Masons in Boston. By the Reverend Brother Marrant, Chaplain*. Boston, 1789.

Martyr, Justin. Horatory Address to the Greeks (trans. Rev. M. Dods). 150 C.E. At http://www.ccel.org/ccel/schaff/anf01.viii.vi.html.

Mather, Cotton, and Zebidiah Boylston. *Some Account of What is Said of Inoculating or Transplanting the Small Pox. By the Learned Dr. Emanuel Timonius, and Jacobus Pylarinus*. Boston, 1721.

Mayhew, Jonathan. *Observations on the Charter and Conduct of the Society for the Propagation of the Gospel*. Boston: Richard and Draper, 1804.

Mr. Whi__d's Soliloquy, or a Serious Debate with Himself what Course He Shall Take. Boston, 1745.

Pateshall, Richard. *Pride Humbled, Mr. Hobby Chastised: Being some Remarks on Said Hobby's Piece, Entitled, a Defence of the Itinerancy and the Conduct of the Rev. Mr. Whitefield. In a Letter to the Reverend Mr. William Hobby, Pastor of the First Church in Reading*. Boston: Draper, 1745.

Bibliography

Penn, William. *The Great Case of Liberty of Conscience.* Pennsylvania, 1670.

Postlethwayt, Malachy. *The Universal Dictionary of Trade and Commerce.* London: H. Woodfall, 1766.

Prescott, Benjamin. *A Letter to the Reverend Mr. Whitefield, An Itinerant Preacher.* Boston, 1745.

Shepard, Thomas. *The Sincere Convert: Discovering the Paucitie of True Believers and the Difficulty of Saving Conversion.* Edinburgh, 1647.

———. *New England's Lamentation for Old England's Present Errours, and Divisions, and their Feared Future Desolations if not Timely Prevented, Occasioned by the Increase of Anabaptists, Rigid Separatists, Antinomians and Familists.* London, 1645.

Smith, Josiah. *The Character, Preach, &c of George Whitefield.* Boston: Rogers for Edwards and Foster, 1740.

Taylor, Jeremy. *The Rules and Exercises of Holy Dying.* N.p., 1651.

Tennent, Gilbert. *The Examiner, Examined. . . .* Philadelphia, 1743.

Tindall, Matthew. *The Rights of the Christian Church Asserted. . . .* N.p., 1709.

"Tractus (and Speculum) Artis Bene Moriendi." 1415.

Tyerman, Luke. *The Life of the Rev. George Whitefield, BA., of Pembroke College, Oxford.* London: Hodor, ca. 1819.

Wesley, John. *A Sermon on the Death of . . . George Whitefield.* New York: Holt, 1771. *A Sermon on the Death of the Rev. Mr. George Whitefield. Preached at the Chapel in Tottenham-Court-Road and at the Tabernacle near Moorfields, on Sunday, November 18, 1770* (London, 1770).

Wheatley, Phillis. *On the Death of that Celebrated Divine, and Eminent Servant of Jesus Christ, the Late Reverend, and Pious George Whitefield.* Boston, 1770.

———. *Poems on Various Subjects, Religious and Moral.* London, 1773.

Wheelock, Eleazar. *A Continuation of the Narrative of the Indian Charity-School, Begun in Lebanon, in Connecticut; Now Incorporated with Dartmouth-College, in Hanover, in the Province of New-Hampshire.* Hartford, CT: Ebenezer Watson, 1773.

Whitefield, George. *The Almost Christian.* Boston, 1739.

———. *A Continuation of Mr. Whitefield's Journal, from his Embarking after the Embargo.* London: 1740.

———. *A Further Account of God's Dealings with the Rev. Mr. George Whitefield . . . from his Ordination to his Embarkment to Georgia. . . .* London, 1747.

———. *A Hymn Composed by the Reverend Mr. Whitefield to be Sung Over his Own Corps Taken from the Original, May 1, 1764.* N.p., 1764?

———. "Hymn XXXVI: The Divine Sovereignty." In *A Collection of Hymns for Social Worship.* 7th ed. London, 1753.

———. *Journal of a Voyage from London to Savannah in Georgia in three Parts.* London: W. Strahan, 1741.

Bibliography

———. *Letter to the Inhabitants of Maryland, Virginia, North and South Carolina, Concerning Their Negroes.* Philadelphia, 1740.

———. *Mr. Whitefield's Sermon on the Benefits of an Early Piety.* London, 1737.

———. *Represented in a Sermon: Preach'd at Philadelphia, on Sunday August 24, 1746. And Occasioned by the Suppression of the Late Unnatural Rebellion.* Philadelphia and London, 1746.

———. *A Sermon by the Reverend Mr. George Whitefield, Being His Last Farewell to His Friends...Preached at the Tabernacle at Moorfield . . . August 30, 1769, Immediately Before His Departure. . . .* London, 1767.

———. *A Short Account of God's Dealings with the Reverend George Whitefield, A.B., Late of Pembroke-College Oxford from His Infancy to His Entering into the Holy Orders.* London, 1740.

———. *The Works of the Reverend George Whitefield.* 7 vols. London: Dilly, 1771–1772.

Woolman, John. *Considerations on Keeping Negroes; Recommended to the Professors of Christianity, of Every Denomination.* Philadelphia: James Chattin, 1754.

Primary Sources: Published

Allies, Mary H., ed. *St. Thomas Damascene. On Holy Images.* London: Thomas Baker, 1898.

Armstrong, Edward, ed. *Correspondence between William Penn and James Logan.* 3 vols. New York: AMS Press, 1872.

Bray, Thomas. *The Reverend Thomas Bray, 1656–1730, Founder of the American Public Library System, The Society for the Propagation of the Gospel in Foreign Parts and the Society for Promoting Christian Knowledge: A Selection of his Papers.* Catalogue 152. New York: H. P. Kraus, 1978.

Brooks, Joanna, ed. *The Collected Writings of Sansom Occom, Mohegan: Leadership and Literature in Eighteenth-Century Native America.* New York: Oxford University Press, 2006.

———, and John Salliant, eds. *"Face Zion Forward:" First Writers of the Black Atlantic.* Boston: Northeastern University Press, 2002.

Carretta, Vincent, ed., *Quoba Ottobah Cugoano: Thoughts and Sentiments on the Evils of Slavery, and Other Writings.* New York: Penguin Books, 1999.

———. *Olaudah Equiano, The Interesting Narrative and Other Writings.* New York: Penguin Books, 2003.

Coleman, Kenneth, ed. *The Colonial Records of the State of Georgia.* 32 vols. Athens: University of Georgia Press, 1986.

Bibliography

Coleman, Kenneth, and Milton Ready, eds. *Colonial Records of the State of Georgia: Original Papers of Governor Wright, President Habersham, and Others.* Athens: University of Georgia Press, 1979.

——. *Colonial Records of the State of Georgia: Trustees' Letter Book, 1732–1738.* 31 vols. Athens: University of Georgia Press, 1985.

Cotton, John. *The New England Way.* New York: AMS Press, 1983.

Damascus, Saint John. *Three Treatises on the Divine Images.* St. Vladimir's Seminary Press, 2003.

Davis, William V., ed. *George Whitefield's Journals (1738–1741).* Gainesville, FL: Scholars' Facsimiles & Reprints, 1969.

Fundamental Constitutions of Carolina. The Avalon Project: Documents in Law, History and Diplomacy. At http://avalon.law.yale.edu.

Gifford, Andrew, ed. *Eighteen Sermons Preached by the Late George Whitefield.* London, 1771.

Gober, Sarah B. Temple, and Kenneth Coleman, eds. *Georgia Journeys: Being an Account of the Lives of Georgia's Original Settlers and Many Other Early Settlers from the Founding of the Colony in 1732 until the Institution of Royal Government in 1754.* Athens: University of Georgia Press, 1961.

Hammer, Philip M., ed. *The Papers of Henry Laurens.* Columbia: University of South Carolina Press, 1968–.

Hening, Walter, ed. *The Statutes at Large: Being a Collection of all the Laws of Virginia, from the First Session of the Legislature in the Year 1619.* Vol. 2. Charlottesville: University Press of Virginia, 1969.

Hewatt, Alexander. *An Historical Account of the Rise and Progress of the Colonies of South Carolina and Georgia, in Two Volumes.* Spartanburg, SC: The Reprint Company, 1962.

Krise, Thomas W., ed. *Caribbeana: An Anthology of English Literature of the West Indies, 1657–1777.* Chicago: University of Chicago Press, 1999.

Lane, Mills, ed. *General Oglethorpe's Georgia: Colonial Letters, 1733–1743.* 2 vols. Savannah, GA: Beehive Press, 1975.

MacKinney, Gertrude. *Pennsylvania Archives, 8th Series: Votes and Proceedings of the House of Representatives of the Province of Pennsylvania.* Philadelphia, 1931.

New England Historical and Genealogical Register 1863. Vol. 17. Westminster, MD: Heritage Books, 1994.

Newman, Richard, Patrick Rael, and Phillip Lapsansky, eds. *Pamphlets of Protest: An Anthology of Early African American Protest Literature, 1790–1860.* New York: Routledge, 2001.

Odella, Margaretta Matilda. *Memoir and Poems of Phillis Wheatley, a Native African and a Slave. Dedicated to the Friends of the Africans.* Chapel Hill:

Bibliography

University of North Carolina Press, 1999. At http://docsouth.unc.edu/neh/wheatley/menu.html.

Penn, William. *Primitive Christianity Revived in the Faith and Practice of the People Called Quakers.* Salem, MA: George F. Read, 1844.

———. *The Select Works of William Penn in Three Volumes.* 4th ed. New York: Kraus Reprint Co, 1971.

Perry, William Stevens, ed. *Historical Documents Relating to the American Colonial Church.* Vol. 1: *Virginia.* New York: AMS Press, 1969.

Ramsay, David M. *The History of the Independent or Congregational Church in Charleston, South Carolina from its Origin till the Year 1814.* Philadelphia: J. Maxwell, 1815.

———. *History of South Carolina from its First Settlement in 1670 to the Year 1808.* 2 vols. Philadelphia: W.J. Duffie, 1858.

Reese, Trevor R., ed. *Our First Visit in America: Early Reports from the Colony of Georgia, 1732–1740.* Savannah, GA: Beehive Press, 1974.

Reverend Thomas Bray: A Section of His Papers, Together with a Group of American Manuscripts. New York: H.P Kraus, 1978.

Simmons, Martha, and Frank A. Thomas, ed. *Preaching with Sacred Fire: an Anthology of African American Sermons, 1750 to the Present.* New York: W.W. Norton, 2010.

Smith, Mark M., ed. *Stono: Documenting and Interpreting a Southern Slave Revolt* (University of South Carolina Press, 2005).

Smith, Joseph, ed. *Fifteen Sermons Preached on Various Important Subjects by George Whitefield, Late of Pembroke College, Oxford.* London: Paisley, 1794.

South Carolina Protest Against Slavery: Being a letter from Henry Laurens, Second President of the Continental Congress, to his Son, Colonel John Laurens; Dated Charles Town, SC, August 14th, 1776. New York: Putnam, 1861.

Tyson, John R., and Boyd S. Schlenther, eds. *In the Midst of Early Methodism: Lady Huntingdon and Her Correspondence.* New York: Scarecrow Press, 2006.

Wesley, Charles. *The Diary of Charles Wesley*, Wesley Center Online. At http://wesley.nnu.edu/charles-wesley/the-journal-of-charles-wesley-1707-1788/the-journal-of-charles-wesley-march-9-august-30-1736/.

Wesley, John. "Sermon 45: The New Birth." The United Methodist Global Ministries website. At http://new.gbgm-umc.org/umhistory/wesley/sermons/45/.

Secondary Literature

Abraham, M. H., and Stephen Greenblatt, eds. *The Norton Anthology of English Literature.* Vol. 1. New York: W.W. Norton, 2000.

Bibliography

Abzug, Robert H. *Cosmos Crumbling: American Reform and the Religious Imagination*. New York: Oxford University Press, 1994.

Adams, Catherine, and Elizabeth H. Pleck. *Love of Freedom: Black Women in Colonial and Revolutionary New England*. New York: Oxford University Press, 2010.

Akers, Charles W. "Religion and the American Revolution: Samuel Cooper and the Brattle Street Church." *William and Mary Quarterly*. Third Series, 35, no. 3 (July 1978): 477–498.

Aldridge, A. Owen, "Natural Religion and Deism in America before Ethan Allen and Thomas Paine," *William and Mary Quarterly*. Third Series, 54, no. 4 (October 1997): 435–448.

Alexander, Leslie M., and Walter C. Rucker, eds. *Encyclopedia of African American History*. Vol. 1. New York: ABC-CLIO, 2010.

Anderson, Benedict. *Imagined Communities: Reflections on the Origins and Spread of Nationalism*. New York: Verso, 1983.

Anderson, Jeffrey E. *Conjure in African American Society*. Baton Rouge: Louisiana State University Press, 2007.

Andrews, Edward E. *Native Apostles: Black and Indian Missionaries in the British Atlantic World*. Cambridge, MA: Harvard University Press, 2013.

Bailyn, Bernard. *The Ideological Origins of the American Revolution*. Cambridge, MA: Harvard University Press, 1991.

Bailyn, Bernard, Donald Fleming, and Stephan Thernstrom, eds. *Perspectives in American History*. Vol. 1: *1967*. Cambridge, MA: Charles Warren Center for Studies in American History at Harvard University, 1967.

———, eds. *Perspectives in American History: New Series*. Vol. 1. New York: Cambridge University Press for the Charles Warren Center for Studies in American History, 1984.

Bainton, Roland H. *Yale and the Ministry: A History of Education for the Christian Minister at Yale, from the Founding in 1701*. New York: Harper and Brothers, 1957.

Banner, Lois W. "Religious Benevolence as Social Control: A Critique of an Interpretation." *Journal of American History* 60, no. 1 (June 1973): 23–41.

Barasche, Moshe. *Icon: Studies in the History of an Idea*. New York: New York University Press, 1995.

Beasley, Nicolas M. *Christian Ritual and the Creation of British Slave Societies, 1650-1900*. Athens: University of Georgia Press, 2010.

Bebbingdon, D. W. *Evangelicals in Modern Britain: A History from the 1730s to the 1980s*. New York: Unwin and Hyman, 2008.

Belcher, Joseph. *George Whitefield: a Biography, with Special References to his Labors in America*. New York: American Tract Society, 1857.

Bibliography

Bellot, Leland J. "Evangelicals and the Defense of Slavery in Britain's Old Colonial Empire." *Journal of Southern History* 37, no. 1 (February 1971): 19-40.

Beneke, Chris. *Beyond Tolerance: The Religious Origins of American Pluralism.* New York: Oxford University Press, 2006.

Beneke, Chris, and Christopher S. Grenda, eds. *The First Prejudice: Religious Tolerance and Intolerance in Early America.* Philadelphia: University of Pennsylvania Press, 2010.

Berry, Steven Russell. "Seaborne Conversions, 1700–1800." PhD diss., Duke University, 2005.

Bogin, Ruth. "Notes and Documents: 'Liberty Futher Extended': A 1776 Antislavery Manuscript by Lemuel Haynes," *William and Mary Quarterly*, third series, 40, no. 1. (January 1983): 85–105.

Boles, John B. *Black Southerners, 1619–1869.* Lexington: University Press of Kentucky, 1983.

Bonomi, Patricia U. *Under the Cope of Heaven: Religion, Society and Politics in Colonial America.* New York: Oxford University Press, 2003.

———. "'Hippocrates Twins': Religion and Politics in the American Revolution." *The History Teacher* 29, no. 2 (February 1996): 137–144.

Bonser, Wilfrid. "The Cult of Relics in the Middle Ages," *Folklore* 73 (Winter 1962): 234–256.

Braund, Kathryn E. Holland. *Deerskins and Duffels: The Creek Indian Trade with Anglo-America, 1685–1815.* Lincoln: University of Nebraska Press, 2009.

Breen, Timothy H. "An Empire of Goods: The Anglicization of Colonial America, 1680–1776." *Journal of British Studies* 25 (1986): 467–499.

———. "'Baubles of Britain': The American and Consumer Revolutions of the Eighteenth Century," *Past and Present*, no. 119 (May 1988): 73–104.

———. *The Marketplace of Revolution: How Consumer Goods Shaped American Independence.* New York: Oxford University Press, 2005.

Breen, Timothy H., and Timothy Hall. "Structuring Provincial Imagination: The Rhetoric and Experience of Social Change in Eighteenth-Century New England." *American Historical Review* 103, no. 5 (December 1998): 51–68.

Bremer, Francis J. *America's Forgotten Founding Father.* New York: Oxford University Press, 2005.

Brewer, John. *The Pleasures of the Imagination: English Culture in the Eighteenth Century.* New York: Routledge, 2013.

Brown, Christopher Leslie. *Moral Capital: Foundations of British Abolitionism.* Chapel Hill: University of North Carolina Press, 2005.

Buckley, Thomas E. *Church and State in Revolutionary Virginia, 1776–1787.* Charlottesville: University of Virginia Press, 1977.

Bibliography

Bumsted, J. M. "Revivalism and Separatism in New England: The First Society of Norwich, Connecticut as a Case Study." *William and Mary Quarterly*, third series, 24, no. 4 (October 1967): 588–612.

———. "Orthodoxy in Massachusetts: The Ecclesiastical History of Freetown, 1683–1776," *New England Quarterly*, 43, no. 2 (June 1970): 274–284.

Burridge, Richard. *Imitating Jesus: An Inclusive Approach to New Testament Ethics*. Grand Rapids, MI: Wm. B. Eerdmans, 2007.

Bushman, Richard L. *From Puritan to Yankee: Character and the Social Order in Connecticut, 1690–1765*. Cambridge, MA: Harvard University Press, 1967.

———. *The Refinement of America: Persons, Cities, Houses*. New York: Knopf, 1992.

Butler, Jon. "Magic, Astrology and the Early American Religious Heritage, 1600–1760." *American Historical Review*, 84, no. 2 (April 1979): 317–346.

———. *Awash in a Sea of Faith: Christianizing the American People*. Cambridge, MA: Harvard University Press, 1990.

Cameron, Richard M. *Methodists and Society*. Vol. 1. Nashville, TN: Abingdon Press, 1961.

Carretta, Vincent. *Phillis Wheatley: Diary of a Genius in Bondage*. Athens, GA: The University of Georgia Press, 2011.

Carretta, Vincent, and Philip Gould. *Genius in Bondage: Literature of the Early Black Atlantic*. Lexington: University Press of Kentucky, 2001.

Chamberlain, Ava. "Self-Deception as a Theological Problem in Jonathan Edwards's 'Treatise Concerning Religious Affections.'" *Catholic History* 63, no. 4 (December 1994): 541–556.

Clark, Charles E. *The Public Prints: The Newspaper in Anglo-American Culture, 1665–1740*. New York: Oxford University Press, 1994.

Coleman, Kenneth. *Colonial Georgia: A History*. New York: Charles Scribner's Sons, 1976.

Coleman, Kenneth, ed. *Colonial Records of the State of Georgia: Trustees' Letter Book, 1745–1752*. 31 vols. Athens: University of Georgia Press, 1986.

Colley, Linda. *Britons: Forging the Nations, 1707–1837*. New York: Yale University Press, 1992.

Cooper, James F., Jr. "Higher Law, Free Consent, Limited Authority: Church Government and Political Culture in Seventeenth-Century Massachusetts." *New England Quarterly* 69, no. 2 (June 1996): 201–222.

———. *Tenacious of Their Liberties: The Congregationalists in Colonial Massachusetts*. New York: Oxford University Press, 1999.

Corkran, David H. *The Creek Frontier, 1540–1783*. Norman: University of Oklahoma Press, 1967.

Cornell, Saul. *The Other Founders: Anti-Federalism and the Dissenting Tradition in America, 1788–1828*. Chapel Hill: University Press of North Carolina, 1999.

Bibliography

Crawford, Michael. "Origins of the Eighteenth-Century Evangelical Revival: England and New England Compared." *Journal of British Studies* 26, no. 4 (October 1987): 361–397.

Cross, Arthur Lyon. *The Anglican Episcopate and the American Colonies.* Cambridge, MA: Harvard University Press, 1924.

Currier, John J. *History of Newburyport.* Vol. 1: *1764–1905.* Newburyport, MA, 1906.

Davis, David Brion. *The Problem of Slavery in the Age of Revolution, 1770–1823.* Ithaca, NY: Cornell University Press, 1975.

De Krey, Gary S. "Rethinking the Case for Restoration: Dissenting Cases for Conscience, 1667–1672." *The Historical Journal* 38, no. 1 (1995): 53–83.

Delbanco, Andrew. *The Death of Satan: How Americans Have Lost the Sense of Evil.* New York: Farrar, Straus and Giroux, 1996.

Donoghue, John. "'Out of the Land of Bondage': The English Revolution and the Atlantic Origins of Abolition." *American Historical Review* 115, no. 4 (October 2010): 943–974.

Dunn, Richard S. *Sugar and Slaves: The Rise of the Planter Class in the English West Indies, 1624–1719.* Chapel Hill: University of North Carolina Press, 1972.

Engel, Katherine Carté. *Religion and Profit: Moravians in Early America.* Philadelphia: University of Pennsylvania Press, 2009.

Eskridge, Larry. "Defining Evangelicalism," Institute for the Study of American Evangelicals (1995). At http://isae.wheaton.edu/defining-evangelicalism.

Eustace, Nicole. *Passion Is the Gale: Emotion, Power, and the Coming of the American Revolution.* Chapel Hill, NC: University of North Carolina Press, 2008.

Fisher, Linford D. *The Indian Great Awakening: Religion and the Shaping of Native Cultures in Early America.* New York: Oxford University Press, 2012.

Flanders, Ralph Betts. *Plantation Slavery in Georgia.* Cos Cob, CT: John E. Edwards, 1967.

Forest, Jim. *Praying with Icons.* New York: Orbis Books, 1997.

Frey, Sylvia R., and Betty Wood. *Come Shouting to Zion: African American Protestantism in the American South and British Caribbean to 1830.* Chapel Hill: University of North Carolina Press, 1998.

Gallay, Alan. "The Origins of Slaveholders' Paternalism: George Whitefield, the Bryan Family, and the Great Awakening in the South." *Journal of Southern History* 53, no. 3 (August 1987): 369–394.

———. *The Formation of a Planter Elite: Jonathan Bryan and the Southern Colonial Frontier.* Athens: University of Georgia Press, 1989.

Gallay, Alan, ed. *Indian Slavery in Colonial America.* Lincoln: University of Nebraska Press, 2009.

Garrigus, John D., and Christopher Morris, eds. *Assumed Identities: The Meanings of Race in the Atlantic World.* College Station: Texas A&M Press, 2010.

Bibliography

Gates, Henry Louis, Jr. *The Trials of Phillis Wheatley: America's First Black Poet and Her Encounters with the Founding Fathers.* New York: Basic Books, 2003.

Gaustad, Edwin. *Liberty of Conscience: Roger Williams in America.* New York: Judson Press, 1999.

Gaustad, Edwin, and Mark A. Noll, eds. *A Documentary History of Religion in America.* Grand Rapids, MI: Wm. B. Eerdmans, 2003.

Glasson, Travis. "Baptism Doth Not Bestow Freedom: Missionary Anglicanism, Slavery and the Yorke-Talbot Opinion, 1701–30." *William and Mary Quarterly* 67, no. 2 (April 2010): 279–318.

———. *Mastering Christianity: Missionary Anglicanism and Slavery in the Atlantic World.* New York: Oxford University Press, 2011.

Goetz, Rebecca Anne. *The Baptism of Early Virginia: How Christianity Created Race.* Baltimore: Johns Hopkins University Press, 2012.

Goldman, Lawrence, ed. *Oxford Dictionary of National Biography.* Online ed. Oxford: Oxford University Press, 2012.

The Good News Bible. 2nd ed. New York: American Bible Society, 1992.

Gould, Eliga H. *Among the Powers of the Earth: The American Empire and the Making of a New World Empire.* Cambridge, MA: Harvard University Press, 2012.

Gould, Philip. *Barbaric Traffic: Commerce and Antislavery in the Eighteenth-Century Atlantic World.* Cambridge, MA: Harvard University Press, 2003.

Grasso, Christopher. *A Speaking Aristocracy: Transforming Public Discourse in Eighteenth-Century Connecticut.* Chapel Hill: University of North Carolina Press, 1999.

Greene, Jack P. *The Intellectual Construction of America: Exceptionalism and Identity from 1492 to 1800.* Chapel Hill: University of North Carolina, 1992.

Gregg, Steven H. "'A Truly Christian Hero': Religion, Effeminacy, and Nation in the Writings of the Societies for Reformation of Manners." *Eighteenth-Century Life* 25, no. 1 (Winter 2001): 17–28.

Grigg, John A. "'How This Shall Be Brought About': The Development of the SSPCK's American Policy." *Itinerario* 32, no. 3 (November 2008): 43–60.

Halbwachs, Maurice. *On Collective Memory.* Chicago: University of Chicago Press, 1992.

Hall, David D. *A Reforming People: Puritanism and the Transforming of Public Life in New England.* New York: Alfred A. Knopf, 2011.

Halliday, Peter D. *Habeas Corpus: From England to Empire.* Cambridge, MA: Belknap Press, 2010.

Hancock, David. *Citizens of the World: London Merchants and the Integration of the British Atlantic Community, 1735–1785.* New York: Cambridge University Press, 1997.

Bibliography

Harold, Frances. "Colonial Siblings: Georgia's Relationship with South Carolina during the Pre-Revolutionary Period." *Georgia Historical Quarterly* 73, no. 4 (Winter 1989): 707–744.

Harris, J. William. *The Hanging of Thomas Jeremiah: A Free Black Man's Encounter with Liberty*. New Haven, CT: Yale University Press, 2009.

Hatch, Nathan O. *The Democratization of American Christianity*. New Haven, CT: Yale University Press, 1991.

Haynes, Stephen R. *Noah's Curse: The Biblical Justification of American Slavery*. New York: Oxford University Press, 2002.

Henretta, James A. *The Evolution of American Society, 1700–1815: An Interdisciplinary Analysis*. New York: DC Heath, 1973.

Hill, Christopher. *Puritanism and Revolution: The English Revolution of the 17th Century*. New York: Schocken Books, 1964.

———. *The World Turned Upside Down: Radical Ideas during the English Revolution*. New York: Penguin Books, 1984.

Hobsbawm, Eric, and Terence Ranger. *The Invention of Tradition*. New York: Canto, 1992.

Hoffer, Peter Charles. *When Benjamin Franklin Met the Reverend George Whitefield: Enlightenment, Revival, and the Power of the Printed Word*. Baltimore: Johns Hopkins University Press, 2011.

Holy Bible: King James Version. New York: American Bible Society, 1980.

Hudson, Alex. "The Secret Code of Diaries," *BBC Today*, August 29, 2008. At http://news.bbc.co.uk/today/hi/today/newsid_7586000/7586683.stm.

Hurd, John Codman. *The Law of Freedom and Bondage in the United States*. New York: Applewood Books, 2009.

Irons, Charles F. *The Origins of Proslavery Christianity: White and Black Evangelicals in Colonial and Antebellum Virginia*. Chapel Hill: University of North Carolina Press, 2008.

Isenberg, Nancy, and Andrew Burstein, eds. *Mortal Remains: Death in Early America*. Philadelphia: University of Pennsylvania Press, 2003.

Jackson, Harvey H. "Hugh Bryan and the Evangelical Movement in Colonial South Carolina." *William and Mary Quarterly*, third series, 43, no. 4 (October 1986): 594–614.

Jones, David Ceri, "'So Much Idolized by Some, and Railed at by Others': Towards Understanding George Whitefield." *Wesley and Methodist Studies* 5, no. 1. (2012): 3–29.

Jones, David Ceri, Boyd Stanley Schlenther, and Eryn Mant White. *The Elect Methodists: Calvinistic Methodism in England and Wales, 1735–1811*. Cardiff, UK: University of Wales Press, 2012.

Kammen, Michael. *Digging Up the Dead: A History of Notable American Reburials*. Chicago: University of Chicago Press, 2010.

Bibliography

———. *Mystic Chords of Memory: The Transformation of American Culture.* New York: Vintage, 1991.

Kidd, Colin. *The Forging of Races: Race and Scripture in the Protestant Atlantic World, 1600-2000.* New York: Cambridge University Press, 2006.

Kidd, Thomas S. *The Great Awakening.* New Haven, CT: Yale University Press, 2009.

Klooster, Wim. "Communities of Port Jews and Their Contacts in the Dutch Atlantic World." Special issue, "Port Jews of the Atlantic." *Jewish History* 20, no. 2 (2006): 129–245.

Kramnick, Isaac, ed. *The Portable Enlightenment Reader.* New York: Viking, 1995.

Lambert, Frank. *The Founding Fathers and the Place of Religion in America.* Princeton, NJ: Princeton University Press, 2003.

———. *Inventing the "Great Awakening."* Princeton, NJ: Princeton University Press, 2001.

———. "'Pedlar in Divinity': George Whitefield and the Great Awakening, 1737—1745." *Journal of American History* 77, no. 3 (December 1990): 812–837.

———. *"Pedlar in Divinity": George Whitefield and the Transatlantic Revivals.* Princeton, NJ: Princeton University Press, 1994.

Landsman, Ned C. *Scotland and Its First American Colony, 1683-1765.* Princeton, NJ: Princeton University Press, 1985.

Langford, Paul. *A Polite and Commercial People: England 1727-1783.* New York: Oxford University Press, 1994.

Law, Robin. *The Slave Coast of West Africa, 1550-1750: The Impact of the Atlantic Slave Trade on an African Society.* New York: Clarendon Press, 1991.

———. "Religion, Trade and Politics on the 'Slave Coast': Roman Catholic Missions in Allada and Whydah in the Seventeenth Century." *Journal of Religion in Africa* 21 (1991): 42–77.

Lee, Francis Bazley. *New Jersey as a Colony and as a State: One of the Original Thirteen.* Vol. 1. New York: Publishing Society of New Jersey, 1902.

Levin, Harry. *Contexts of Criticism.* Cambridge, MA: Harvard University Press, 1958.

Lincoln, C. Eric, and Lawrence H. Mamiya. *The Black Church in the African American Experience.* Durham, NC: Duke University Press, 1990.

Love, W. DeLoss. *Sansom Occom and the Christian Indians of New England.* Syracuse, NY: Syracuse University Press, 2000.

Lovejoy, David S. *Religious Enthusiasm in the New World: Heresy to Revolution.* Cambridge, MA: Harvard University Press, 1985.

Macartney, Clarence Edward Noble. *Six Kings of the American Pulpit.* New York: Ayer, 1971.

Mahaffrey, Jerome Dean. *The Accidental Revolutionary: George Whitefield and the Creation of America.* Waco, TX: Baylor University Press, 2011.

Bibliography

———. *Preaching Politics: The Religious Rhetoric of George Whitefield and the Founding of a New Nation*. Waco, TX: Baylor University Press, 2007.

Malcolmson, Robert W. *A Set of Ungovernable People: The Kingswood Colliers in the Eighteenth Century*. Kingswood History Series. N.p.: Robert W. Malcolmson and Kingswood Borough Council, 1986.

Mansfield, Stephen. *Forgotten Founding Father: The Heroic Legacy of George Whitefield*. New York: Cumberland, 2001.

Marsden, George M. *Jonathan Edwards: A Life*. New Haven, CT: Yale University Press, 2008.

Massey, Gregory D. "Limits of Antislavery Thought in the Revolutionary Lower South: John Laurens and Henry Laurens," *Journal of Southern History*, 63, no. 3 (August 1997): 495-530.

Mathews, Donald G. *Slavery and Methodism: A Chapter in American Morality, 1780–1845*. Princeton, NJ: Princeton University Press, 1965.

McGann, Mary E., and Eva Marie Lumas. "The Emergence of African American Worship." Special issue, "African American Spirituality and Liturgical Renewal." *U.S. Catholic Historian* 19, no. 2. (Spring 2001): 27–65.

Miller, Perry. *The New England Mind: The Seventeenth Century*. New York: Macmillan, 1939.

Mitchell, Henry H. *Black Church Beginnings: The Long-Hidden Realities of the First Years*. Grand Rapids, MI: Wm. B. Eerdmans, 2004.

Morgan, David T., Jr. "The Consequences of George Whitefield's Ministry in the Carolinas and Georgia, 1739–1740." *Georgia Historical Quarterly* 55 (1971): 62–82.

Morgan, Philip D. *Slave Counterpoint: Black Culture in the Eighteenth-Century Chesapeake and Lowcountry*. Chapel Hill: University of North Carolina Press, 1998.

Muldoon, James. "Papal Responsibility for the Infidel: Another Look at Pope Alexander VI's 'Inter Caetera.'" *Catholic Historical Review* 64, no. 2 (April 1978): 168–184.

Nash, R. C. "South Carolina and the Atlantic Economy in the Late Seventeenth and Eighteenth Centuries." *Economic History Review*, new series, 45, no. 1 (January 1995): 677–702.

———. "Trade and Business in Eighteenth-Century South Carolina: The Career of John Guerard." *South Carolina Historical Magazine* 96, no. 1 (January 1995): 6–29.

Newman, Richard S. *Freedom's Prophet: Bishop Richard Allen, the AME Church, and the Black Founding Fathers*. New York: New York University Press, 2009.

Noll, Mark A. *America's God: From Jonathan Edwards to Abraham Lincoln*. New York: Oxford University Press, 2002.

Bibliography

———. "The American Revolution and Protestant Evangelism." *Journal of Interdisciplinary History* 23, no. 3 (Winter 1993): 615–638.

Noll, Mark A., David W. Bebbington, and George A. Rawlyk, eds. *Evangelicalism: Comparative Studies of Popular Protestantism in North America, the British Isles, and Beyond*. New York: Oxford University Press, 1994.

Oatis, Steven J. *A Colonial Complex: South Carolina's Frontier in the Era of the Yamasee War, 1680–1730*. Lincoln: University of Nebraska Press, 2004.

Olson, Alison G. "Rhode Island, Massachusetts, and the Question of Religious Diversity in Colonial New England." *New England Quarterly* 65, no. 2 (March 1992): 93–116.

Onuf, Peter S. *Jefferson's Empire: The Language of American Nationhood*. Charlottesville, VA: University of Virginia Press, 2000.

Outwin, Charles P. M. "Securing the Leg Irons: Restriction of Legal Rights for Slaves in Virginia and Maryland, 1625–1791." *Archiving Early America* (Winter 1996). At http://www.earlyamerica.com/review/winter96/slavery.html.

Piper, John. *Tested by Fire: The Fruit of Suffering in the Lives of John Bunyan, William Cowper, and David Brainerd*. Downers Grove, IL: InterVarsity Press, 2001.

Pestana, Carla Gardina. *Protestant Empire: Religion and the Making of the British Atlantic World*. Philadelphia: University of Pennsylvania Press, 2010.

Pettit, Norman. "Prelude to Mission: Brainerd's Expulsion from Yale." *New England Quarterly* 59, no. 1 (March 1986): 28–50.

Pocock, J. G. A. *The Machiavellian Moment: Florentine Political Thought and the Atlantic Republican Tradition*. Princeton, NJ: Princeton University Press, 1975.

Pomfret, John E. *The Province of East New Jersey, 1609–1702*. Princeton, NJ: Princeton University Press, 1962.

"Profile: Hervey, Rev. James (1714–1758)." In *Spenser and the Tradition: English Poetry 1569–1830: A Gathering of Texts, Biography, and Criticism*, comp. David Hill Radcliffe. At http://spenserians.cath.vt.edu/Welcome.php.

Raboteau, Albert J. *Canaan Land: A Religious History of African Americans*. New York: Oxford University Press, 2001.

———. *Slave Religion: The "Invisible Institution" in the Antebellum South*. New York: Oxford University Press, 2004.

Ramsey, William L. *The Yamasee War: A Study of Culture, Economy, and Conflict in the Colonial South*. Lincoln: University of Nebraska Press, 2010.

Remer, Gary. *Humanism and the Rhetoric of Toleration*. University Park: Pennsylvania State University Press, 1996.

Riley, I. Woodbridge. "The Rise of Deism in Yale College." *America Journal of Theology* 9, no. 3 (July 1905): 474–483.

Ross, Kathy W., and Rosemary Stacy. "John Wesley and Savannah." At http://www.sip.armstrong.edu/Methodism/wesley.html.

Bibliography

Ruttenburg, Nancy. "George Whitefield: Spectacular Conversion, and the Rise of Democratic Personality." Eighteenth-Century Cultural Studies series. *American Literary History* 5, no. 3, (Autumn 1993): 429–458.

Schlereth, Eric R. *An Age of Infidels: The Politics of Controversy in the Early States.* Philadelphia: University of Pennsylvania Press, 2013.

Schmidt, Leigh Eric. "'The Grand Prophet,' Hugh Bryan: Early Evangelicalism's Challenge to the Establishment and Slavery in the Colonial South." *South Carolina Historical Magazine* 87, no. 4 (October 1986): 238–250.

Schwartz, Sally. *"A Mixed Multitude": The Struggle for Toleration in Colonial Pennsylvania.* New York: New York University Press, 1987.

Scott, Arthur P. *Criminal Law in Colonial Virginia.* Chicago: University of Chicago Press, 1930.

Seeman, Erik R. *Death in the New World: Cross-Cultural Encounters, 1492–1800.* Philadelphia: University of Pennsylvania Press, 2010.

Sensbach, Jon F. *Rebecca's Revival: Creating Black Christianity in the Atlantic World.* Cambridge, MA: Harvard University Press, 2006.

Sernett, Milton. *Black Religion and American Evangelicalism: White Protestants, Plantation Missions, and the Flower of Negroe Christianity, 1787–1865.* Metuchen, NJ: Scarecrow Press and American Theological Library Association, 1975.

Shammas, Carole. "Anglo-American Household Government in Comparative Perspective." *William and Mary Quarterly*, third series, 52, no. 1 (January 1995): 104–144.

Skinner, Quentin. *The Foundations of Modern Political Thought.* New York: Cambridge University Press, 1969.

Slavery/Antislavery in New England: The Dublin Seminar for New England Folklife. In *Annual Proceedings*, June 20–22, 2003. Smallwood, Stephanie E. *Saltwater Slavery: A Middle Passage from Africa to American Diaspora.* Cambridge, MA: Harvard University Press, 2008.

Sprague, William Buell. *Annals of the American Pulpit: Unitarian Congregational, 1865.* New York: Robert Carter and Brothers, 1865.

Stannard, David E. *The Puritan Way of Death: A Study in Religion, Culture, and Social Change.* New York: Oxford University Press, 1977.

Stein, Stephen J. "George Whitefield on Slavery: Some New Evidence." *Church History* 42, no. 2 (June 1973): 243–256.

Stevens, Abel. *The Women of Methodism: Its Three Foundresses, Susanna Wesley, the Countess of Huntingdon, and Barbara Heck: With Sketches of the Female Associates and Successors in the Early History of the Denomination.* New York: Carlton and Porter, 1866.

Stout, Harry S. *The Divine Dramatist: George Whitefield and the Rise of Modern Evangelicalism.* Grand Rapids, MI: Wm. B. Eerdmans, 1991.

Bibliography

———. *The New England Soul: Preaching and Religious Culture in Colonial New England*. New York: Oxford University Press, 2011.

Stowell, Daniel W. *Balancing Evils Judiciously: The Proslavery Writings of Zephaniah Kingsley*. Gainesville, FL: University Press of Florida, 2001.

Stratton, Margaret. *The Living and the Dead: The Neapolitan Cult of the Skull*. Chicago: Columbia College Press, 2010.

Sweet, James Wood. *Bodies Politic: Negotiating Race in the American North, 1730-1830*. Baltimore, MD: Johns Hopkins University Press, 2003.

Sweet, Julie Anne. "Bearing the Feathers of the Eagle: Tomochichi's Trip to England." *Georgia Historical Quarterly* 86, no. 3 (Fall 2002): 339—371.

———. *Negotiating for Georgia: British-Creek Relations in the Trustee Era, 1733-1752*. Athens: University of Georgia Press, 2005.

———. *William Stephens: Georgia's Forgotten Founder*. Baton Rouge: Louisiana State University Press, 2010.

Tomkins, Stephen. *John Wesley: A Biography*. Grand Rapids, MI: Wm. B. Eerdmans, 2003.

Tomlins, Christopher L., and Bruce H. Mann, eds. *The Many Legalities of Early America*. Chapel Hill: University of North Carolina Press, 2003.

Toulouse, Teresa. *The Art of Prophesying: New England Sermons and the Shaping of Belief*. Athens: University of Georgia Press, 1987.

Tyerman, Luke. *The Life of the Reverend George Whitefield*. 2 vols. London: Anson D.F. Randolph, 1876.

Underwood, James Lowell, and W. Lewis Burke, eds. *The Dawn of Religious Freedom in South Carolina*. Columbia, SC: University of South Carolina Press, 2006.

Valeri, Mark. *Heavenly Merchandize: How Religion Shaped Commerce in Puritan America*. Princeton, NJ: Princeton University Press, 2010.

Van Cleve, George. "Somerset's Case and Its Antecedents in Imperial Perspective." *Law and History Review* (Fall 2006). At http://www.historycooperative.org/journals/lhr/24.3/cleve.html.

Wabuda, Susan. *Preaching during the English Reformation*. New York: Cambridge University Press, 2002.

Wacker, Peter O. *Land and People: A Cultural Geography of Preindustrial New Jersey: Origins and Settlement Patterns*. New Brunswick, NJ: Rutgers University Press, 1975.

Wainwright, William. "Jonathan Edwards." In *The Stanford Encyclopedia of Philosophy*, ed. Edward N. Zalta. 2009. At http://plato.stanford.edu/archives/win2012/entries/edwards.

Walker, Emery, Charles Robert, Leslie Fletcher, and Harold Beresford Butler, eds. *Historical Portraits . . . 1700-1800*. London: Clarendon Press, 1919.

Walzer, Michael. *The Revolution of the Saints: A Study in the Origins of Radical Politics*. Cambridge, MA: Harvard University Press, 1965.

Bibliography

Washington, Booker T., and W. E. Burghardt Dubois. *The Negro in the South: His Economic Progress in Relation to His Moral and Religious Development*. Philadelphia: George W. Jacobs, 1907.

Webb, Clive, and David Brown. *Race in the American South: From Slavery to Civil Rights*. Gainesville: University Press of Florida, 2007.

Weis, Frederick Lewis. *The Colonial Clergy of Virginia, North Carolina, and South Carolina*. Baltimore, MD: Genealogical Publishing Co., 1976.

Wheeler, Roxann. *The Complexion of Race: Categories of Difference in Eighteenth-Century British Culture*. Philadelphia: University of Pennsylvania Press, 2000.

Whiting, Robert. *The Reformation of the English Parish Church*. New York: Cambridge University Press, 2010.

Wilbanks, Charles. *The American Revolution and the Righteous Community: Selected Sermons of Bishop Robert Smith*. Columbia, SC: University of South Carolina Press, 2007.

Williams, Robert V. "George Whitefield's Bethesda: The Orphanage, the College, and the Library." *Library History Seminar*, no. 3, Proceedings. 1969.

Winslow, Ola Elizabeth. *Jonathan Edwards, 1703–1758: A Biography* New York: Macmillan, 1940.

Witzig, Fred. "'Coining Dupes and Catching Fools' or 'A Little Heaven on Earth?': Philanthropy and Rhetoric in the Great Awakening." Paper presented at the Annual Meeting of the American Studies Association, Baltimore, MD, October 23, 2011.

Wiznitzer, Arnold, "The Jews and the Sugar Industry in Colonial Brazil." *Jewish Social Studies* 18, no. 3 (July 1956): 189–198.

Wood, Betty. *Slavery in Colonial Georgia: 1730–1775*. Athens: University of Georgia Press, 2007.

Wood, Gordon S. *The Americanization of Benjamin Franklin*. New York: Penguin, 2005.

Zabriske, Alexander C., ed. *Anglican Evangelicalism*. Philadelphia: Church Historical Society, 1943.

INDEX

Abbot, John, 35
Abercrombie, Robert, 91
abolitionism, 64, 179, 218
abolitionists, 8, 109, 146–51, 154, 204, 206, 211
Adams, John, 109, 138
Africans, 3, 61, 149, 150, 152, 153, 215
Alexander, Archibald, 131
Almost Christian, The, 203, 213
American Revolution, 10, 107–11, 126, 127, 135–46, 152, 153
American Weekly Mercury, 44, 172, 174, 210
anti-Catholicism, 4, 55, 125, 137, 139, 141, 142
antinomianism, 97, 213
Aristotle, 95
Arminius, Jacob, 58; Arminianism, 59, 82, 88
Arnold, Benedict, 126, 131
Arnold, Jonathan, 44, 45
Ars Moriendi, 196n55
Austrian War of Succession, 140

Bacon, Francis, 149
baptism, 3, 61, 75, 112, 163, 182, 183, 221
Baptists, 9, 40, 90, 213
Barbados, 66
Battle of Culloden, 140
Beecher, Lyman, 107
Belcher, Jonathan, 84
Belcher, Joseph, 83, 186, 217
Bell Inn (Gloucester, England), 12–13

Benefits of Early Piety, 142, 203, 214
Benezet, Anthony, 10, 80, 109, 147, 205, 210
Benson, Martin, 17, 20, 32, 33, 53, 89
Bethesda Orphan House (Georgia), 56, 59, 77–78, 79, 94, 130, 197n74
Boltzius, Johan Martin, 73
Book of Common Prayer, 36
Book of Genesis, 152, 180
Book of John, 20
Book of Romans, 54, 177
Boston Evening Post, 92
Brainerd, David, 88, 102–3
Brainerd, John, 88, 102–3
Brattle Street Church (Boston, Massachusetts), 85, 124, 202, 211, 217
British Mercies, 140
Bryan, Andrew, 6, 220, 222
Bryan, Hugh, 52, 79, 177, 184, 185, 222, 226
Bryan, Jonathan, 79, 169
Burning Bush, 142, 203

Calvinism, 48, 59, 118, 130, 201, 222
Causton, Thomas, 17, 169
Chauncy, Rev. Charles, 97, 100, 139, 149, 190, 191, 211
Chickasaw Indians, 67
Choctaw Indians, 67, 68
Christ Church (Oxford, England), 31
Christ Church (Philadelphia, Pennsylvania), 45

Index

Christian Liberty, 60
Christian Unity, 37, 44, 45, 46, 86, 114
Christie, Thomas, 24
Church Governance, 6, 27, 47
Church of England (Anglican Church), 14–18, 19, 21, 27, 28, 31–34, 36, 38, 43, 45, 46, 48–50, 54, 56–60, 62, 67, 79, 82, 83–87, 90, 91, 92, 96–98, 109, 113, 114, 135, 138, 139, 141
Church of Scotland, 51, 112, 129, 141, 223
Clapham Sect, 146
Clarkson, Thomas, 146, 211
Colman, Benjamin, 82, 84–86, 90, 91, 94, 99, 100
Congregationalists, 6, 31, 81, 85, 86, 88, 93, 115, 132
Constitutions: American, 108, 111, 144; British, 27
Cooper, Samuel, 136
Cotton, John, 82, 186
Cowper, William, 121, 130, 192, 225
Cox, Rev. F. A., 132
Creek, 66–67
Cugoano, Quobna Ottobah, 151–52
Cummings, Archibald, 45, 46, 174, 201, 211
Curse of Ham, 150, 152
Cushing, Caleb, 99
Cushing, John, 99
Cutler, Timothy, 84, 91, 186

Damascus, St. John of, 5, 31, 168, 170, 171, 173–75, 177–80, 184, 187, 188, 190, 191, 199, 201, 203
Dartmouth, Earl of (William Legge), 150
Dartmouth College, 88, 104, 150, 187
Davenport, Rev. James, 88
deism, 49, 175, 176, 217, 225
Delaware, 176; Newcastle, 59

Delaware River, 65
Durrell, Rev. Dr. David, 112, 194, 195
Dutch Reform Church, 43, 58, 81

Edict of the Governor of Spanish Florida (1738), 68, 69, 73
Edwards, Jonathan, 6, 31, 37, 84–86, 88, 93, 94–95, 102, 115, 116, 139
Edwards, Thomas, 94
Elizabeth, 36, 38
Emerson, Rev. Joseph, 96
England: Basingstoke, 35; Bristol, 13, 20, 33, 35, 77, 172, 184; Durham, 132; Gloucester, 12, 13, 17, 20, 32, 33, 35, 53, 89; Liverpool, 35; London, 3, 17, 18, 20, 23, 27, 28, 29, 34, 36, 40, 45, 47, 51, 53–57, 59, 62, 74, 77, 101, 102, 103, 105, 112, 122, 132, 133, 139, 145; Oxford, 13, 14, 16, 17, 20, 25, 31, 34, 112, 129
English Civil War, 19, 39, 53, 136, 137, 141
Enlightenment, 31, 48, 49, 85, 95, 143
enthusiasm, 4, 31, 36, 52, 53, 56, 58, 82, 85, 94, 96, 99, 101, 102, 117, 157
Equiano, Olaudah, 10, 64, 80, 148, 149, 151, 185
Erskine, James, 40
Eveleigh, Samuel, 69
Examiner Examined, The (1743), 60, 179

Falconar, Magnus, 44, 45
First Amendment, 111, 144
First Religious Society of New England (Massachusetts), 115
Florida, 24, 55, 68, 69, 73, 163; governor of, 68, 73; Saint Augustine, 68, 73
Foxcroft, Thomas, 91, 94, 100, 189
France, 4, 139

230

Index

Franklin, Benjamin, 49
Freemasons, 26
French and Indian War. *See* Seven Years War
Fundamental Constitutions of Carolina, 19, 169

Garden, Alexander, 26, 27, 28, 36, 51, 62–63, 67; dispute with Whitefield, 52–60, 62, 71, 77–79, 94, 98, 112, 114; Guerard family, 67
General Magazine, 42, 78
Georgia, 17–25, 28, 29, 34, 38, 47, 51, 59, 62, 64, 66–70, 72, 74, 102, 112, 124, 128, 147; Altahama River, 23; and James Oglethorpe in, 24–25, 47, 62, 68–70; Savannah, 17, 23–25, 47, 70, 76, 124; trustees of, 24–25, 47, 62, 68–70, 74–76; slavery in, 66–70, 72, 74–78; Wesleys in, 17–18
Germans, 39, 69
Gibson, Edmund, 17, 18, 20, 28, 45, 47, 53–57, 59, 101, 105
Gifford, Andrew, 128, 203
Gillies, John, 129, 130, 200, 201
Glorious Revolution, 141
Godwyn, Morgan, 62
good works, 15, 54
Gookin, Charles, 40
Gookin, Nathaniel, 99
Gospel, 3, 12, 27, 42, 44, 47, 50, 54, 92, 95, 98, 115, 134, 153
Great Awakening, 117, 123, 135, 143; first, 6, 7, 8, 31, 38, 44, 100–101, 109, 115, 156; second, 9, 10, 41, 44, 111, 156; third, 157
Great Britain, 8, 14, 15, 17–19, 22, 25, 27, 30, 35, 37, 55, 57, 89, 101, 103, 110–12, 123, 128, 132, 136–38, 140, 141, 145, 146, 155

Guerard, John, 67
Guerard Family, 52, 67

habeas corpus, 147, 204
Habersham, James, 70, 80, 145, 148
Harman, James, 111
Harris, Howell, 191
Harvard College, 82, 93, 99
Hastings, Selina. *See* Huntingdon, Countess of
Haynes, Lemuel, 152–53, 206, 218
Hobby, William, 91, 93, 94, 98, 100, 189
Hoby, James, 132
Holyoke, Edward, 99
Huguenots, 26, 67
Hume, David, 80, 149, 185
Huntingdon, Countess of (Selina Hastings), 76, 80, 89, 121, 128–30, 145, 147, 151
Hutchinson, Thomas, 136, 149
Huygens, Christiaan, 82

iconoclasm, 10, 53, 112, 179, 184
idolatry, 86
Imitatio Christi, 5, 13, 108
Ingham, Benjamin, 26
Ireland, 28, 132, 140, 141

Jacobites, 4, 26, 140
Jamaica, 69
Jenny, 112
Johnson, Robert, 68, 181
Johnson, William, 99
justification by faith, 21, 40, 54, 61, 98

Kant, Immanuel, 80, 149
Keen, Robert, 102
Koch, George Byron, 15

Latitudarianism, 22, 27
Laurens, Henry, 64

Index

Law, William, 5, 14, 15, 38
Lee, Jesse, 131
Leile, George, 6
Letter to the Inhabitants . . . (1739), 71–72, 92, 174, 177
liberty of conscience, 19, 39, 40, 88, 136, 173
Locke, John, 19, 95
Logan, James, 40
London Magazine, 127, 128
London Tabernacle at Moorfields, 122, 145, 166
Luther, Martin, 54
Lutherans, 26

Maine, York Harbor, 96
Makemie, Francis, 46
Mansfield, Lord (William Murray), 147
Marks, David, 132
Marrant, James, 10, 80, 104, 150–51
Martyn, Benjamin, 68–69
Maryland, 67, 71, 101, 147; Fort Cumberland, 114
Massachusetts: Boston, 33, 57, 81–82, 84–85, 90–93, 96–97, 99–101, 104, 112, 114, 116–17, 129, 133, 149; Boxford, 99; Bradford, 99; Charlestown, 99; Deerfield, 86; Ipswich, 133; Malden, 96; Newbury, 99; Newburyport, 11, 99, 113–16, 120–21, 124, 127, 133, 155, 156, 160; Northampton, 31, 86, 93, 95; Reading, 100; Salem, 92; Salisbury, 99
Mather, Cotton, 49, 82, 84
Mather, Nathaniel, 82
Matheson, James, 132, 133
Mayhew, Jonathan, 136
memory, 12, 80, 96, 105–6, 108–9, 115, 118, 121, 123, 124, 129, 132, 135–36, 156

methodically mad, 34, 65
Methodism, 14, 20, 112, 130, 135
Minerva, 59
Mohegans, 88, 103
Moir, Robert, 51
Monthly Advertiser, 128
Monthly Review, The, 112, 128
Moody, Samuel, 96
Moravians, 26, 38
Mr. Jack Wilkes, 137
Muhammad, 59

Native Americans, 61, 63, 67, 88, 102, 103, 104, 151, 153. *See also specific names*
Netherlands, Utrecht, 59
New Birth, 20, 21, 30–32, 41, 43, 48, 85, 95–96, 100, 122, 129, 148, 157; as understood by Whitefield, 15–16
New England, 6, 7, 11, 20–21, 38, 48, 57, 60, 80–102, 105, 112–15, 119, 129, 145, 150
New England Weekly Journal, 89
New Hampshire, 99, 101, 119, 152
New Jersey, 43, 44, 52, 102, 128; Burlington, 44
New Lights, 6, 21, 40, 91
New Testament, 12
New York, 36, 46, 51, 96, 114, 152; commissary of, 36, 46–48
New York Gazette, 113
New-Jersey Magazine, 128
Newport Mercury (Massachusetts), 114, 136
Newton, Isaac, 82
North Briton, The, 137

Obeah, 74
Occom, Sansom, 88, 103–4

Index

Oglethorpe, James, 17–18, 20, 23, 24, 26, 68, 69, 70
Old Lights, 6, 40
Old South Church (Reading, Massachusetts), 93
Old South Presbyterian Church (Newburyport, Massachusetts), 6, 11, 113–15, 119–20, 127, 131–33, 155–57
On the Dangers of an Unconverted Ministry, 157
Oxford Castle, 14

Parsons, Jonathan, 88, 115–16, 129, 132
Parsons, Moses, 119
paternalism, 64–66
Pateshall, Richard, 93–94, 98
Pemberton, Ed, 129, 149
Pembroke College (University of Oxford), 13–16, 129
Penn, William, 29
Pennsylvania, 34, 38–40, 43, 45, 48, 51, 59, 65, 101, 102, 112; Delaware River, 65; German Town, 48; Philadelphia, 36, 39–41, 43–48, 51, 78, 103, 116, 140, 141, 148
Pennsylvania Gazette, 43, 59, 102, 112, 164
Periam, Joseph, 34, 65
Pharisees, 12, 14, 55
Philadelphia synod, 43, 48, 51
Pickering, Theophilus, 101
pilgrims, 10, 110, 134
Pomeroy, Benjamin, 88
Presbyterians, 9, 38, 40–43, 51, 86, 113, 114; New Siders, 40
Primitive Christianity, 29, 142
Prince, Thomas, 91
Prince Hall Masons, 104
Pringle, Robert, 73

Protestant Reformation, 8, 110, 141
Puritans, 83, 84, 118

Quakers, 30, 38, 39, 40, 41, 50, 81, 90

race, 3, 5, 56, 61, 70, 73, 88, 103, 105, 107–8, 148–54
Reed, Andrew, 132
refinement, 26, 51–52, 61, 67, 73, 76, 78, 83, 85, 118, 126
regeneration, 12, 13, 40
religion: democratization of, 8, 107; freedom, 3–4, 9, 10, 19, 21, 29, 31–32, 34, 37, 39, 49, 56, 59, 66, 99, 100, 108, 111, 131, 136–38; toleration, 7–9, 19, 22, 25–27, 29–30, 37, 40, 45, 66, 85, 101, 105, 106, 108, 111, 137, 139, 141–44, 146
religious societies, 29, 32, 40, 108, 115; Crooked Lane Society, 29; Crutched Friars' Society, 29; First Religious Society, 115
Rhode Island, 26, 90, 101; Newport, 90
Roman Catholics, 39, 43, 50, 86, 117, 125, 141
Roundheads, 53
Royal Line of Proclamation, 137
Rush, Benjamin, 107–9, 138
Ryle, J. C., 157

Saint John's Church (Bristol, United Kingdom), 20
Saint Mary de Crypt Church (Oxford, United Kingdom), 14
Saint Stephen's Church (Bristol, United Kingdom), 20
Salzburger Lutherans, 26
Scotland, 16, 36, 39, 40, 51, 112, 129, 141
Scots Magazine, 128

Index

Scougal, Henry, 15
Selwyn, Lady, 17
seraphim, 132
Seven Years War, 138, 139, 203, 204
Sewall, Samuel, 100
Seward, Benjamin, 35
Sharpe, Granville, 80, 146, 147
Siege of Louisbourg, 139
slavery, 5, 8, 10, 61–70, 76–80, 88, 89, 103–5, 109–11, 126, 134, 146–53; and the law, 3, 68, 69, 73, 75, 147; legalization in Georgia, 62–64, 66–70, 71–77, 147; Whitefield's views on, 3–5, 8, 10, 25, 52, 61–77, 79, 88–89, 103, 147–48
slaves, 3–5, 8, 10, 25, 52, 61–77, 79, 80, 88–89, 103, 143, 147–52; in Georgia, 62–64, 66–70, 71–77, 147; in South Carolina, 52, 66, 67, 71
smallpox, 82
Smith, Richard, 120
Society for the Propagation of the Gospel (SPG), 3, 27, 43, 50, 51, 62, 67, 79, 91
Somerset, James, 146, 147
Somerset Case (1772), 146, 147
South Carolina, 24, 26, 27, 36, 38, 51, 52, 55, 57, 58, 64, 66–69, 71–76, 79, 98, 102, 147, 157; Charles Town, 27, 28, 51, 52, 59, 62, 63, 66–69, 73, 75, 79, 99, 112, 114, 150–51; commissary of, 26, 27, 28, 36, 51, 62–63, 67; Slave Code of 1740, 73
South Carolina Gazette, 52, 58, 74, 78
Spain, 25, 55
Spanish Florida, 24, 55, 68, 73
Stephens, Thomas, 75
Stevens, Abel, 131
Stoddard, Esther, 94–95
Stoddard, Solmon, 31, 95

Stono Rebellion (South Carolina), 52, 66, 68, 69, 72
Stuart, Charles, 147
Stuart, Charles Edward (Young Pretender), 140
Stuart, James Francis Edward (Old Pretender), 140, 141
Swedes, 39
Switzerland, 48

Talbot, Charles, 75
Tappan, William B., 133
Tennant, Gilbert, 37, 40, 44, 48, 59, 60, 96, 102, 107, 114, 157
Tennant, William, 40, 44, 91, 114
Terry, John, 24
Thirty-Nine Articles of the Church of England, 98
Tillotson, John, 54, 59
Tindall, Matthew, 43
Tories, 136
Trinity Church (New York), 46

van Leeuwenhoek, Antonie, 82
Vermont, 153
Vessey, William, 36
Virginia, 49–51, 63, 67, 71, 147; charter, 49–50; Roman Catholics in, 50; Upper Marlborough, 49

War of Jenkins Ear, 35
Watts, Isaac, 152
Wesley, Charles, 14–19, 122–23, 130
Wesley, John, 14–20, 25, 26, 29, 32
Wheatley, Phillis, 88–89, 104, 121, 135, 144–45, 149–50, 151
Wheatley, Susanna, 88
Wheelock, Eleazar, 88, 103, 104
Whigs, 136
Whitaker (ship), 22, 23

Index

Whitaker, Nathaniel, 146
Whitefield, Elizabeth Jenk, 12, 13
Whitefield, George: accusations of bigotry, 21, 34, 35, 47, 53, 54, 56, 60, 90, 92, 96, 121, 122, 129; accusations of hypocrisy, 5, 30, 32, 39, 47, 53, 61, 118, 119; autobiographies, 32; childhood, 12–13; as Christlike figure, 9, 12, 29; comparisons with St. Paul, 130; conversion experience, 15–16; conversion of slaves, 4, 62–63, 71, 82, 103, 150; crypt, 9, 120, 124, 125, 133, 134, 155; death of, 12, 105–6, 115–16; defense of slavery, 61–80; dispute with Alexander Garden, 52–60, 62, 71, 77–79, 94, 98, 112, 114; funeral, 107–8; journals, 9, 28, 29, 35, 38, 44, 49, 57, 89, 113, 128; meets the Wesleys, 14–16; memorialization, 107–58; ordination, 17; Oxford, 13–16, 129; paternalism, 64–66; relationship with Benjamin Franklin, 49; sermons, 40–41, 46, 48, 51, 59–60, 91; as source of religious disunity, 97–99; theft of humerus bone, 19; use of scripture, 12, 14, 16, 31, 54, 55, 65, 132
Whitefield, Thomas, 12
Whittelsey, Chauncey, 103
Wilberforce, William, 146

Yale College, 31, 86, 96, 97, 102, 103, 114
Yamasee, 25, 67, 68
Yeamans, John, Jr., 66
Yorke, Philip, 75
Yorke-Talbot Opinion (1729), 3, 75, 147
Young, Edward, 152

www.ingramcontent.com/pod-product-compliance
Lightning Source LLC
Chambersburg PA
CBHW022009220426
43663CB00007B/1018